Teaching the Causes of the American Civil War 1850–1861

Caroline R. Pryor, Erik Alexander, Charlotte Johnson,
James Mitchell, and Whitney Blankenship
General Editors

Vol. 2

The Teaching Critical Themes in American History series
is part of the Peter Lang Education list.
Every volume is peer reviewed and meets the highest
quality standards for content and production.

PETER LANG
New York • Bern • Berlin
Brussels • Vienna • Oxford • Warsaw

Teaching the Causes of the American Civil War 1850–1861

Edited by
Michael E. Karpyn

PETER LANG
New York • Bern • Berlin
Brussels • Vienna • Oxford • Warsaw

Library of Congress Cataloging-in-Publication Data
Names: Karpyn, Michael E., editor.
Title: Teaching the causes of the American Civil War, 1850–1861 /
edited by Michael E. Karpyn.
Description: New York: Peter Lang Publishing, 2020.
Series: Teaching critical themes in American history; v. 2
ISSN 2576-0718 (print) | ISSN 2576-0726 (online)
Includes bibliographical references and index.
Identifiers: LCCN 2019053374 (print) | LCCN 2019053375 (ebook) ISBN
978-1-4331-7431-5 (hardback: alk. paper)
ISBN 978-1-4331-7417-9 (paperback: alk. paper)
ISBN 978-1-4331-5528-4 (ebook pdf)
ISBN 978-1-4331-5529-1 (epub) | ISBN 978-1-4331-5530-7 (mobi)
Subjects: LCSH: United States—History—Civil War, 1861–1865—Causes. |
United States—History—Civil War, 1861–1865—Study and teaching.
Classification: LCC E459 .T43 2020 (print) | LCC E459 (ebook) |
DDC 973.7/11—dc23
LC record available at https://lccn.loc.gov/2019053374
LC ebook record available at https://lccn.loc.gov/2019053375
DOI 10.3726/b16178

Bibliographic information published by **Die Deutsche Nationalbibliothek**.
Die Deutsche Nationalbibliothek lists this publication in the "Deutsche
Nationalbibliografie"; detailed bibliographic data are available
on the Internet at http://dnb.d-nb.de/.

© 2020 Peter Lang Publishing, Inc., New York
29 Broadway, 18th floor, New York, NY 10006
www.peterlang.com

All rights reserved.
Reprint or reproduction, even partially, in all forms such as microfilm,
xerography, microfiche, microcard, and offset strictly prohibited.

For my parents

For Lauren and Anna

Table of Contents

Images and Tables — ix

Acknowledgments — xi

Foreword — xiii
    CAROLINE R. PRYOR, ERIK ALEXANDER, JAMES MITCHELL,
    CHARLOTTE JOHNSON AND WHITNEY BLANKENSHIP

Introduction — 1
    MICHAEL E. KARPYN

SECTION 1: Historical Analysis

1. *Struggling to "Remember" the Causes of the American Civil War* — 13
    KEVIN CAPRICE, RICKY DALE MULLINS
    AND DAVID HICKS

2. *Slavery Was God's Will: How Abolitionists Challenged Social and Theological Justifications for the Civil War* — 23
    DAVID CHILDS

3. *Through the Heart: "Jim Brown" and the Murder of Dr. Walter Alves Norwood in Henderson County, Kentucky* — 35
    EMILY D. MOSES

4. *A Historical Inquiry into John Brown and His Raiders* — 43
    JOHN H. BICKFORD AND BONNIE LAUGHLIN-SCHULTZ

5. *1860: The Election That Started the War* — 77
    ELIZABETH BARROW

SECTION 2: Pedagogical Issues

6. *Facing Hard History: Confronting the Disconnect in Student Understanding of the Causes of the Civil War* — 91
   BONNIE LAUGHLIN-SCHULTZ

7. *Why Did the South Secede? Using Inquiry to Confront Contentious History* — 105
   CARLY MUETTERTIES AND RYAN A. LEWIS

8. *Civil War Memories: Untangling the Long and Difficult History of the Causes of the Civil War* — 117
   KEVIN CAPRICE, RICKY DALE MULLINS AND DAVID HICKS

9. *Collective Memory of Secession: On Outbreaks and Moral Acts* — 127
   GABRIEL A. REICH, MELANIE L. BUFFINGTON AND WILLIAM R. MUTH

10. *The Civil War and the Inquiry Design Model* — 135
    S.G. GRANT, KATHY SWAN AND JOHN LEE

SECTION 3: Lesson Plans and Resources

Resources for Classroom Teachers — 147
   CAROLINE R. PRYOR, CHARLOTTE JOHNSON, WHITNEY BLANKENSHIP AND AMY WILKINSON

Appendix: Teaching the Causes of the American Civil War Using Inquiry Design Model: Lesson Plans and Resources for Classroom Teachers — 167

Contributors — 185

Index — 191

Images and Tables

Image 1.1:	Thomas Drayton wearing his Confederate army uniform	2
Image 1.2:	Percival Drayton, photographed in 1864	3
Image 1.3:	Map showing the distribution of the slave population of the southern states of the United States, compiled from the census of 1860	5
Image 1.4:	Abraham Lincoln raises the new 34-star American flag at Independence Hall on February 22, 1861	6
Image 1.5:	The inauguration of Jefferson Davis, February 18, 1861	8
Image 3.1:	Wanted poster for Jim Brown, April 4, 1861	37
Image 4.1:	Tragic Prelude. United Missouri Bank of Kansas City, 1938	63
Image 4.2:	John Brown. 1899	64
Image 4.3:	John Brown. 1859	65
Image 4.4:	John Brown. Meeting the slave-mother and her child on the steps of Charlestown jail on his way to execution. 1863	66
Image 4.5:	John Brown—the martyr. 1870	67
Image 4.6:	John Brown exhibiting his hangman. 1865	68
Image 4.7:	Death warrant of John Brown. 1906	69
Image 4.8:	John Brown ascending the scaffold preparatory to being hanged. 1859	69
Image 4.9:	The last moments of John Brown leaving the jail on the morning of his execution. 1885	70

Image 4.10:	John Brown riding on his coffin to the place of execution Charlestown, W. Va. 1859	71
Image 4.11:	John Brown, full-length portrait, lying wounded on floor beside his son. 1859	72
Image 4.12:	En route for Harper's Ferry. 1859	73
Image 5.1:	1860 electoral vote and popular vote map	83
Table 4.1:	The Importance of John Brown's Raid	47
Table 4.2:	Primary Source Observations, Inferences, Connections & Significance	49
Table 6.1:	Standards Implicated in Teaching Civil War Memory	98
Table 8.1:	Description of Options for Beginning the Lesson	119
Table 8.2:	Features Sources Pre-Civil War, Features Sources Post-Civil War	120
Table 8.3:	Position A: Slavery was the cause of the American Civil War; Position B: Slavery was NOT the cause of the American Civil War	123
Table 8.4:	Description of Options for Follow-Up Activities	123
Table 10.1:	IDM Blueprint of an Inquiry about Southern Secession	137
Table A1:	Why Did the South Secede?	168
Table A2:	Can Words Lead to War?	171
Table A3:	Caught in the Middle: Kentucky and Causes of the Civil War	173
Table A4:	Slavery and Justice	175
Table A5:	Passmore Williamson and the Fugitive Slave Act	177
Table A6:	The Election of 1860 by the Numbers	179
Table A7:	Who Voted for Abraham Lincoln?	181
Table A8:	The Economic Causes of the Civil War	183

Acknowledgments

With appreciation and acknowledgment to the Series Editorial Advisory Board for their invaluable insights and contributions to this volume and their dedication to teachers, students and the production of this series.

Erik Alexander, Adam Atwoof, Whitney Blankenship, Laura Milsk Fowler, Brian Gibbs, Andrew Hostetler, Stephen Hansen, Charlotte Johnson, Julianna Kershen, Stephanie McAndrews, James Mitchell, Jack Sevin, Mary Stockwell and Dennis Urban

Special appreciation and acknowledgment to *Caroline Pryor* for the incredible opportunity to edit this volume, and for her guidance and encouragement throughout this process, and to *Whitney Blankenship* and *Charlotte Johnson* for their invaluable assistance.

I also appreciate and acknowledge:

Patty Mulrane, Monica Baum, and Jackie Pavlovic, Peter Lang Publishing, for their flexibility and support in bringing this volume to print.

Michael J. Birkner, Gettysburg College and *Stephen Petrus,* for 25 years of friendship, mentorship and inspiration.

Meg Garey, for everything.

To my teaching colleagues who do incredible work to expand the frontiers of our craft.

Foreword

Caroline R. Pryor, Erik Alexander, James Mitchell, Charlotte Johnson and Whitney Blankenship

In his introductory essay to this volume, editor Michael Karpyn notes the importance of historical analysis about which teachers might reflect as they examine the pedagogical challenges of their teaching. This foundational challenge begins when we question—as suggested by the first essay in this volume—the objectives of our teaching:

> Why do we as a nation struggle so much to understand the cause of the American Civil War? There is no simple answer to this question, but our lack of understanding is at least partially due to both sides contesting the memory of the war before the guns had time to cool. (Caprice, Mullins and Hicks, Chapter 1)

This volume continues to explore the enduring question of this book series: How have we as a nation addressed our civic life and, provided—over time—for the liberties we envision. In this volume Michael Karpyn leads contributing authors to grapple with this question.

Karpyn's remarks in his opening preface foreshadow his own essay on the causes of the civil war explaining that "causes" is no simple matter. His preface begins with a scenario familiar to many, the story of brothers separated by familial circumstances in the early 19th century and told to us in part by letters that provide us with insight into and the prediction of the "imminent secession" and coming of the war. Here Karpyn reminds us that primary sources alone pale in comparison to the collective memory of what these resources represent—the long-term suffering of war and the complex effort to explain its cause(s).

Karpyn's focus in this preface is not—surprisingly, the topic of slavery—its morality and the debate and contention that slavery is less a moral issue than an economic one. Rather, Karpyn is resolved to bring clarity to the war's causes by offering essays in this volume that range from efforts to face "hard history" (see Schultz essay) to efforts to "remember" the war's causes (see Caprice, Mullins and Hicks); other of the volume's essays (Moses, Bickford, Barrow, Muetterties, and Grant, Swan and Lee) further illuminate these main themes. This important volume is less a history lesson than a dynamic of inquiry. Here teachers may read essays that help to "untangle" (see Caprice, Mullins and Hicks) difficult history—the history of codified incivility and the resistance to dissolve it and substantiate the undoing of slavery.

The resource section of this volume (see Pryor, Blankenship, Johnson and Wilkinson) offers teachers a range of media sources, video, media links, books and essays from which they might model for students how to evaluate the veracity of sources and use these evaluations to respond to a complexity of questions typically not found in classroom textbooks. The Appendix section augments the use of these and others resources as it describes the Inquiry Design Model (IDM) and presents sample lesson plans to help teachers frame IDM lessons.

It is therefore Karpyn's remarks in his opening essay—that collective memory is taken for granted—that suggest the importance of this volume. It is not the teaching of the causes of the civil war as factoids or the many heart-breaking stories that is prescient in planning to teach. Rather the importance of planning to teach the causes of the civil war lies in the need for authentic remembrance, a task of unease that even with the best of resources can appear out of reach.

We urge our collective teaching profession to reach beyond this unease and challenge ourselves and our students to examine the war's causes and respond to "hard history" as a statement of civil right.

Caroline R. Pryor, with Erik Alexander,
James Mitchell, Charlotte Johnson and
Whitney Blankenship, 2019

Introduction

Michael E. Karpyn

If two brothers ever embodied the powerful and tragic forces that led to the American Civil War, it is Thomas and Percival Drayton.

Born in Charleston, South Carolina, in 1809 and 1812, the brothers were separated in 1833, when their father William relocated to Philadelphia in response to the Nullification Crisis. William, a unionist, planned to take his whole family north. Thomas, a believer in states' rights and a supporter of slavery, instead chose to stay behind in South Carolina.

Thomas (Image 1.1), an 1828 graduate of West Point, embarked on a career path that ranged from service in the U.S. Army, a civil engineer, a representative in the South Carolina legislature, and then the owner of over 100 slaves at his 1100-acre Fish Hill Plantation near the Port Royal Sound. Percival (Image 1.2) entered the U.S. Navy in 1827, earning promotion to commander in 1855.

On November 7, 1860, Thomas was still living in Charleston, South Carolina, while Percival was stationed at the Philadelphia Navy Yard. Processing the results of the previous day's presidential election, Thomas wrote to his brother with a dire prediction. "Well, Lincoln is elected," he wrote, adding, "and now for the end."

Thomas meant "the end" of the country as it existed, correctly predicting that several Southern states would secede within the next few months. Despite his Southern roots, Thomas seemed despondent about the tragedy of this conflict, telling Percival that

> None deplores it more than I do, particularly as it will involve, what I had hoped never to have lived to see—divisions between brothers—who up to this moment, have been one in sentiment and devotion to each other. (Drayton, 1860, November 7)

Image 1.1: Thomas Drayton wearing his Confederate army uniform. Internet Archive

Reading further, what is also interesting about this letter is not only its frank prediction of imminent secession but also the reasons behind such an action. Thomas, as he wrote, was "in no temper for toast or celebration" about the secession of his home state, but he was also clear about why, in his view, his native South Carolina was forced to take such a drastic action.

> I now go for separation as the only security of the South. My judgement [sic] and feelings may have led me to think and decide erroneously. But I shall not waiver. I have no hope of new guaranties [sic] to protect us against a fanatical and unscrupulous majority. Misrule, contempt of law, word and religion crop out of the body politic, to the exclusions of honor, decency and truth. There is no sober … thought strong enough to do justice, if appealed to. I shall attempt to [in]criminate no one Section. The whole people are to blame—and must suffer together. (Ibid.)

And suffer the nation did. While each generation in American history has faced its own challenges and crises, all seem to pale in comparison to the many horrors of the American Civil War. Four years of bitter fighting led to

Image 1.2: Percival Drayton, photographed in 1864. Wikipedia

over 750,000 deaths in both armies, billions of dollars in property damage and immeasurable hardships on civilian populations throughout the entire country.

The Challenge of Teaching the Causes of the Civil War

The events of the American Civil War are so steeped in the collective memory of this country and so taken for granted that it is sometimes difficult to take a step back and consider *why* such a tragic war occurred. This volume will attempt to provide classroom teachers with the resources and strategies to thoughtfully inquire, evaluate and assess this critical and complex period in American history.

The inspiration for the structure of this volume is rooted in my own experience as a classroom teacher. My first full time teaching job was in an economically and racially diverse public high school. I was ecstatic to teach U.S. History, especially the American Civil War. It was, and still is, one of my favorite areas of American history and my mind reeled at all of the wonderful content that laid at my fingertips.

Thomas Drayton's letter, however, hints at the unique challenges faced by secondary classroom teachers charging their students to grapple with the causes of the American Civil War. He was discouraged about the onset of the war, but also felt that blame was shared fully by the entire country—not just the South. Herein lies the challenge: when one begins to peel back the layers of Drayton's letter and consider what he means by "protection," "misrule," and the "contempt of law" by "fanatical and unscrupulous majority," the raw fault lines of this conflict become uncomfortably clear.

At this point, teachers and students of this critical era of American history cannot ignore or deemphasize the ghastly specter of slavery (Image 1.3) as the central cause of this conflict. The chronological focus of this volume—1850 to 1861—represents a clear turning point where the issue of slavery evolved from an uneasy series of compromises between North and South into the unstoppable force that led to armed conflict.

As a new teacher in a diverse community, I quickly became aware of the magnitude of this challenge for a classroom teacher. As I worked my students towards the events and ideas that led to secession and war, I became aware of how, in many ways, completely unprepared I was to teach this topic. It wasn't a matter of my content knowledge; it instead was something much more challenging, something that I had not considered until that point in time. The reality of slavery as an institution and a cause of the American Civil War was not a dusty, distant set of facts from a long ago era. It was instead a painful, fresh reality of my students' present existence. It was a perspective that I had not previously considered and did not understand. As a new teacher, I tried the best that I could, but I struggled mightily with teaching the antebellum era and the Civil War that followed.

To go beyond a cursory examination of the practice of slavery in the United States is an uncomfortable necessity for many classroom teachers. While students and educators should take care to not judge actions and ideas of the past through the benefit of hindsight, evaluating American slavery within the context of the time is not for the faint of heart. The many horrors of this practice are well known; the beliefs that a race of people was inferior to others, that they were viewed as property and that they lived and worked in backbreaking and squalid conditions.

And, most troubling to modern audiences, many Americans—even in the North—believed that this practice was justified and legal where allowed

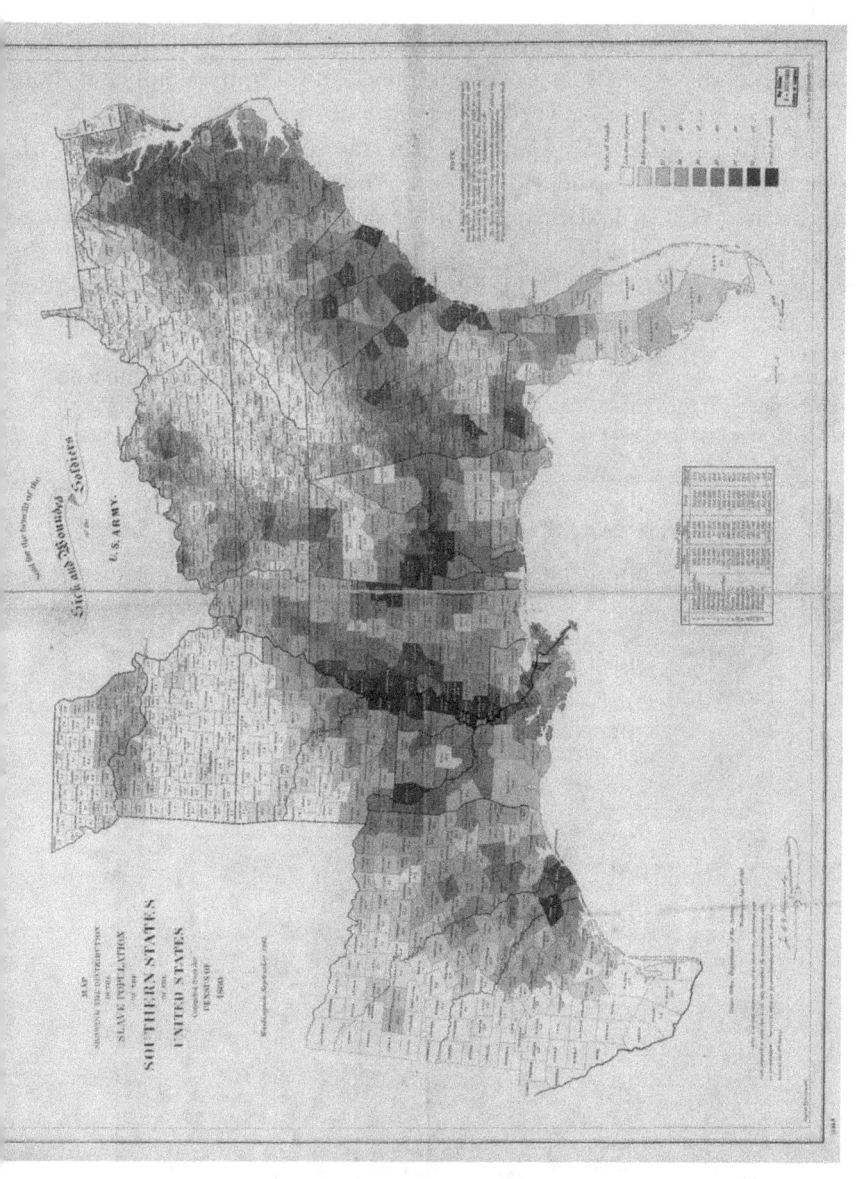

Image 1.3: Map showing the distribution of the slave population of the southern states of the United States. Compiled from the census of 1860. Library of Congress

by state law and was outside of the reach of the federal government. Beyond that, defenders of slavery claimed that owning slaves was a right protected by the U.S. Constitution and that this "property," in their view, could not be taken without due process of the law.

Further muddying the waters of this exploration is the reality that *both* sides in this conflict—those who favored preservation of the union and those who favored secession—believed that their side best embodied the principles and ideals of America's founding. For example, on February 22, 1861, President-Elect Lincoln paid a visit to the very site of America's founding—Independence Hall in Philadelphia. Observing both the birthday of George Washington and the raising of a U.S. flag that included a 34th star for the new state of Kansas (Image 1.4), Lincoln was unambiguous in stating that preserving the nation was critical to preserving the spirit of its founding

> I have never had a feeling politically that did not spring from the sentiments embodied in the Declaration of Independence. I have often pondered over the dangers which were incurred by the men who assembled here, and framed

Image 1.4: Abraham Lincoln raises the new 34-star American flag at Independence Hall on February 22, 1861. Library of Congress

and adopted that Declaration of Independence. I have pondered over the toils that were endured by the officers and soldiers of the army who achieved that Independence.... It was not the mere matter of the separation of the Colonies from the motherland; but that sentiment in the Declaration of Independence which gave liberty, not alone to the people of this country, but, I hope, to the world, for all future time. It was that which gave promise that in due time the weight would be lifted from the shoulders of all men. This is a sentiment embodied in the Declaration of Independence. Now, my friends, can this country be saved upon that basis? If it can, I will consider myself one of the happiest men in the world, if I can help to save it. If it cannot be saved upon that principle, it will be truly awful. But if this country cannot be saved without giving up that principle, I was about to say I would rather be assassinated on this spot than surrender it. (Lincoln, 1861, February 22)

On February 18, three days before Lincoln's Philadelphia speech, Jefferson Davis, the president of the Confederate States of America, gave his inaugural address from the balcony of the Alabama State Capitol in Montgomery (Image 1.5). Like Lincoln, Davis also invoked the spirit and ideas of our founding documents as justification for their secession from the union forged in Philadelphia

> The declared purpose of the compact of Union from which we have withdrawn was "to establish justice, insure domestic tranquility, provide for the common defense, promote the general welfare, and secure the blessing of liberty to ourselves and our posterity;" and when, in the judgment of the sovereign States now composing this Confederacy, it had been perverted from the purposes for which it was ordained, and had ceased to answer the ends for which it was established, a peaceful appeal to the ballot-box declared that so far as they were concerned, the government created by that compact should cease to exist. In this they merely asserted a right which the Declaration of Independence of 1776 had defined to be inalienable; of the time and occasion for its exercise, they, as sovereigns, were the final judges, each for itself.... The right solemnly proclaimed at the birth of the States, and which has been affirmed and reaffirmed in the bills of rights of States subsequently admitted into the Union of 1789, undeniably recognize in the people the power to resume the authority delegated for the purposes of government. Thus the sovereign States here represented proceeded to form this Confederacy, and it is by abuse of language that their act has been denominated a revolution. (Davis, 1861, February 18)

Both speeches clearly illustrate the difficulty of bringing this critical era to life in our classrooms. The essential questions to this examination are both challenging and extremely painful to consider: How did secession and war arise from the arguments over the horrible and inhuman institution of human bondage? How did both sides in this conflict feel that they best were preserving and exhibiting the ideals of the American founding? This volume will hopefully assist classroom teachers and students of this critical era in American history.

Image 1.5: The inauguration of Jefferson Davis, February 18, 1861. Wikimedia Commons

The Need for Inquiry in Social Studies Classrooms

Inquiry is the key to any meaningful examination of any time period in U.S. history. Innovations in social studies education, most recently embodied the National Council for the Social Studies C3 (College, Career and Civic Life) Framework have rightfully moved the classroom teaching of history and social studies content away from an endless barrage of memorized facts to pedagogical approaches that encourage teachers and students to ask critical questions and examine relevant primary and secondary sources to reach their own conclusions about the course content. Building these skills is not just important to reach a fuller appreciation of our discipline's content and methodology, but is also required for the complex challenges faced by all citizens in a participatory democracy (National Council for the Social Studies, 2013).

To provide classroom teachers with the tools to navigate this challenging, but critical, era in American history, this volume is separated into three distinct parts. The first two sections provide teachers with historical analysis for and examination of the pedagogical challenges of their classroom teaching.

From the historical perspective, Kevin Caprice's opening essay analyses the three different strands that comprise our nation's collective memory of the Civil War. With this foundation established, the next essays in this section focus on both national and local events that underscore the many forces that fractured this country into open conflict. David Childs illustrates the complex record of religious beliefs on both sides of the slavery debate. John Bickford III addresses the complex historical memory of John Brown's Raid at Harper's Ferry, Virginia, while Emily Moses brings to light how a little known murder in the border state of Kentucky paralleled the nationwide debate over slavery. Elizabeth Barrow closes this section by analyzing the importance of the election of Abraham Lincoln in 1860—the very event that signaled "the end" for Thomas Drayton in South Carolina.

It is essential for classroom teachers to not only understand the complex social, political and economic forces that led to the conflict, but also need assistance in navigating the pedagogical challenges found within the content. The next four essays not only touch upon different aspects of these challenges, but also provide concrete examples of how teachers can successfully deliver classroom instruction that asks meaningful questions and allows for student inquiry in a culturally sensitive manner. Bonnie Laughlin-Shultz's essay comprehensively addresses the challenge of facing the "hard history" related to the coming of the Civil War and Gabriel Reich specifically addresses the connection of this hard history to our collective understanding the issue of Southern secession.

Taking these issues and content down to the classroom level, Ricky Mullins provides several specific approaches for addressing controversial issues with secondary students, specifically the Structured Academic Controversy format. Carly C. Muetterties, who has also authored one of the inquiry-based units in the third section of this volume, reflects on the challenge of writing that inquiry and how she navigated the many issues faced by educators who teach this critical and controversial era.

The third section provides inquiry-based units ready for implementation into secondary classrooms. Each inquiry is built around the Inquiry Design Model (IDM), designed by Professors S.G. Grant, Kathy Swan and John Lee. Building off of the C3 Framework the IDM allows for the meaningful examination of complex historical topics by providing a blueprint that contains essential questions, classroom activities and resources, summative and formative assessments and guidelines for students to take informed action based on the content of the inquiry (Grant, Swan, & Lee, 2017) The essay not only examines each section of the IDM in depth, but also discusses its specific connections to the teaching of this era.

The inquiries included this volume will allow classroom teachers to effectively challenge and engage their students with critical questions about the political, social and economic forces that veered this nation into a long and bloody civil war. Inquiries by Carly Muetterties, Christina Palo and Janine Draschner address the broader political, economic and social issues that lead to war, while Elizabeth Barrow tackles two different, but equally important aspects of the crucial presidential election of 1860. Emily Moses provides two fascinating glimpse on how issues in the critical border state of Kentucky reflected growing national tensions. Alaina McNaughton and the educational staff of Pennsylvania's Chester County Historical Society bring to life a direct challenge to the Fugitive Slave Act. Last, an inquiry from C3 Teachers asks to what extent the publication of *Uncle Tom's Cabin* by Harriet Beecher Stowe played a role in the coming of the war.

It is my hope that these collected resources will provide classroom teachers with the tools to meaningfully guide their students through the critical questions of a critical time period in American history. To understate and ignore these critical and often painful questions is a gross disservice to our students as budding historians and future citizens.

References

Davis, J. (1861, February 18). *First inaugural address*. Retrieved from https://jefferson-davis.rice.edu/archives/documents/jefferson-davis-first-inaugural-address

Drayton, T. (1860, November 7). *Thomas Drayton to Percival Drayton, 7 November 1860*. [Letter]. Retrieved from https://hsp.org/sites/default/files/attachments/handout_1_drayton_letter_transcription.pdf

Grant, S. G., Lee, J., & Swan, K. (Eds.). (2017). *Inquiry based practice in social studies education*. London, England: Routledge.

Lincoln, A. (1861, 22 February). *Address in Independence Hall*. Retrieved from http://www.abrahamlincolnonline.org/lincoln/speeches/philadel.htm

National Council for the Social Studies. (2013). *The college, career, and civic life (C3) framework for social studies state standards: Guidance for enhancing the rigor of K–12 civics, economics, geography, and history*. Silver Spring, MD: Author.

Section 1: Historical Analysis

1. Struggling to "Remember" the Causes of the American Civil War

KEVIN CAPRICE, RICKY DALE MULLINS AND DAVID HICKS

Why do we as a nation struggle so much to understand the cause of the American Civil War? There is no simple answer to this question, but our lack of understanding is at least partially due to both sides contesting the memory of the war before the guns had time to cool. As Warren (1961) famously wrote, "The Civil War is our only 'felt' history—history lived in the national imagination" (p. 4). The way in which people remember the Civil War still has relevance today, because memory is active by its very nature. Janney (2014) points out that:

> [t]he war generation understood what historians have come to grasp only in the past few decades: memory is not a passive act. People actively shaped what was remembered—and omitted—from the historical record for social, cultural, and political purposes. (p. 1139)

In the immediate post-war period, three memory strands emerged: (1) the Lost Cause Memory; (2) the Unionist Memory; (3) the Emancipationist Memory. Yet these memories proved fluid in the minds of individuals living in this era. As Janney (2013) notes, these memories were "never clear-cut, nor did they remain static" (p. 10). The memory of the war grew even more complex when a desire for reconciliation between the North and the South began to affect which memories were given primacy. In many ways, it is because of the nebulous nature of memory that we struggle today to fully understand the causes of the Civil War. The various intersections of these memories have muddied our understanding. In order to grasp why the war began, we have to untangle these threads of memory. In this chapter, we will sort these threads by explaining the importance of context in historical analysis through explicating these three Civil War memories, showing the importance of these memories in achieving historical understanding within and beyond the classroom. The inclusion of memory studies in our historical analysis will in turn help us to answer the compelling question: "How can we as educators and historians understand and then explain the multi-faceted causes of the American Civil War to students?"

The Importance of Context

"The Civil War was not fought over slavery!" This mantra tends to be the starting point of many when positing arguments about the cause of the American Civil War. Subtler forms of this idea, pushing against the notion that slavery was the cause of the Civil War, have appeared in such publications as a fourth-grade textbook in Virginia, which made the claim that, "African Americans fought for the Confederacy during the Civil War, a claim that nearly all historians of the era reject" (Sutherland, 2010, para. 1). Deliberating slavery's role in the coming of the Civil War is of special relevance in our current democracy. From public forums to classrooms, historians and teachers are seizing the opportunity to replace one mantra with another: "No, slavery was the cause of the Civil War." But is a new mantra enough? Suppose the next piece of evidence a student hears is the following quotation from Abraham Lincoln (1862), "If I could save the Union without freeing *any* slave I would do it" (p. 205). How can this be true if slavery was the singular cause of the war? In order to achieve greater understanding, we as educators and historians should strive to move the debate beyond mantras and toward contextualized historical analysis.

The current public debate over the causes of the Civil War is trapped in a binary of it either was or was not caused by slavery, thus speaking to the notion of Dewey's (1938a) either/or proposition. Dewey (1938a) argues, "Mankind likes to think in terms of extreme opposites. It is given to formulating its beliefs in terms of Either-Ors, between which it recognizes no intermediate possibilities" (p. 17). Therefore, while many people argue that the Civil War was either about slavery or it was not, a more accurate response requires elaboration beyond these boundaries. Dewey (1938b) further argues, "Categories of selection and order, having an implicit esthetic quality, are involved in the writing of history. These categories when liberated from their original context gave rise to the historical novel" (p. 181). When a source, or evidence, is taken out of context, the argument moves into the realm of fiction. It is then paramount to introduce students to a manner of historical thinking that does not allow historical events, quotations, or evidence to be considered without context. Historical analysis cannot exist in a vacuum. Dewey (1931) posits, "But I can see how analysis falsifies when its results are interpreted as complete in themselves apart from any context" (p. 208; see also Garrison, 1994 for more on Dewey and context). In other words, without context, results are invalid. Let us, then, attain some context by analyzing the development of different Civil War memories.

Memories of the Civil War

Southern Memory: The Lost Cause Memory

Perhaps the most well-known Civil War memory is the Southern memory of the war, known as the Lost Cause. According to Gallagher (2000), during the formulation of the Lost Cause, "ex-Confederates denied the importance of slavery in triggering secession" (p. 4). The Lost Cause instead put forth a number of other reasons why the South seceded, usually state rights or tariff disputes, but never slavery. There is much more to the Lost Cause, but for our purposes, slavery is the focus. The Lost Cause Memory is why debates continue over whether or not the Confederacy fought to preserve slavery, and is simply untrue.

Vast amounts of contemporary evidence exist that show the Southern states seceded to protect the institution of slavery, but for brevity's sake, we will consider one example. First, when considering the Lost Cause, we must always consider the context of when evidence was created. Secessionists writing after 1865 came up with far different reasons for forming the Confederacy than they did in 1860–1861. The architects of the Lost Cause fabricated their narrative in such a way that would protect the legacy of their failed experiment. Few better exemplify this than Alexander Stephens, the Vice President of the Confederacy. In an 1861 address known popularly as the "Cornerstone Speech," Stephens (1861) proclaimed:

> Our new government is founded upon exactly the opposite idea; its foundations are laid, its corner-stone rests, upon the great truth that the negro is not equal to the white man; that slavery—subordination to the superior race—is his natural and normal condition. (p. 721)

Remembering the Confederacy seven years later, however, Stephens (1868) imagined slavery's role in secession differently: "I repeat that this whole subject of Slavery, so-called, in any and every view of it, was, to the Seceding States, but a drop in the ocean" (p. 542). In 1861, slavery was the cornerstone of the Confederacy, but by 1868, it was a mere drop in the ocean; this shift in memory is a microcosm for the formation of the Lost Cause, and can also be found in documents such as the "Declaration of the Immediate Causes Which Induce and Justify the Secession of South Carolina from the Federal Union," "A Declaration of the Immediate Causes which Induce and Justify the Secession of the State of Mississippi from the Federal Union," and many others.

As Nolan (2000) suggests, members of the defeated South put forward the Lost Cause following the war in order to "foster a heroic image of secession and the war so that the Confederates would have salvaged at least their honor from the all-encompassing defeat. Thus the purpose of the legend was to hide the Southerners' tragic and self-destructive mistake" (pp. 13–14). Contested during the lifetime of the Civil War generation, the Lost Cause memory achieved national prominence by the end of the 1930s, aided by a desire for reconciliation, and due in no small part to the success of *Gone with the Wind*, notorious for its propagation of Confederate memory, as well as earlier pro-Confederate films, such as *Birth of a Nation* (Janney, 2014, p. 1151). As Nolan (2000) points out, since this period, "[i]n the popular mind, the Lost Cause represents the national memory of the Civil War; it has been substituted for the *history* of the war" (p. 12). Nolan's (2000) claims have come to seem overstated, as greater attention has shed light on the dark underbelly of the Lost Cause. However, far too many are still living in the darkness.

Northern Memory: The Unionist Memory

In Northern memory there exist two strands of memory: The Unionist Memory and the Emancipationist Memory. The Unionist Memory most accurately depicts the reason the northern states went to war: preservation of the Union. Gallagher (2011) excellently sums up the Unionist Memory when he writes:

> Maintenance of the Union … always ranked first among war aims for most citizens in the United States. Anyone interested in why the mass of northern people supported crushing the rebellion, even at a hideous cost, must come to grips with this crucial fact. (p. 34)

It was preserving the Union, then, and not destroying slavery, that inspired the North to take up arms.

The Unionist Memory is not completely devoid of any acknowledgment of emancipation, but the Unionist Memory recognizes preserving the Union as the cause of the war above emancipation. Gannon (2017), in her study of the memory of the Civil War, explains that "closer examination of the federal supporters' memory demonstrated the primacy of Union over emancipation"

(p. 21). While Gannon (2017) finds that Union soldiers were proud of their role as harbingers of freedom for African Americans, they still remembered that their original war aim was reuniting the country. Janney (2013), too, argues that while "[e]mancipation had been a crucial means and happy result of Union victory," ultimately "reunion *was* the Union cause" (p. 5, 7). The importance of emancipation as a result of the war clouds the memory of 1861, but close review shows emancipation was not in the hearts of most when the war started; it was reunion that stirred the men.

To view contemporary evidence of this reunion spirit, we need only to return to our letter from Lincoln to Horace Greeley, the abolitionist editor of the popular *New-York Tribune*. The reason this letter is so antithetical to our understanding of slavery as being the cause of the war is because Lincoln expressed the reason the *North* went to war: to preserve the Union, not to destroy slavery. Lincoln certainly hated slavery, and hoped to see it end, but he did not think it in his powers to make it end, nor did he initially go to war aiming to end it. After a letter from Greeley prodded Lincoln to pursue emancipation, Lincoln (1862) replied:

> As to the policy I 'seem to be pursuing' ... I would save the Union. ... My paramount object in this struggle *is* to save the Union, and is *not* either to save or to destroy slavery. If I could save the Union without freeing *any* slave I would do it, and if I could save it by freeing *all* the slaves I would do it. (pp. 204–205)

This point is further exemplified by Lincoln's decision in the 1864 election to run on a "Union" ticket, rather than the "Republican" ticket he ran on in 1860 (Gallagher, 2011, p. 52). But this creates a problem. If, according to the evidence, the North fought only for reunion, then why do we have the Emancipation Proclamation and the Thirteenth Amendment (1865)?

Northern Memory: The Emancipationist Memory

The answer to the previous question involves the Emancipationist Memory. The Emancipationist Memory is arguably the most difficult to fully understand, and is likely the reason behind much of the confusion regarding slavery's role in the coming of the Civil War. The Emancipationist Memory takes two forms, which we refer to as Emancipationist Memory (A) and Emancipationist Memory (B). Emancipationist Memory (A) views emancipation as having been a great result of the war, but accepts that it was ultimately a war strategy, rather than a war aim. We understand a strategy as a means to end the war, and an aim as a reason to start the war. For example, as strategy, the Emancipation Proclamation aided in freeing slaves, resulting in a weaker Confederacy, while the Thirteenth Amendment (1865) abolished slavery, thus ensuring there would not be a second war over the same issue as the first. Combining the Emancipationist Memory (A) and the Unionist Memory of the war allows us to get closer to the reality of the causes and result of the Civil War.

The second form of the Emancipationist Memory, Emancipationist Memory (B), takes a teleological approach to the Civil War, using the outcome to define the aim of the event. The Civil War ended slavery, therefore the aim of the Civil War must have been to end slavery. Emancipationist Memory (B) confuses the cause of the Civil War with the result; as Crofts (2016) suggests:

> Today we assume that the Civil War was fought to end slavery, but we forget that no Republican supported in advance using armed force to bring about such an 'astounding' result ... The Union army went south to quell the rebellion, not to emancipate slaves—only to find that the two were inextricably interconnected. (p. 7)

For most Northerners emancipation was a result of the conflict; a result of which they were proud. They therefore often connected the Unionist Memory to the Emancipationist Memory (A). Gannon (2017) finds that "[m]en and women who supported the federal government linked Union with emancipation together because the former could not have been saved without the destruction of the latter" (pp. 19–20). As time wore on, however, it appears the teleological understanding of Emancipationist Memory (B), emancipation as an aim, began to take primacy. Blight (1989) notes in his study of Frederick Douglass, a key figure behind Emancipationist Memory (B), that Douglass "labored to shape the memory of the Civil War, then, as a skilled propagandist," "often neglected the complex, reluctant manner in which emancipation became the goal of the Union war effort," and frequently "criticized the claim that emancipation came only by 'military necessity' during the war" (pp. 98, 111, 112). Douglass, along with many African Americans living in this period, viewed this emancipationist memory as the best hope for protecting the rights of African Americans, especially as he saw African American successes slipping away during the period of reconciliation between North and South. For Douglass, if the country could be convinced it went to war to free the black man, then it had a stake in protecting that freedom. In order to protect African Americans, then, emancipation *had* to be the dominant memory of the war.

The memory of Douglass, Emancipationist Memory (B), outlived him, and appealed to the sensibilities of later generations. Gannon (2017) shows that following the post-war generation, emancipation as an aim "resonated in later decades when 'the liberation of others became understood as a critical objective for which an American military fights,'" and that, ultimately, "twentieth-century wars shaped Civil War memory" (p. 24). Going to war to free a race of people, then, became more and more alluring a memory.

Emancipation continued to eclipse reunion during the second half of the 20th century; according to Janney (2014):

> As historians began to reassess emancipation and black participation in the war in the 1970s, they simultaneously began to dismiss loyal white citizens' devotion to the Union as the most powerful motivator for the war, and in doing so, they lost sight of the true meaning of 'union' for nineteenth-century Americans. In subsequent years, historians tended to conflate the *cause* for which soldiers fought (union) with the *strategies* they employed to achieve their goal (emancipation). (pp. 1146–1147)

During the late 20th century, as the Unionist Memory fell out of favor, and more Americans identified with the Emancipationist Memory (B), the statement "the Civil War was fought over slavery" grew to represent the sole cause of the conflict, but as a result, allowed memory to take the place of history.

Conclusion: Bringing Memory and Context into the Classroom

Let us, one final time, reconsider the words of Mr. Lincoln (1862), "If I could save the Union without freeing *any* slave I would do it" (p. 205). Lincoln's words, absent of context, undermine the argument that slavery was the sole cause of the war. These words could leave our students confused, or perhaps even convinced, that slavery did not play a substantive role in the coming of the Civil War. But, provided with the context of the North's war aims, Lincoln's words serve to further explain why, in fact, the war came. Loewen (1995) uses this Lincoln letter to Horace Greeley as an example of how one could misconstrue Lincoln's message if the quotation is not extended to provide the whole context of the argument. Loewen (1995) did an analysis of 12 different textbooks to identify ways in which history has been misrepresented. As such, Loewen (1995) identifies how 9 of the 12 U.S. textbooks leave out the last sentence of the letter: "I have here stated my purpose of *official* duty, and I intend no modification of my oft-expressed *personal* wish that all men, everywhere could be free" (p. 174). Furthermore, if we consider the end of his letter, Lincoln's words provide insight into his personal hatred of slavery at the time of his writing, and his desire to see the institution abolished. Taken in totality, Lincoln's letter sheds light on his inner turmoil, desiring at once to both preserve the Union and its Constitution, and see a nation in which everyone was free. Regardless of his personal desires, however, Lincoln made clear his dedication, first and foremost, to the cause he believed his role as president demanded, the preservation of the Union.

The Civil War was, and is, messy, and without context it can be incomprehensible. A single letter, such as Lincoln's to Greeley, can confound us if we do not have a working knowledge of the memories of the Civil War. Much like the numerous gears working together to run a clock, the various memories of the Civil War are always at play beneath every piece of evidence we present to our students. When the gears fall out of sync, the clock stops. When we lose our grasp on the memory of the Civil War, our understanding stops. Lincoln's words can seem completely foreign when out of context, but when seen through the proper lens of memory, they tick right along, and we can see the thought process behind his sentiment.

Our students are doing their best without a full assortment of gears. Some students are finally coming to grips with the idea that the Civil War was fought over slavery, but when pressed further, they struggle to elaborate on what that means. We are not blameless in regard to this struggle, because we as educators and historians often fail to contextualize the depths that lie beneath that statement. With sufficient evidence, students have an opportunity to notice the same contradictions that haunted Warren (1961) when he wrote:

> [I]t is forgotten that the Republican platform of 1860 pledged protection to the institution of slavery where it existed, and that the Republicans were ready, in 1861, to guarantee slavery in the South, as bait for a return to the Union. (pp. 60–61)

With all of this in mind, how could the war have only been about slavery? The simple and accurate answer is that it was not *only* about slavery, at least not when considering both sides of the conflict. Whether talking with our students or with the public, we need to be more accurate when we answer the question "was slavery the cause of the Civil War?" The evidentiary explorations of memory in this chapter allow us to emphatically say, "Yes, slavery caused the Civil War in that the South seceded because they feared that Lincoln's election meant the end of slavery. After the secession of the South, however, the North went to war only in order to preserve the Union. During the war, the North learned that in order to defeat the South and bring them back into a lasting Union, they also had to defeat slavery." By studying the memory of the Civil War, we build a foundation that allows us to make this claim, and from that foundation we can build up a greater understanding of why exactly the war came in 1861.

References

Blight, D. W. (1989). "For something beyond the battlefield": Frederick Douglass and the struggle for the memory of the Civil War. *The Journal of American History, 75*(4), 1156–1178.

Crofts, D. W. (2016). *Lincoln and the politics of slavery: The other thirteenth amendment and the struggle to save the Union*. Chapel Hill: The University of North Carolina Press.

Dewey, J. (1931). Context and thought. In L. A. Hickman & T. M. Alexander (Eds.), *The essential Dewey: Pragmatism, education, and democracy* (Vol. 1, pp. 206–216). Bloomington/Indianapolis: Indiana University Press.

Dewey, J. (1938a). *Experience and education*. New York, NY: TOUCHSTONE.

Dewey, J. (1938b). Mathematical discourse. From logic: The theory of inquiry. In L. A. Hickman & T.M Alexander (Eds.), *The essential Dewey: Ethics logic, and psychology* (Vol. 2, pp. 180–193). Bloomington/Indianapolis: Indiana University Press.

Dew, C. (2001). *Apostles of disunion: Southern secession commissioners and the causes of the Civil War*. Charlottesville: University of Virginia Press.

Gallagher, G. W. (2011). *The Union war*. Cambridge: Harvard University Press.

Gallagher, G. W. (2000). Introduction. In G. W. Gallagher & A. T. Nolan (Eds.), *The myth of the Lost Cause and Civil War history* (pp. 1–10). Bloomington: Indiana University Press.

Gannon, B. A. (2017). *Americans remember their Civil War*. Santa Barbara, CA: Praeger.

Garrison, J. (1994). Dewey, contexts, and texts. *Educational Researcher, 23*(1), 19–20. Retrieved from http://www.jstor.org.ezproxy.lib.vt.edu/stable/1176283

Janney, C. E. (2014). Memory. In A. Sheehan-Dean (Ed.), *A companion to the U.S. Civil War* (pp. 1139–1154). West Sussex, UK: Wiley.

Janney, C. E. (2013). *Remembering the Civil War: Reunion and the limits of reconciliation*. Chapel Hill: The University of North Carolina Press.

Lincoln, A. (1862). Letter to Horace Greeley. In M. P. Johnson (Ed.), *Abraham Lincoln, slavery, and the Civil War: Selected writings and speeches* (pp. 204–205). Boston, MA: Bedford/St. Martin's.

Loewen, J. W. (1995). *Lies my teacher told me: Everything your American history textbook got wrong*. New York, NY: The New Press.

Nolan, A. T. (2000). The anatomy of the myth. In G. W. Gallagher & A. T. Nolan (Eds.), *The myth of the Lost Cause and Civil War history* (pp. 11–34). Bloomington: Indiana University Press.

Stephens, A. H. (1861). Speech delivered on the 21st March 1861, in Savannah, known as "The Corner Stone Speech," reported in the Savannah Republican. In H. Cleveland (Ed.), *Alexander H. Stephens, in public and private, with letters and speeches, before, during, and since the war* (pp. 717–729). Philadelphia, PA: National Publishing Company.

Stephens, A. H. (1868). *A constitutional view of the late war between the states* (Vol. 1). Philadelphia, PA: National Publishing Company.

Sutherland, J. J. (2010). VA textbook claims blacks fought for south in Civil War. Source? *The Internet*. Retrieved from https://www.npr.org/sections/thetwoway/2010/10/20/130693482/va-textbook-claims-blacks-fought-for-south-in-civil-war-source-the-internet.

Warren, R. P. (1961). *The legacy of the Civil War*. New York, NY: Random House.

2. Slavery Was God's Will: How Abolitionists Challenged Social and Theological Justifications for the Civil War

DAVID CHILDS

> Princes shall come out of Egypt; Ethiopia shall soon stretch out her hands unto God.
> —Psalm 68:31 (KJV)

Introduction

Psalms 68:31 is a bible passage that has been quoted by African American writers often throughout history. For some, the Ethiopian embodies the person of African descent in general, they have "stretched out their hand to God" even in the midst of struggle (Raboteau, 1983). It symbolizes the African and African American triumph over adversity and hardship, capturing their spiritual strength. Noted Princeton historian and theologian Albert Raboteau stated that this is the most quoted verse in black religious history (Fulop & Raboteau, 1997). This bible passage hearkens to black struggle and triumph. That black struggle and triumph was at the center of the war between the states.

The American Civil War is one of the most researched historical events in U.S. history. Many books, articles, lectures and films have been created surrounding the subject matter. The factors that led to the bloodiest conflict in U.S. history are varied and consist of a confluence of cultural, societal, economic, political and theological forces (McPherson, 2003; Stamp, 1991). But the primary issue that triggered a war between the states was slavery. After a long, hard battle the Union forces ultimately became the victor in the Civil War making further arguments to justify slavery pointless, as the peculiar institution had now been abolished. What were some of the ideological undertones that caused the south to embrace slavery and ultimately the Civil War? How was slavery, the Civil War and its results viewed by the 19th century religious community in the United States?

Today with the luxury of being able to look back in history it is very easy to see that anti-slavery proponents were correct in denouncing chattel slavery and all of its ugly trappings in America. However, in 19th century Southern society context, pro-slavery voices made strong arguments that often swayed the southern masses to even see slavery as God's will. There were compelling socio-religious arguments from both sides of the slavery debate. Many clergy and public intellectuals argued in support of the right to own slaves just as articulately as those that refuted it. Their endorsement of American racialized slavery was rooted in their own defense of the southern social order (Dill, 1994).

Although there were compelling theologically based arguments offered for and against slavery, in this essay I argue that the South's insistence on defending slavery and racism at all costs, tainted their scriptural analysis. This ultimately lead them to secede, thus leading to a Civil War. This chapter builds on Mark Noll's (2006) idea that the Civil War posed a "theological crisis" to religious America involving the Bible and slavery. Based on Noll's work, the essay will examine various scriptural arguments for and against slavery and the Civil War.

In the first section I will outline Noll's basic idea of how the Civil War posed a theological crisis for the South. This will allow us to establish the conceptual framework of the essay. The second section will examine the ideology and rationale behind the south's stubborn adherence to slavery. In the third section I will discuss the theological arguments for and against slavery in antebellum times. I will do this primarily by comparing and contrasting sermons, speeches and other writings that supported and refuted slavery. I will conclude by briefly highlighting implications the work has for modern discussions about race in society and in social studies classrooms.

How the Civil War Posed a Theological Crisis for the South

In Mark Noll's (2006) text entitled "The Civil War as a Theological Crisis" he explains that when the South lost the Civil War it posed a major theological crisis for them. After the war's end Southerners were at a loss because they were confident that it was God's will for them to win (Dill, 1994). Fueling this mindset were the foremost religious thinkers of the day. They told Southerners that the Confederate cause was guided by the hand of providence. Northerners felt the same way about the union cause, and seemed to be proven right at the war's end. Noll (2006) points out that "confident pronouncements about what God was 'doing' in and through the war arose in profusion from all points on the theological compass" (pp. 4–5). However, interpretations of what aspects of the events were considered "divine providence differed materially depending on the standpoint of the one who identified how God was at work" (p. 5). But much of the debate centered on the question of whose side of the conflict God was on, the North or the South.

Noll's basic premise was that these theological "clashes over the meaning of the Bible and the workings of providence ... revealed a significant theological crisis (p. 12)." Americans in the 19th century were deeply religious. In 1850, ten million (40%) of the total population were active evangelical Christians attending church regularly. This was the largest subculture in U.S. society at the time. These figures do not include other religious groups such as Catholics, Mormons and Jews. In this way, religious ideology had a great influence on public opinion. To further demonstrate this point the ratio of U.S. mail carriers to clergy was 1 to 1 in 1860, "in 2006 the ratio was nine to one" (p. 12).

Both sides of the debate tried to make sense of slavery and the Civil War from a scriptural lens, which created a crisis of sorts. Noll argues that this theological crisis had several components.

- Firstly, He points out that there was "a failure to examine biblically the Southern charge that individualistic consumer capitalism was an ethnically dangerous economic system" (p. 74). That is, because the theological debate was so focused on whether or not the Bible defended or refuted slavery, clergy did not give enough attention to what scripture might have to say about the evils of individualistic consumer capitalism. From a moral standpoint the economic system had many perils, for example, it helped to justify the existence of chattel slavery, which made Southern critiques of Northern consumer capitalism hypocritical.
- Secondly, "abolitionists flight to the idea of the "spirit of Scripture" served as a blow to Christian orthodoxy." Many abolitionists such as Lloyd Garrison did not necessarily fully look to the Bible for justification, but instead looked to a sort of Christian humanism or republican ideals (pp. 35–36). Traditional Protestants saw this as an attack on biblical authority. This in turn weakened the anti-slavery biblical argument, thereby making pro-slavery arguments more popular with the Bible believing South.

- Thirdly, much of the theological debate centered on whether or not the Bible supported or justified slavery of any kind. But this seemed to create "an inability to act on biblical teaching about the full humanity of all people, regardless of race." The theological debate on both sides did not adequately address the "Negro question" and America's particular brand of racist, chattel slavery (p. 51).
- Lastly, there seemed to be "a confusion about principles of interpretation between what was in the Bible and what was in the common sense of culture" (p. 74). Pro-slavery minister's lengthy literalist biblical exegesis was corrupted by their staunch adherence to the Southern ideals and their commitment to the institution of slavery. Anti-slavery ministers more often than pro-slavery proponents overly relied on humanistic and altruistic arguments when interpreting the Bible to refute slavery.

For the remainder of this chapter I will primarily draw from Noll's last three points concerning racial equality as taught in the Bible and the confusion about scriptural interpretation between biblical passages and common sense of culture. I will also make some brief references to the first two points in a limited way in the remainder of the essay as well. Although Southerners were dissuaded by anti-slavery arguments that adhered to the "the spirit of scripture," strong and articulate cases were made that sufficiently challenged the pro-slavery arguments, as we will see later in the essay (p. 35).

Key Factors of Southern Ideology that Influenced Clergy Views on slavery

At the beginning of the 19th century most of the ministers in the South would have at least given that slavery was "to be tolerated" and eventually abolished in the United States. This included Presbyterian clergy who were generally Calvinists. In fact, most southern Calvinists agreed with churches in the North whose "hope and assumption" was "that slavery would be a temporary institution, believing as mankind progressed toward the millennium, institutions that were harmful would fall to the wayside" (Dill, 1994, pp. 79–80). However, as the south became more and dependent on slavery for economic success the position of southern clergy began to "move toward a more affirmative conception of slavery in general, and in favor of the variety practiced in the American South in particular" (p. 80).

Dill outlines several key factors that influenced Southern minister's views on slavery and the Bible, which brought about a shift in their theology. Firstly,

Slavery Was God's Will

the basis for the South's economic strength was agriculture. The geographic location and climate of the south made it possible to harvest a variety of crops in large quantity. The North was limited in its agricultural abilities due to colder climates and geographic properties that did not lend itself to the harvesting of certain crops. In the south "Slavery became very profitable in conjunction with growing staple crops, especially cotton ... southern clergy, particularly Presbyterians, went by the wayside with the onslaught of the cotton boom" (p. 81). In this way, Southern ministers faced a theological crisis in that the economic wellbeing of Southern society as a whole was being propped up by slavery.

Secondly, Southerners felt their "sense of honor and morality" being challenged by the increased attacks on the institution of slavery by abolitionists. These ideas began to influence the sermons and theology of clergy. From this thinking "Southern Presbyterian ministers were inspired to find scriptural justifications to defend and confirm the South's honor, morality, and peculiar institution" (p. 81). Edward Crowther (1952) in his doctoral dissertation argued that the shift in clergy views on slavery were influenced by an increase in Abolitionist activity. Crowther went on to say that Southern minister's views went from slavery as a "tolerated evil" to being considered a "positive good" (p. 129).

Thirdly, Noll argues that the "South suffered from certain phobias concerning its culture and social structure. Every white person in the South knew his position in society." Americans of European decent belonged to the "white aristocracy," and all black slaves were by nature inferior and even subhuman. In this way, "no matter what financial standing a white person had in the antebellum South, there was always "white equality" because the slaves were at the bottom of the southern social stratification." Noll also went on to say that "Southerners feared slave uprisings and rebellions would incite the slave population to revolt against the southern social order, though very few uprisings actually occurred." Southern Presbyterians (one of the leading denominations in the south) generally "feared any change in their social structure that might alter the South's white equality and racial unity" (Noll, 1994, p. 82).

Lastly, this shift in clergy views on slavery from being an evil that was tolerated to a positive institution ordained by God "was solidified by the scriptural literalism espoused by Old School Calvinism in the South." Presbyterian ministers in the south who supported slavery began putting forth the argument that the "Scriptures acknowledged the existence of slavery as a legitimate system without evaluating it as bad or temporary." This is an example of the "confusion about principles of interpretation" that Noll has observed as a part of the theological crisis that existed (p. 74). In this way pro-slavery clergy never properly addressed the specific sins of American slavery, such as rape, murder, kidnapping and adultery. Most of the sermons (with some exceptions) made blanket arguments in support of slavery in general. In fact "The Bible, they believed, was purposefully silent as to slavery being a sin or an evil to be extinguished" (pp. 81–82).

Sermons and Writings for and Against Slavery of the Nineteenth Century

The sermons, speeches and writings of ministers from both sides of the argument were often so popular they were published widely. Debates were very public affairs and well attended. One of the best examples was the four day debate between two clergymen; the moderate emancipationist Nathaniel Rice and abolitionist Jonathan Blanchard. The debate lasted eight hours each day (Noll, p. 41). I will examine writings and speeches from both sides to get an idea of the arguments given. The historical background, speeches, sermons and writings will highlight the theological crisis that emerged as a result of the Civil War and slavery.

One of the earliest defenders of American slavery from a biblical perspective was the Reverend James Smylie of the Presbytery of Mississippi. In Reverend Smylie's (1836) published sermon entitled "A Review of the Letter from the Presbytery of Chillicothe to the Presbytery of Mississippi, on the Subject of Slavery" he stated, "I have, years ago, entered seriously on the investigation of the question, is slavery in itself sinful." He states that upon his "examination of the scriptures" and historical research he "arrived at the conviction, that slavery, itself, is not sinful." He goes on to say that "the evils of slavery, like the evils of matrimony, may be traced to the neglect of duties incumbent upon the individuals sustaining the relation" (pp. 15–16). Later in his sermon he evokes the curse of Ham theology, that was widely used as a justification for the subjugation of the black race. Pro-slavery advocates and proponents of racist theology have longed used Genesis 9:21–25 to justify slavery. Verse 25 states "And he said, Cursed be Canaan; a servant of servants shall he be unto his brethren." This view has since been disputed as the text does not say Ham (from whom some scholars believe Africans descended) was cursed. But Canaan, Ham's son was to be cursed. In short, this was the sort of theology that influenced the everyday mindset of the southerner in the 1860s. The Southern Presbyterians of South Carolina took an official position in support of slavery in October 1836 stating that:

> The church has no right to prescribe rules and dictate principles which can bind or affect the conscience in reference to slavery; and any such attempt would constitute ecclesiastical tyranny; ... and whosoever has a conscience too tender to recognize this relation as lawful ... has submitted his neck to the yoke of man, sacrificed his Christian liberty of conscience, and leaves the infallible word of God for the fancies and doctrines of men. (Minutes of the Harmony Presbytery in Zebulon Crocker, 1837, as cited in Dill, 1994, p. 78)

Theologically Presbyterians were staunch predestinationists. Therefore, these clergy "concluded that some had been placed in authority over others by the providential hand of God" (78).

Pro-slavery sermons are plentiful throughout the 19th century. Even some ministers that preached in the North were supporters of the slave system in the United States. Reverend Van Dyke (1861) of the First Presbyterian Church in Brooklyn supported the institution of slavery. In his Fast Day sermon entitled "The Character and Influence of Abolitionism," Van Dyke drew his text from I Timothy 6:1–5, which states in verse 1 "Let as many servants as are under the yoke count their own masters worthy of all honour, that the name of God and his doctrine be not blasphemed." He used this verse to make the case that slavery is biblical. Van Dyke draws four main conclusions about abolitionism in his sermon and they are as follows:

1. Abolitionism has no foundation in the Scriptures.
2. Its principles have been promulgated chiefly by misrepresentation and abuse.
3. It leads in multitudes of cases, and by logical process, to utter infidelity.
4. It is the chief cause of the strife that agitates, and the danger that threatens, our country (p. 9).

Although Van Dyke was a learned man, he was still blinded by the anti-slavery rhetoric of his time. This prevented him from making a proper scriptural analysis of the unique brand of American chattel slavery that was racist in nature.

As we have noted, there were also many clergy that openly critiqued the institution of slavery. Reverend Henry Ward Beecher (brother of *Uncle Tom Cabin* author Harriet Beecher Stowe) was the most renowned preacher in the North in 1860s. He was also noted for his strong anti-slavery stance. On the same day Van Dyke preached a sermon in support of slavery in New York, Beecher strongly denounced the institution. He stated that slavery was a "national sin." He went on to say that "where the Bible has been in the household, and read without hindrance by parents and children together—there you have an indomitable yeomanry, a state that would not have a tyrant on the throne, a government that would not have a slave or a serf on the field" (Beecher, 1861, as cited in Noll, 2006, p. 2). Beecher argued in the spirit of the great awakening, believing that if bibles are present in people's homes the literate can read and find out for themselves that God condemns slavery. This was a contradiction to traditional worship, where clergy played a central role in controlling the religious narrative (Noll, 2006).

The African American Theological Argument Against Slavery

It is probably not surprising that some of the most bold and clear theological arguments against slavery came from black clergy. In the early 19th century African American ministers had begun challenging the pro-slavery arguments using scripture. By the advent of the Civil War there had already arisen a well-established tradition of biblical commentary on slavery from the black community (Noll, 2006).

The African Methodist Episcopal (AME) church was noted for its open anti-slavery stance. Several AME clergy during the 19th century were well-known for their unabashed anti-slavery stance. Bishop Richard Allen (1833), founded the AME church as a protest against the racist practices of the Methodist Episcopal Church in Philadelphia. In his memoir *The Life, Experience, and Gospel Labours of the Rt. Rev. Richard Allen*, he includes a chapter entitled "An Address to Those Who Keep Slaves, and Approve the Practice" where he uses scripture in a sort of common sense tone to attack the American slave system. Allen urges white America "to consider how hateful slavery is, in the sight of that God who hath destroyed kings and princes, for their oppression of the poor slaves." Moving into biblical references he states that "Pharaoh and his princes with the posterity of king Saul, were destroyed by the protector and avenger of slaves. Would you not suppose the Israelites to be utterly unfit for freedom, and that it was impossible for them, to obtain to any degree of excellence?" Allen boldly rails against slave masters stating that "Men must be willfully blind, and extremely partial, that cannot see the contrary effects of liberty and slavery upon the mind of man." Using a well-known analogy among black clergy he compares white slave masters to pharaoh, which makes African Americans by default Israel (God's chosen people). But Allen remarkably assures American oppressors that he does not hate them. He states "that God who knows the hearts of all men ... hath strictly forbidden it [hatred] to his *chosen people*, 'Thou shalt not abhor an Egyptian, because thou wast a stranger in his land.' Deut. 23:7" (Allen, 1833, p. 45). Allen was very active abolitionist, the church he founded was an Underground railroad station until his death in 1831 (Childs, 2009).

Other noteworthy anti-slavery AME ministers included Bishop Daniel Payne and Rev. Daniel Coker. Bishop Daniel Payne (1839) was the first president of the historically black Wilberforce University. He was a learned man, seminary trained and had mastered the languages of Greek, Latin and French (Payne, 1888). An outspoken opponent of slavery, he used his oratorical skills and status to attack the institution. In his sermon entitled "Slavery Brutalizes a Man" he argues that slavery leads humans to sin and rebel against God. In an elaborate sermon he argues that the nature of slavery as it is manifested in the United States leads to sinful practices such as adultery and urges slaves to serve their white masters and not God. He ends his sermon with a thunderous conclusion stating:

> In a word, slavery tramples the laws of the living God under its unhallowed feet–weakens and destroys the influence which those laws are calculated to exert over the mind of man, and constrains the oppressed to blaspheme the name of the Almighty.

In urging his Christian brethren to denounce slavery he states "Awake to the battle and hurl the hottest thunders of divine truth at the head of this cruel monster, until he shall fall to rise no more, and the groans of the enslaved are converted into the songs of the free!!" (Payne, 1839).

One of the most elaborate and articulate biblical arguments against slavery came from AME minister Daniel Coker (1810). In his widely circulated pamphlet "A Dialogue Between a Virginian and an African Minister" Coker offers a clearly constructed point-by-point refutation of pro-slavery arguments. He uses the format of a friendly dialog between a white Virginian slave owner and a African American Minister. The tone of the text is not radical or revolutionary but offers reasonable solutions. Coker proposes the idea of a type of gradual emancipation where slaves are paid for their labor so that they may ultimately buy back their freedom. Perhaps more pertinent to this study is Coker's masterful scripture analysis. Under the guise of the Virginia slave owner's questions he cites scripture that were commonly used to defend slavery. And in a systematic careful way he carefully refutes each argument.

The Virginia slave owner used the scripture oft quoted by pro-slavery proponents "Servants, obey in all things your masters according to the flesh" (Colossians 3:22, KJV). However, the minister refuted his argument by placing the scripture in context. He also provided a lengthy defense against the claim that Abraham had slaves and thus Americans are justified in having black slaves. For example, he expounds upon Genesis 17 where foreigners that were slaves in Abraham's house were to be circumcised and become a part of the family of God. Coker states:

Abraham was commanded to circumcise all that were born in his house or bought with money; We find in the sequel of the chapter, that he obeyed the command without delay ... By Divine appointment, not only Abraham, and his seed, but *he that was bought with money*, of any stranger that was not of his seed ... received the token of the covenant (which was circumcision). Coker goes on to say that "these persons bought with money, were no longer looked upon as uncircumcised and unclean; as aliens and strangers; but were incorporated with the church and nation of the Israelites." Therefore "they should be properly educated, made free and enjoy all the common privileges of citizens."

Coker in his extensive argument to further solidify his point cites Leviticus 25:42 "For they are my servants, which I brought forth out of the land of Egypt: they shall not be sold as bondmen." He concludes this section of the argument by stating that these passages of scripture which the slave owner used to support slavery does not support the American enslavement of Africans but in fact "they evidently forbid it" and does not at all support the "lawfulness of your enslaving the children of Africa" but clearly "condemns the practice as criminal" (Coker, p. 58).

In contrast to Coker's friendly, reasonable dialog David Walker (1829) brought a radical message of rebuke against slaveholding America. He called for immediate emancipation. Walker, a black minister in Boston and son of a slave, in his "Appeal ... to the Colored Citizens of the World" used scripture to attack the hypocrisy of a slaveholding nation that speaks of freedom and characterizes themselves as Christians. He urged African Americans to rebel, terrifying Southern White society. But Walker was perhaps prophetic when he predicted that violence will come to the United States (read Civil War) as a result of its sinful practice of slavery. Other noteworthy African American clergy and spokesmen such as Frederick Douglass and Christian writer Daniel Ruggles made similar arguments against slavery.

African Americans who spoke against slavery had a unique perspective. Because they were both African and American they were not blinded by the racism that was often inherent in the arguments of Southern White clergy. As W.E.B. Dubois pointed out nearly a half a century after slavery:

> It is a peculiar sensation, this double-consciousness ... One ever feels his twoness, an American, a Negro; two souls, two thoughts, two unreconciled strivings; two warring ideals in one dark body, whose dogged strength alone keeps it from being torn asunder. (Dubois, 1903, p. 2)

In this way, the black community did not suffer as much from a theological crisis as their white counterparts. They read the Civil War as being divinely ordained by God to bring about their freedom.

Conclusion

Based on the resources mentioned throughout this chapter it is clear that clergy on both sides of the slavery debate were often articulate and very learned men. With pro-slavery arguments so carefully crafted and rooted in scripture, it is no wonder that much of the South (as religious as they were) vehemently supported slavery, secession and by default the Civil War. However, as we have pointed out, the South's insistence on defending slavery and racism at all costs, tainted their scriptural understanding of the issue. Therefore, the South could justify secession and the Civil War because after all, they felt that God was on their side. Although the end of the Civil War and the passage of the 13th, 14th and 15th amendments effectively abolished slavery and gave African Americans their freedom the historic pro-slavery arguments fueled much of the racist ideology throughout the Jim Crow era and even into modern times.

Using This Material in Social Studies Classrooms

The study of the American Civil War is a broad topic that is multi-faceted and complex. It is a historical topic that is covered in high school classrooms across the country. Studying a topic such as the theological debate over slavery and the Civil War can help students understand the ideological and philosophical roots that divided the United States in the 1860s. By exploring this topic in-depth students can make larger connections about accepting difference and learning how dangerous ideas can fuel hate and prejudice even in modern times.

References

Allen, R. (1833). *The life, experience, and gospel labours of the Rt. Rev. Richard Allen. To which is annexed the rise and progress of the African Methodist episcopal church in the United States of America. Containing a narrative of the yellow fever in the year of our lord 1793: With an address to the people of colour in the United States.* Philadelphia, PA: Martin & Boden, Printers.

Barnes, A. (1857). *The church and slavery.* Philadelphia, PA: Parry & McMillan.

Childs, D. J. (2009). *The black church and African American education: The African Methodist Episcopal Church educating for liberation, 1816–1893* (Ph.D. dissertation). Miami University.

Coker, D. (1810). *A dialogue between a Virginian and an African minister (1810).* Baltimore, MD: Printed by Benjamin Edes.

Crowther, E. R. (1986). *Southern protestants, slavery and secession: A study in religious ideology, 1830–1861* (Ph.D. dissertation). Auburn University.

Dill, R. P. (1994). *A rhetorical analysis of selected pro-slavery sermons by Presbyterian clergy in the antebellum south* (Dissertation). Louisiana State University.

Du Bois, W. E. B. (1903). *The souls of black folk*. New York, NY: Dover.

Dyke, H. V. (1861). *The character and influence of abolitionism*. Washington, DC: Henry Polkinhorn.

Fulop, T. E., & Raboteau, A. J. (Eds.). (1997). *African-American religion: Interpretive essays in history and culture*. New York, NY: Routledge.

Maddex, J. P., Jr. (1979, Fall). The southern apostasy revisited: The significance of Proslavery Christianity. *Marxist Perspectives*, p. 134.

McPherson, J. (2003). *Battle cry of freedom: The civil war era*. Oxford: Oxford University Press.

Noll, M. (1994). *The scandal of the evangelical mind*. Grand Rapids: Eerdmans.

Noll, M. (2006) The Civil War as a Theological Crisis. Chapel Hill: University of North Carolina Press.

Presbytery of Mississippi. (1836). *On the subject of slavery*. Woodville, MS: Wm. A. Norris.

Payne, D.A. (1839). Slavery Brutalizes Man. Fort Plain, NY: Lutheran Herald and Journal.

Payne, D. A. (1888). *Recollections of seventy years*. Nashville, TN: Publishing House of the AME Sunday School Union.

Raboteau, A. (1983). *Ethiopia shall soon stretch forth her hands: Black destiny in nineteenth-century America*. Phoenix: Arizona State University.

Smylie, J. (1836). *A review of a letter from the Presbytery of Chillicothe to the Presbytery of Mississippi, on the subject of slavery*. Woodville, MS: Wm. A. Norris.

Stampp, K. (1967). *The peculiar institution: Slavery in the antebellum south*. New York, NY: Alfred A. Knopf.

Stampp, K. (1991). *The causes of the civil war*. New York, NY: Simon and Schuster.

Thornwell, J. H. (1852). *Report on the subject of slavery presented to the synod of South Carolina*. Columbia, SC: Steam-power Press of A.S. Johnston.

Walker, D. (1829). *Walker's appeal, in four articles; together with a preamble, to the coloured citizens of the world, but in particular, and very expressly, to those of the United States of America*. Boston, MA: David Walker.

3. Through the Heart: "Jim Brown" and the Murder of Dr. Walter Alves Norwood in Henderson County, Kentucky

EMILY D. MOSES

On April 1, 1860, just south of Henderson, Kentucky, Dr. Walter Alves Norwood lay on the ground of his stable, dead. Moments prior, a runaway slave, known to those in the town as "Jim Brown," pulled a gun on the doctor and "shot [him] through the left breast," through the heart (Major, 1861). What pushed Jim Brown to murder a respected white male of the Henderson County community? All evidence points towards one reason: slavery.

Born in North Carolina, Walter Norwood attended the University of North Carolina to study medicine (Dialectic Society, 1890, p. 70). Some years later, Dr. Norwood, moved to Henderson County, Kentucky. He served the city of Henderson with the practice of Dr. Robert P. Letcher; they grew the office to be the largest in the city. By 1856, Dr. Norwood had married Mary Lambert, with whom he later had two children (Mary Lambert, 1856). The new family retreated to the country to raise their children, open a private practice, and cultivate crops. Like most white people in Kentucky, Dr. Norwood owned slaves. At the time of his death in 1860, Norwood was well respected in the county, partly to do with his medical practice. So how did the county physician die at the hands of a runaway slave? It is likely he was at the wrong place at the wrong time; however, his death should not shock historians. Tension over the abolition of slavery meant that any white man shot by an African American, whether enslaved or free, would elicit a hasty emotional and irrational response. The bigger issue here is how tensions became so volatile.

Historians have charged the role of slavery as the cause of the Civil War for years. Due to the Lost Cause narrative established by former confederates and sympathizers, educators find themselves in a position to set the record straight and teach slavery as the cause of the war. Even so, secondary educators cannot do this alone. The field of Civil War history continues to change and uncover new evidence illuminating the causes of the war. Scholars of this era need to find ways to reach out to secondary teachers and give them the resources to teach the new material in their classrooms. The Civil War Governors of Kentucky Digital Documentary Edition (CWGK), housed at the Kentucky Historical Society, is trying to do just that. CWGK promotes scholarly research while forging lasting connections in the classroom. Most importantly, the project promotes the value of primary source research in leading to new understandings of timeless topics. The murder of Dr. Norwood by Jim Brown in 1860 shows how essential slavery was to the war by highlighting the legal parameters that those enslaved persons navigated and how a state chose "armed neutrality" instead of a side—especially critical in a nationwide battle where it sat geographically in the dead middle.

Students of this era often think of Kentucky as a Union state, that because it was farther north it therefore supported abolition. This is false. Kentucky, admitted to the United States in 1792, was a slave state. While it did not support as many large plantations as states in the Deep South, Kentucky's economy was still deeply invested in the institution of slavery. The Commonwealth held the unique position of bordering the Deep South's plantations and the free North. The citizens of the Commonwealth of Kentucky wanted to protect slavery and believed they could do so on their own, at least for a time. Most Kentuckians in 1861 agreed with Senator Archibald Dixon when he stated, "I think the true ground for Kentucky is either in the Union or an armed neutrality" (Arnett, 1976, p. 51). Though Kentucky took up "armed neutrality," when confederate troops invaded the state in 1861, neutrality ended in Kentucky, and the state aligned with the Union (Harris, 2011, p. 93). However, Kentucky had another reason for remaining in the Union. By 1860, it was not yet the intention of the federal government to dismantle and outlaw slavery. The Commonwealth wanted to preserve the institution and believed that aligning itself with the Union would permit them to do so. White slaveholding Kentuckians armed themselves to show both the North and the South that they would not be persuaded to choose a side. Citizens were heavily armed for that purpose before the start of the Civil War but had to give up neutrality, under pressure from the federal government to remain in the Union. With the installation of the Louisville and Nashville Railroad (L&N) in 1850, it was ever important for Kentucky to remain neutral: it served as the gate to trade for both the Union and Confederacy. Nevertheless, in the years to come, Kentuckians would begin to speak out against what they considered overreach by the federal government, in the hopes of preserving the slaveholding institution (Magoffin, 1860, pp. 4–15).

The death of Dr. Norwood details how committed white Kentuckians were to slavery. But more than that, it highlights the lengths to which they would go to preserve their power. "Armed Neutrality" allowed for white citizens to hold onto their authority and slavery. Blood spattered the floor of the Norwood barn, and a dark shadow lingered upon the body and "after leisurely viewing the dead body of the murdered man—made for the woods" (Major, 1861). With the town doctor dead, members of the community wrote to Kentucky's Governor Beriah Magoffin requesting he take action, while others headed to the woods in search of the suspect (Image 3.1). Alex H. Major, a farmer in Henderson County, stated, "it is the universal opinion, that if taken, he will be immediately punished without a moments hearing … those in search of him are armed with double barrel shotguns and will in all probability shoot him down upon sight" (Major, 1861). The problem here and in other places revolved around the fact that Kentucky bordered the slaveholding Deep South and the free North. It was unlikely that Brown

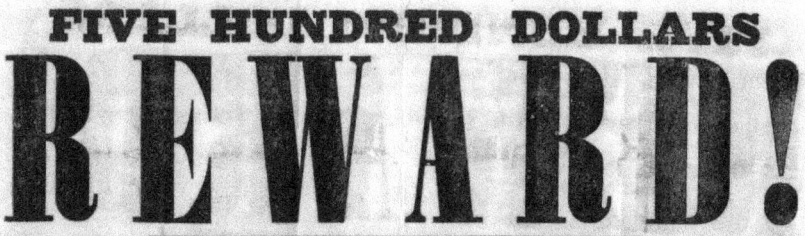

Image 3.1: Wanted poster for Jim Brown, April 4, 1861. Kentucky Historical Society. Reprinted with permission

would run farther south. Henderson County lies along the Ohio River, bordering Indiana, and for slaves, it thus rested on the border of freedom. There were two areas for these so-called bounty hunters to search: first, Henderson County and second, across the Ohio River in Indiana.

Rhetoric of the 1850s shows that anti-slavery leaders believed that the federal government sought to promote the agenda of slaveholders and disregarded white males who were not slaveholders. Abolitionists were proven correct when Congress passed the Fugitive Slave Law (or Act) as part of the Compromise of 1850 on September 18. This law allowed the federal government to allow private citizens to arrest fugitive slaves and, ultimately, to bring the national problem of slavery to every doorstep, extending the grasp of slavery from slaveholders to non-slaveholders. Slaves were denied basic trial, and northern courts could not interfere in the capture of a fugitive. However, this law also meant that free African Americans were just as susceptible to these roundups. To assist in the return of fugitives, those in search of runaway slaves could insist that northern citizens aid them in the capture. Jim Brown already escaped once from his mistress's home prior to the incident in 1860: In 1859, Brown fled the state for the freedom of Indiana for more than three months before returning to his mistress.[1] Robert Glass referred to the instance in his letter Governor Magoffin in 1861 stating that, "It is feared that he [Jim Brown] has gone to Indiana (where the stepfather of his mistress lives & who harbored him for four months last year while runaway)" (Glass, 1861). Nevertheless, what brought Jim back to Kentucky was the love he held for his wife.

Accounts indicate that Jim Brown had a wife, whom on multiple occasions he requested to see but was continually denied by her owner, Furna A. Cannon. While Seraphine Pentecost owned Jim Brown, Furna Cannon owned Brown's wife. Determined to be with his wife, Brown once again ran away in hope that he could get to his wife and that they could escape together.[2] Being on this border of freedom, "The [Ohio] river held both terror and hope for slaves and made slavery in Henderson County more

---

1. Please note that the letter indicates that the slave was brought back to his owner, Seraphine Pentecost, but it does not state if he came back on his own volition or if bounty hunters captured him.
2. While there are no accounts written by Brown himself, the documents, and secondary literature, all point to this being the cause for Brown's escape. Because Brown and his wife were enslaved by different persons, there is no record of their marriage. The 1850 and 1860 censuses do show that both Pentecost and Furna owned slaves. Once again, the census did not record the names of slaves, just the quantity owned by slaveholder.

complicated" (King & Thurman, 1991). Slaves in Henderson County could see their freedom but could not have it. Though freedom was in sight, the river harbored fear too—the constant apprehension of being sold down river. For any fugitive, it was paramount that they should continue to move north as fast as possible. In several instances, runaway slaves were hunted down with no cost spared, making Brown again distinctive because he left bondage once only to return and then run away again. Due to his extensive knowledge of the land in Henderson County, he was able to evade his pursuers.

Jim Brown spent days hiding in the woods and surrounding areas after his most recent escape from his mistress, which led to him hiding in the barn of Dr. Walter Norwood. In correspondence from Alex H. Major to Governor Magoffin, Major described how on the evening of April 1 upon being told that there "was a man in the stable loft," Dr. Norwood went to the stable to inquire after the man. The letter read, "Upon seeing the man there he asked his name business &c to which the Negro replied, that he had run away some days before from his mistress." Dr. Norwood then told the man to come down, to which Jim Brown replied that he would not come down. The doctor called for a slave to bring him his gun, and upon that action, Brown "sprang towards him, at the same time shot him through the left breast, with a large [dueling] pistol" (Major, 1861). Brown fled to the woods once again. Upon hearing the news of the death of Dr. Norwood, Captain Bill Quinn, a member of the community, led a search party, equipped with bloodhounds, into the woods and fields to locate Brown. Their initial search proved unsuccessful. Wanting to capture the murderer, the citizens of Henderson County issued a reward of $300 for the "capture, 'dead or alive' of the slave 'Jim Brown'… In addition it is expected that the Governor of the state will offer a reward for his apprehension" (Cannon et al., 1861). The citizens of Henderson County got their wish and on April 12, 1860 Governor Magoffin offered a reward of $250 for the capture of Brown. After continued search of the county, citizens John Quinn, Bunk Hurt, and John H. Marshall discovered Brown hiding in the barn of William J. Marshall, where John H. Marshall "fired, the ball striking him [Brown] in the right temple, causing instant death" (Starling, 1965, pp. 560–561). His murderers were exonerated on the consensus that they did what was best for the community.

Henderson County's experience with the deaths of Brown and Dr. Norwood highlights the distinctiveness of Kentucky as a border state and a unique piece of the larger picture of the nation in the Civil War. CWGK continues to examine the place Kentucky held during the war years. It is important to understand the causes of the Civil War, but it is equally important to grasp how everyday Kentuckians and Americans reacted to growing dissonance across the nation. While Kentucky decisively attempted "armed neutrality," in the end it failed. Slavery remained at the core of the Commonwealth's economy, politics, and culture. The state believed that by remaining with the Union the institution of slavery would continue to be preserved. The Civil War and "Armed Neutrality" created chaos across Kentucky. There should be no doubt that the cause of the Civil War should and is attributed to the institution of slavery. With the implementation of the Fugitive Slave Law in 1850, slavery became an issue for every individual in the United States, Henderson County's story is a prime example of that. Scholars and students at all levels should take micro-histories, such as Jim Brown, and use them to support a more intensive and comprehensive learning experience that is not afraid of asking the difficult questions.

References

Primary Sources

Dialectic Society. (1890). *Catalogue of the members of the dialectic society instituted in the University of North Carolina* (p. 70). Baltimore, MD: Isaac Friedenwald Press.

Cannon, F. A., et al. (1861, April 4). *Five hundred dollars reward!* (Office of the Governor, Beriah Magoffin: Governor's Official Correspondence File, Petitions for Pardons and Remissions, 1859–1862, MG19-518). Frankfort: Kentucky Department for Libraries and Archives. Accessed via the *Civil War Governors of Kentucky Digital Documentary Edition*, discovery.civilwargovernors.org/document/KYR-0001-020-0958.

Robert Glass to Beriah Magoffin. (1861, April 4). Office of the Governor, Beriah Magoffin: Governor's Official Correspondence File, Apprehension of Fugitives from Justice Papers, 1859–1862, MG8-112 to MG8-113. Frankfort: Kentucky Department for Libraries and Archives. Accessed via the Civil War Governors of Kentucky Digital Documentary Edition, discovery.civilwargovernors.org/document/KYR-0001-021-0028.

Robert Glass to Unknown. (1861, April 4). Office of the Governor, Beriah Magoffin: Governor's Official Correspondence File, Apprehension of Fugitives from Justice Papers, 1859–1862, MG8-110 to MG8-111. Frankfort: Kentucky Department for Libraries and Archives. Accessed via the *Civil War Governors of Kentucky Digital Documentary Edition*, discovery.civilwargovernors.org/document/KYR-0001-021-0027

"Mary Lambert". (1856, April 29). Kentucky Birth, Marriage and Death Records, Microfilm (1852–1910). *KDLA*, Roll #994035, Henderson County Marriages, p. 113.

Alex H. Major to Beriah Magoffin. (1861, April 3). Office of the Governor, Beriah Magoffin: Governor's Official Correspondence File, Apprehension of Fugitives from Justice Papers, 1859–1862, MG8-114 to MG8-115. Frankfort: Kentucky Department for Libraries and Archives. Accessed via the Civil War Governors of Kentucky Digital Documentary Edition, discovery.civilwargovernors.org/document/KYR-0001-021-0029.

Letter of Beriah Magoffin, Governor of the Commonwealth of Kentucky. (1860, December 28). *The war of the rebellion: A compilation of the official records of the union and confederate armies.* Washington, DC, 1880–1902, Ser.4, I: 4–15.

L.W. Trafton to Beriah Magoffin. (1861, April 9). Office of the Governor, Beriah Magoffin: Governor's Official Correspondence File, Apprehension of Fugitives from Justice Papers, 1859–1862, MG8-108. Frankfort: Kentucky Department for Libraries and Archives. Accessed via the *Civil War Governors of Kentucky Digital Documentary Edition*, discovery.civilwargovernors.org/document/KYR-0001-021-0025

Unknown, Note. (n.d.). Office of the Governor, Beriah Magoffin: Governor's Official Correspondence File, Apprehension of Fugitives from Justice Papers, 1859–1862, MG8-109. Frankfort: Kentucky Department for Libraries and Archives. Accessed via the *Civil War Governors of Kentucky Digital Documentary Edition*, discovery.civilwargovernors.org/document/KYR-0001-021-0026

Unknown, Note. (1861, April 12). Office of the Governor, Beriah Magoffin: Governor's Official Correspondence File, Apprehension of Fugitives from Justice Papers, 1859–1862, MG8-116. Frankfort: Kentucky Department for Libraries and Archives. Accessed via the *Civil War Governors of Kentucky Digital Documentary Edition*, discovery.civilwargovernors.org/document/KYR-0001-021-0030

U.S. Census Bureau. (1860). *Eighth manuscript census of the United States, population schedules* (p. 85). Henderson County, KY.

Secondary Sources

Arnett, M. (1976). *The annals and scandals of Henderson County, Kentucky, 1775–1975* (p. 51). Corydon, KY: Fremar Publishing Company.

Astor, A. (2017). *Rebels on the border: Civil War, emancipation, and the reconstruction of Kentucky and Missouri.* Baton Rouge: Louisiana State University Press.

Blight, D. (2002). *Race and reunion: The Civil War in American memory.* Cambridge, MA: Harvard University Press.

Emberton, C. (2013). *Beyond redemption: Race, violence, and the American south after the Civil War.* Chicago, IL: University of Chicago Press.

Gallagher, G. W. (2012). *The Union War.* Cambridge, MA: Harvard University Press.

Harris, W. C. (2011). *Lincoln and the Border States: Preserving the Union* (p. 93). Lawrence: University of Kansas.

Johnson, W. (2017). *River of dark dreams: Slavery and empire in the Cotton kingdom.* Cambridge, MA: Harvard University Press.

King, G., & Thurman, S. (1991). *Currents: Henderson's river book.* Henderson, Ky.: Mail orders to Henderson county public library. Frankfort: Kentucky Historical Society.

Lewis, P. (2015). *For slavery and union: Benjamin Buckner and Kentucky loyalties in the Civil War*. Lexington: University of Kentucky Press.

Marshall, A. E. (2010). *Creating a Confederate Kentucky. The Lost Cause and Civil War memory in a Border State*. Chapel Hill: University of North Carolina Press.

Starling, E. (1965). *History of Henderson County, Kentucky: Comprising history of county and city, precincts, education, churches, secret societies, leading enterprises, sketches and recollections, and biographies of the living and dead* (pp. 560–561). Evansville, IN: Unigraphic Inc.

Varon, E. (2008). *Disunion!: The coming of the American Civil War: 1789–1859*. Chapel Hill: University of North Carolina Press.

4. A Historical Inquiry into John Brown and His Raiders

John H. Bickford and Bonnie Laughlin-Schultz

Federal determination to resupply—and Confederate blockade of—a federal arsenal in Fort Sumter sparked the Civil War, yet the conflict originated over slavery. No matter the subsequent revisionist rebranding of the conflict as about states' rights, slavery's import to the American South is evidenced in contemporaneous historical documents such as Confederate states' declarations of secession and Confederate politicians' and generals' speeches. The plantation aristocracy—few, fearful of losing their wealth's foundation, and politically powerful—used racial solidarity calls, fears of miscegenation, and a patriarchal order turned upside down to rouse rural masses to support political departure (Isenberg, 2016; McCurry, 1995). Southerners' trepidation of Northern restriction of slavery had brimmed for decades with sectional flare-ups over territorial acquisitions and statehood from Missouri to California to Kansas. While Haiti, Denmark Vesey, Nat Turner, Amistad, and other revolts alarmed chattel slave owners, John Brown's raid was particularly troubling as it was led by a white abolitionist within a slave state and came amidst growing sectional tension and the rise of a new political party opposed to slavery, the first in American life explicitly committed to banning the extension of slavery (Carton, 2002; DeCaro, 2002; Horwitz, 2011; McGlone, 2009; Nudelman, 2004; Oates, 1970; Reynolds, 2005). Brown's raid lived on in American life: Brown was a controversial figure, depicted alternately as madman or saint, as a terrorist or Christ-like, and not just in 1859 but for a solid 100 years after Appomattox (e.g., Finkelman, 1995; Peterson, 2002; Russo & Finkelman, 2005). Here, we articulate one way to position history students to answer the question: How should Brown and his raiders be remembered?

Born into an anti-slavery-leaning family, John Brown's abolitionist beliefs sharpened throughout the 1830s and 1840s against the backdrop of territorial expansion and a shifting abolitionist ideology labeling slavery a sin and demanding immediate emancipation. In the late 1840s, Brown moved his large family to upstate New York to live among an African American community founded by abolitionist Gerrit Smith. Scholars—John Stauffer (2001) and David Reynolds (2005) in particular—argue Brown was not just abolitionist but anti-racist in a way that stood out even among 19th-century white radicals. Brown had become an advocate of violent self-defense, advocating African American armed self-defense in the wake of the renewed Fugitive Slave Act, part of the Compromise of 1850. In North Elba, Brown heard reports about growing tensions between pro-slavery and free state settlers from his sons who had gone to territorial Kansas, and he soon followed them to Bleeding Kansas. There, Brown adopted a proactive violence stance, both in his fighting with free state forces and with his extralegal violence at Pottawatomie Creek in May of 1856 (Carton, 2002; DeCaro, 2002; McGlone, 2009; Oates, 1970). In the years after Kansas, Brown traveled widely throughout the country and Canada, courting abolitionist-funders and recruiting men to participate in his planned attack on the institution of slavery. After freeing 11 Missouri slaves in 1858, Brown moved to seize the federal arsenal at Harper's Ferry and arm area enslaved and free African Americans. To make slavery so hard to sustain that it would collapse from within, Brown recruited 21 men to join his cause, and they arrived to the Virginia countryside in the summer of 1859 (Horwitz, 2011; Laughlin-Schultz, 2013; Lubet, 2015).

Brown's raid—launched on October 16, 1859—quickly failed, and he became a notorious figure in its aftermath. Abolitionists struggled over how to characterize Brown, with many expressing admiration for his ideas if not his actions. Only radicals such as Henry David Thoreau were willing to admire both, with Thoreau famously comparing Brown to Christ: "Some eighteen hundred years ago Christ was crucified; this morning, perchance, Captain Brown was hung. These are the two ends of a chain which is not without its links. He is not Old Brown any longer; he is an angel of light" (Thoreau, 1859). Other Northerners distanced themselves, though during Brown's six weeks in jail his letters and careful self-presentation, what Paul Finkelman (1995) refers to as his work to "manufacture martyrdom," drew more admiration than had the initial reports of his raid. Appreciative Northerners—especially abolitionists and African Americans—raised money for Brown's family and the families of other raiders, and his wife Mary's trip to visit him prior to his execution was reported on in newspapers throughout the north (Laughlin-Schultz, 2013). Other Northerners saw him as the worst of abolitionism realized. Horrified white Southerners envisioned Brown as symbolic of all that the new Republican party would bring, should a Republican capture the presidency, with then-Mississippi Senator Jefferson Davis (1859) proclaiming that if the Republicans came to power, then "a thousand John Browns" could invade the south without fear of federal intervention. It is no wonder so many scholars credit Brown's raid as a prominent causal factor for the Civil War; South Carolina and the Deep South seceded soon after Republican candidate Abraham Lincoln's electoral vote majority seemed to bring Jefferson Davis' fears to life.

John Brown's uncompromising methods, unbending resolve, and cataclysmic end compel his place in secondary history curriculum, yet the evolution of Brown's ideals and his raiders—a variegated crew of Canadians and Americans, white and black folk, men and women, Northerners and Southerners, free and escaped enslaved African Americans, close family members and drifters—are oft-neglected. Brown, his raiders, and their place in history ground this guided inquiry (Gilpin, 2011; Laughlin-Schultz, 2013; Peterson, 2002; Russo & Finkelman, 2005; Taylor & Herrington, 2005), which are included, but minimized, in curricular resources. In commonly used American history textbooks, Brown's evolution is disregarded, his raiders' voices are absent, the implications of the raid are limited in scope, and the disputed, shifting meaning of Brown's significance is overlooked or omitted (Appleby, Brinkley, Broussard, McPherson, & Ritchie, 2014; Berson, Howard, & Salinas, 2009; Davis, 2011; Foner, 2017; Garcia, Ogle, Risinger, & Stevos, 2005). Scholars have examined the historical representation of chattel slavery within textbooks (Loewen, 2007; Roberts, 2015) and trade books (Bickford & Rich, 2014; Bickford & Schuette, 2016; Connolly, 2013), but textbook and trade book authors have not thoroughly incorporated historians' work on the evolution of Brown's ideals, the perspectives of his raiders, and the historical memory of the raid (Gilpin, 2011; Horwitz, 2011; Laughlin-Schultz, 2013; Peterson, 2002). Simplifications deny students the chance to consider the very nature of history, which is contested and bound to historians' subjectivity and inquiries. The subsequent sources and strategies fill these figurative gaps in teachers' history curriculum. The artifacts, which are as much about memory as they are about history, position students explicitly and concretely to confront the nature of historiography. The texts and tasks, when coupled, spark critical thinking and disciplinary literacy (NCSS, 2013; NGA & CCSSO, 2010). Criticality appears as students analyze, evaluate, and creatively express newly constructed ideas (Anderson & Krathwohl, 2001; Benassi, Overson, & Hakala, 2014). Disciplinary literacy emerges through close readings and text-based writing about historical sources (e.g., Lesh, 2010; Monte-Sano, De La Paz, & Felton, 2014; Nokes, 2011, 2013; VanSledright, 2014; Wineburg,

Martin, & Monte-Sano, 2011). Diverse sources, like primary and secondary sources, give educators various ways to teach about the raid on Harper's Ferry. Slavery-based teaching guides include space for Brown and his raiders within the growth of the Abolitionist movement (Jay & Lyerly, 2016; Shuster, Jay, & Lyerly, 2017; Swan, Lee, & Grant, 2018), which we highlight here using the Inquiry Design Model with recognition of the research and advice on teaching difficult topics (Middendorf et al., 2016; Miller, 2016; Sheppard, 2010; Swan, Lee, & Grant, 2015; Teaching Tolerance, n.d.).

History Literacy and Historical Thinking

Prior to this exercise, students should have the necessary background on American chattel slavery, which can be accomplished using the previously mentioned research and slavery-based curricular framework (e.g., Bickford & Rich, 2014; Bickford & Schuette, 2016; Connolly, 2013; Jay & Lyerly, 2016; Shuster et al., 2017; Swan et al., 2018). Teachers should also include a narrative on 1850s America and John Brown, like the secondary summary provided (Appendix A). The compelling question—How should Brown and his raiders be remembered?—has three supporting questions that spark consideration of people, actions, intents, and how they changed: (1) How did Brown's anti-slavery ideals and actions evolve? (2) What were the raiders' motivations and views on Brown? (3) How do citizens oppose laws they find unjust? Carefully selected, abridged primary sources accompany each supporting question, to which the teacher can return for a formative assessment that builds towards the summative performance task. Teachers must move students beyond simplistic representations of Brown, such as invoking mental illness to explain the violence, or avoid indeterminable tasks, such as trying to ascertain if he had delusions of grandeur. Students should scrutinize each piece of evidence when considering its import to and impact on Brown's raid (Table 4.1).

The first query—How did Brown's anti-slavery ideals and actions evolve?—prompts students to consider how Brown's reasoning shifted. The Abridged Sources for Supporting Question One (Appendix B) illuminates the progression of Brown's ratiocination. Students can extract meaning about his early anti-slavery beliefs and work (Source 1), early indignation and profound, yet peaceful, opposition to slavery (Source 2), initial response to the 1850 Fugitive Slave Act (Source 3), justification of self-defense (Source 4), impact on his sons who beckon their father towards Kansas (Source 5), words that conceal culpability but justify the violence in Pottawatomie and Kansas (Sources 6 and 7), letter—for an audience beyond the recipient—to raise funds for upcoming raids (Source 8), and speech prior to receipt of the

A Historical Inquiry into John Brown and His Raiders

Table 4.1: The Importance of John Brown's Raid

Document Number:

Questions	Answers
What kind of document is this? (Letter, journal, interview, etc.) Why was it written?	
Who wrote this? What do we know about this person?	
Who is this written to? What did the author want to convey to the audience?	
What is the most important thing to learn from this? Why did I have you read this?	

death sentence (Source 9). As students grapple with the texts using Table One, the teacher can ask questions about the source (who wrote this?), audience (was this written to a single person, the public, or posterity?), context (when was this written?), intent (why was this written?), medium (was this a letter, speech, or something else?), and preparation (extemporaneous or with forethought?) to prompt students' history literacy and historical thinking. Students' text-based writing on the graphic organizer can inform their answers to the first supporting question, a formative assessment that contributes later to summative performance task.

The second question—What were the raiders' motivations and views on Brown?—evokes deliberations about the accompanying raiders' demography, motivations, culpability, views on slavery, and perceptions about Brown. Important background precedes excerpts of letters written years before and immediately after Harper's Ferry (Appendix C). As students extract meaning, they contextualize and weigh the credibility of the source, corroborate claims through intertextual comparison, and determine historical significance, all of which are key elements to history literacy and historical thinking. Students can refine initial ideas (Table 4.1) as they answer the second supporting question, a formative task that builds towards a summative assessment.

The third query—How do citizens oppose laws they find unjust?—melds consideration of history and current events. Students may appreciate comparisons to the 1970s group the Weather Underground which invoked Brown in its journal *Osawatomie* (Berger, 2006), though they may find troubling that anti-abortion activists have also done so—especially Paul Hill, who murdered an abortion provider (Chowder, 2000; Schoen, 2015). Students may themselves invoke modern antifascist groups (Watt, 2017). Civics-oriented dialogue about modern laws and disputable actions emerge from this history-based query. During initial processing, students might let 21st century understandings about slavery's brutality, enslaved African Americans' humanity, and the South's ultimate defeat, to mention a few, influence judgment about Brown. Hindsight and modern assumptions, which manifest as presentism, obscure understanding the past. Students, after considering the previous supporting questions, have ample source material to answer the third question, yet Brown's actions *prior* to Harper's Ferry refine and complicate understandings. First-hand testimony and newspaper accounts speak to terror in Pottawatomie, Kansas (Appendix D). Regional tension manifested for decades prior to 1856, when Brown entered Kansas to battle slavery advocates. At Pottawatomie, pro-slavery citizens were killed by Brown's group (McGlone, 2009; Oates, 1970; Reynolds, 2005). Though Brown was not likely the executioner, his leadership, his raiders' actions, and the collective implications were symptoms of tensions that would not quell until long after the Civil War ended. To encourage complex thinking, the teacher can give students history literacy and historical thinking tasks such as: What can be learned from each source? What are each source's limitations? How did radical advocacy confront reactionary responses? As students engage in a text-based response to the third supporting question, a formative assessment, they are pushed to deeply consider the moral and civic duties of citizens.

Students analyzed each source and synthesized understandings to answer each question. They critically evaluated an ambiguous situation using the best available evidence. They are now positioned to consider and articulate how Brown and his raiders should be remembered.

Historical (and Civic) Argumentation

After investigations into the sources surrounding the supporting questions, the class can return to the compelling question—How should John Brown and his raiders be remembered?—for a summative performance task. As adolescents resist routine, requiring yet another text-based assignment may elicit indifference. Secondary students, experience informs us, crave novel tasks. Teachers can complicate understandings and elicit attention by tasking students with analysis of artistic representations of Brown. Students might perceive artistic depictions as original and evocative. The teacher could prepare students by saying, "Class, you have an emerging idea about how Brown and his raiders should be judged; let's look at how artists from different areas and eras have represented Brown and his raiders." Each artistic representation, like John Steuart Curry's famous *Tragic Prelude* in particular, constructs Brown using contextually contingent nuance and symbolism (Appendix E). Students can extract meaning when appropriately directed. The first two

A Historical Inquiry into John Brown and His Raiders

columns target history literacy tasks; the far-right column funnels students towards historical thinking (Table 4.2).

Artists' views, like the general public's, were shaped by region and demography. Artists expressed understandings using implicit messages and explicit symbols (Appendix E). An extremist himself, Brown would not expect to be viewed evenhandedly. Brown was artistically represented as either a fanatical terrorist or determined patriot. Analyzing others' artistic representations enables students to consider how he *has been* be depicted, which positions them to answer the compelling question, How should John Brown and his raiders be remembered? Doing so engages students in the very nature of history and historiography. With no definitive answer, students' evidence-based justification is the intent of this summative performance task.

Students' scrutiny of professional artists' symbolism and encoded messages can spark ideas for similar artistic creations. Students can critically and creatively exhibit their newly generated understandings through what has been termed original political cartooning (OPC) but is perhaps better characterized as a meme (Bickford, 2010a, 2010b, 2016). As students meld and modify images with complementary text to creatively communicate ideas, they engage in the highest tiers of critical thinking (Anderson & Krathwohl, 2001; Benassi, Overson, & Hakala, 2014). Creating OPCs, or memes, can be completed in an efficient four-step process.

First, students should develop a thesis about how John Brown should be viewed. Was he an inspired martyr, a domestic terrorist, or something in between? Brown's feet will be figuratively fixed in 1850s America, but his shadow can loom as long as the student deems necessary. Individual students'

Table 4.2: Primary Source Observations, Inferences, Connections & Significance

Primary Source Document #:	Observations	Inferences	Connections & Significance
Questions	Describe everything. What are details others might not see? What do you see? What questions do you have? What might you see encoded in the messages? Explain.	How did this person likely feel about Brown and slavery? What messages are conveyed? Why might this have been created? Be specific.	How is this document similar to others? How is this artifact distinct? How does the artist shape how Brown is viewed?
Answers			

theses, of course, originate from understandings developed during analysis of historical documents associated with the supporting questions. Students' articulations, thus, are grounded in understandings derived from close readings of the primary and secondary material.

Second, students should create a concept map with their thesis at the center and evidence-based ideas extending appropriately. Diagramming one's understandings identifies gaps and areas of convergence, while ensuring all tangents are explored. If students struggle to visually convey an abstract concept, the class can cooperatively brainstorm appropriate substitutions to unclog the creative juices. Collaboration on a substitution list can help students use concrete imagery in place of complex, nonfigurative concepts.

Third, students use the Internet and basic software to develop an OPC or meme. Adolescent students are adept at locating and modifying web-based imagery. They can do much or all of the work on a smartphone, actually.

Finally, it might be problematic or appear arbitrary to assess students' creativity or originality, as each are admittedly subjective. Teachers can assess complexity, intent, effort, and the criticality and historical thinking manifest within the text-based explanation of their meme or OPC. To reward intent and effort, students should detail their intended message(s), how it was encoded through symbolism, visual representations, and textual depictions, and which sources were integrated. In other words, students should detail *what* they intended to convey and *how* they did so. Contemporary education initiatives encourage such text-based writing (NCSS, 2013; NGA & CCSSO, 2010) and doing so enables the teacher to reward effort and intent on this summative performance task.

Appendix A

On October 16, 1859, John Brown and 21 armed "raiders" took control of the U.S. arsenal at Harper's Ferry, Virginia. They killed several people and took others hostage. They sought a localized spark to ignite regional rebellion to end slavery. The uprising collapsed in two days. No larger revolt emerged, though it is hard to measure African Americans' response with certainty, given the desire of white southerners to downplay slave resistance and the necessity for African Americans to seek safety by returning to normalcy. U.S. forces quickly subdued the raid, killed ten, and captured Brown and six others as four escaped. Brown was tried, convicted, and hanged on December 2, 1859. With a thousand weapons stored, the potential participation of nearby enslaved African Americans, the raiders' plans for a preliminary government and to launch a long guerrilla war, Brown's actions and intents terrified Southern imaginations, particularly the slave-owning aristocracy. Many contemporary figures and modern historians assert that Brown's raid contributed to the inevitability of the American Civil War, which later ended slavery.

Brown's story is more complicated when prior beliefs and actions. Born in 1800 to a deeply religious family, Brown long abhorred slavery, was anti-racist in a way that far exceeded most contemporary abolitionists, and sharply criticized the Fugitive Slave Act of 1850. In 1855, he went to the Kansas Territory to help "free-state" settlers fight pro-slavery forces. One evening, five pro-slavery men were executed in cold blood. Brown's actions in Kansas and Harper's Ferry, like the 1850 Fugitive Slave Act and the Supreme Court's 1857 Dred Scott decision, contributed to a timeline that culminated in the Civil War.

Appendix B: Abridged Sources for Supporting Question One

Question One: Source One

John Brown to Frederick Brown, November 21, 1834, in Franklin Sanborn, ed., *Life and Letters of John Brown* (1885), digitized by google at http://books.google.com/books/about/The_life_and_letters_of_John_Brown.html?id=Kb_k-2SyTx4C, pp. 40–41

Since you left me I have been trying to devise some means whereby I might do something in a practical way for my poor fellow-men who are in bondage, and having fully consulted the feelings of my wife and my three boys, we have agreed to get at least one negro boy or youth, and bring him up as we do our own,—viz., give him a good English education, learn him what we can about the history of the world, about business, about general subjects, and, above all, try to teach him the fear of God. We think of three ways to obtain one: First, to try to get some Christian slaveholder to release one to us. Second, to get a free one if no one will let us have one that is a slave. Third, if that does not succeed, we have all agreed to submit to considerable privation in order to buy one. This we are now using means in order to effect, in the confident expectation that God is about to bring them—all out of the house of bondage. ... Affectionately yours,
John Brown

Question One: Source Two

Ruth Brown Thompson, reminiscence, in Franklin Sanborn, ed., *Life and Letters of John Brown* (1885), digitized by google at http://books.google.com/books/about/The_life_and_letters_of_John_Brown.html?id=Kb_k-2SyTx4C, pp. 37–40

Ruth, the only daughter of the first marriage, gives me these incidents of her early recollections:

"Father used to hold all his children, while they were little, at night, und sing his favorite songs, one of which was, 'Blow ye the trumpet, blow!' One evening after he had been singing to me, he asked me how I would like to have some poor little black children that were slaves (explaining to me the meaning of slaves) come and live with us; and asked me if I would be willing to divide my food and clothes with them. He made such an impression on my sympathies, that the first colored person I ever saw (it was a man I met on the street in Meadville, Penn.) I felt such pity for him that I wanted to ask him if he did not want to come and live at our house.

When I was six or seven years old, a little incident took place in the church at Franklin, Ohio (of which all the older part of our family were members), which caused quite an excitement. Father hired a colored man and his wife to work for him,—he on the farm, and she in the house. They were very respectable people, and we thought a great deal of them. One Sunday the woman went to church, and was seated near the door, or somewhere back. This aroused father's indignation at once. He asked both of them to go the next Sunday; they followed the family in, and he seated them in his pew. The whole congregation were shocked; the minister looked angry; but I remember father's firm, determined look. The whole church were down on him then. ... My brothers were so disgusted to see such a mockery of religion that they left the church, and have never belonged to another."

Question One: Source Three

John Brown to Mary Brown, November 28, 1850, in Franklin Sanborn, ed., *Life and Letters of John Brown* (1885), digitized by google at http://books.google.com/books/about/The_life_and_letters_of_John_Brown.html?id=Kb_k-2SyTx4C, pp. 106–107

Springfield, Mass., Nor. 28, 1850.

"I heard from Ohio a few days since; all were there well. It now seems that the fugitive slave law was to be the means of making more abolitionists than all the lectures we have had for years. It really looks as if God had his hand in this wickedness also. I of course keep encouraging my friends 'to trust in God and keep their powder dry.' I did so today at thanksgiving meeting publicly."

Question One: Source Four

"League of Gileadites" (1851), in Richard Hinton (1894) *John Brown and His Men: With Some Accounts of the Roads They Traveled to Reach Harper's Ferry* New York: Funk & Wagnalls Company, pp. 586–587.

Should one of your number be arrested, you must collect together as quickly as possible, so as to outnumber your adversaries who are taking an active part against you. ... Do not delay one moment after you are ready; you will lose all your resolution if you do. Let the first blow be the signal for all to engage, and when engaged do not do your work by halves, but make clean work with your enemies, and be sure you meddle not with any others. ... Be firm, determined, and cool; but let it be understood you are not to be driven to desperation without making it awful job to others as well as to you. ... A lasso might possibly be applied to a slave-catcher for once with good effect. Hold on to your weapons, and never be persuaded to leave them, part with them, or have them far away from you. Stand by one another, and by your friends, while a drop of blood remains; and be hanged, if you must, but tell no tales out of school. Make no confession.

Question One: Source Five

John Brown Jr. to John Brown (1855), in Wilson, H. (1913). *John Brown, soldier of fortune: A critique.* Boston: The Cornhill Company. pp. 52–53

Now the remedy we propose is, that the Anti-slavery portion of the inhabitants should IMMEDIATELY, THOROUGHLY ARM AND ORGANIZE THEMSELVES IN MILITARY COMPANIES. ... Here are 5 men of us who are not only anxious to fully prepare, but are thoroughly determined to fight. We can see no other way to meet the case. As in the language of the memorial lately signed by the people here and sent to Congress petitioning help, 'it is no longer a question of negro slavery, but it is the enslavement of ourselves.' ... The General Government may be petitioned until the people here are grey, and no redress will be had so long as it makes slavery its paramount interest. ... We have among us 5, 1 Revolver, 1 Bowie Knife, 1 middling good Rifle, 1 poor Rifle, 1 small pocket pistol and 2 slung shot. What we need in order to be thoroughly armed for each man is ...

Question One: Source Six

John Brown to wife and children, June 1856, in Franklin Sanborn, ed., *Life and Letters of John Brown* (1885), digitized by google at http://books.google.com/books/about/The_life_and_letters_of_John_Brown.html?id=Kb_k-2SyTx4C, pp. 236–241

We were immediately after this accused of murdering five men at Pottawatomie, and great efforts have since been made by the Missourians and their ruffian allies to capture us. ... Since then we have, like David of old, had our dwelling with the serpents of the rocks and wild beasts of the wilderness; being obliged to hide away from our enemies. We are not disheartened, though nearly destitute of food, clothing, and money. God, who has not given us over to the will of our enemies, but has moreover delivered them into our hand, will, we humbly trust, still keep and deliver us. We feel assured that He who sees not as men see, does not lay the guilt of innocent blood to our charge. ...

May God bless and keep you all!

Your affectionate husband and father,

John Brown.

Question One: Source Seven

John Brown to Family, September 7, 1856, folder 17, box 1, John Brown Collection, Kansas State Historical Society, posted on *Kansas Territorial Online*, http://www.territorialkansasonline.org/~imlskto/cgi-bin/index.php?SCREEN=show_document&document_id=102547&SCREEN_FROM=keyword&selected_keyword=Brown,%20Frederick&startsearchat=0

Dear Wife & children every one

I have one moment to write you to say that I am yet alive that Jason & family were well yesterday John; & family I hear are well; he being yet a prisoner. On the morning of the 30th Aug an attack was made by the ruffians on Osawatomie numbering some 400 by whose scouts our dear Fredk was shot dead without warning he supposing them to be Free State men or near as we can learn. One other man a Cousin of Mr. Adair was murdered by them about the same time. At this time I was about 3 miles off where I had some 14 or 15 men over night that I had just enlisted to serve under me as regulars. There I collected as well as I could with some 12 or 15 more & in about ¾ of an Hour attacked them from a wood with thick undergroth, with this force we threw them into confusion for about 15 or 20 minutes during which time we killed & wounded from 70 to 80 of the enemy as they say & then we escaped as well as we could with one killed while escaping; two or three wounded; & as many more missing. Four or Five Free State men were butchered during the day as well. Jason fought bravely by my side during the fight & escaped with me he unhurt. I was struck by a partly spent Grape Canister, or Rifle shot which bruised me some but did not injure me seriously. "Hitherto the Lord both helped me" notwithstanding my afflictions. Things now seem rather quiet just now; but what another Hour will bring I cannot say—I have seen Three or Four letters from Ruth & One from Watson of July or Aug which are all I have seen since in June. I was very glad to hear once more from you & hope you will continue to write to some of the friends so that I may hear from you. I am utterly unable to write you for most of the time May the God of of [sic] our Fathers bless & save you all

Your Affectionate Husband & Father

JOHN BROWN

Question One: Source Eight

Autobiographical Letter: John Brown to Henry Stearns, July 15, 1857, in Franklin Sanborn, ed., *Life and Letters of John Brown* (1885), pp. 12–17, digitized by google at http://books.google.com/books/about/The_life_and_letters_of_John_Brown.html?id=Kb_k-2SyTx4C

During the war with England a circumstance occurred that in the end made him a most *determined Abolitionist: &* led him to declare, *or Swear: Eternal war* with Slavery. He was staying for a short time with a very gentlemanly landlord since a United States Marshall who held a slave boy near his own ago very active, inteligent and good feeling; & to whom John was under considerable obligation for numerous little acts of kindness. *The master* made a great pet of John: brought him to table with his first company; & friends; called their attention to every little smart thing he said *or did: &* to the fact of his being more than a hundred miles from home with a company of cattle alone; while the *negro boy* (who was fully if not more than his equal) was badly clothed, poorly fed; *& lodged in cold weather;* & beaten before his eyes with Iron Shovels or any other thing that came first to hand. This brought John to reflect on the wretched, hopeless condition, of *Fatherless* & *Motherless* slave *children:* for such children have neither Fathers or Mothers to protect, & provide for them. He sometimes would raise the question is *God their Father?* ...

J. Brown

P. S. I had like to have forgotten to acknowledge your contribution in aid of the cause in which I serve. God Almighty *bless you;* my son.

Question One: Source Nine

The Life, Trial, and Execution of Captain John Brown, Known as "Old Brown of Ossawatomie," with a Full Account of the Attempted Insurrection at Harper's Ferry, Compiled from Official and Authentic Sources (1859). New York, NY: R.M. DeWitt, digitized at http://avalon.law.yale.edu/19th_century/john_brown.asp

"I believe that to have interfered as I have done, as I have always freely admitted I have done in behalf of His despised poor, is no wrong, but right. Now, if it is deemed necessary that I should forfeit my life for the furtherance of the ends of justice, and mingle my blood farther with the blood of my children and with the blood of millions in this slave country whose rights are disregarded by wicked, cruel, and unjust enactments, I say let it be done."

Appendix C: Abridged Sources for Supporting Question Two

Raider 1. Aaron Stevens

Source: , Boston, MA

Born in Connecticut, Aaron Stevens (1831–1860) ran away at sixteen to serve in the Mexican War before becoming a Free State fighter in Kansas, which is where he met John Brown. Stevens fought with Brown in Kansas and in an 1858 Missouri raid in which he killed a slave owner. He joined Brown's raiders in Maryland, where he led the men in drills. He was trapped with Brown in the Engine House during the Harper's Ferry raid and was captured, tried, and executed. The excerpts are from letters to his brother.

Aaron Stevens to Henry Stevens, August 28, 1856 [from Kansas]: "I am devoted to the freedom of slaves. Any person that would refuse to fight to end slavery is worse than a traitor. Life is Sweet but Liberty is Sweeter. We in Kansas have struggled against every kind of wickedness that man created with the power of the Devil. From the beginning to the present time we have been attacked by a foreign enemy. First the slave holders came to vote to elect our leaders, then to make our laws, and now they force us to obey those laws. We can either live and die shamefully with slavery or fight and die to become freemen."

Aaron Stevens to Henry Stevens, August 2, 1858 [from Iowa]: "I think I told you before that I was fighting for human freedom. We left Kansas to strike down slavery at the heart. I tell you slavery will never be ended except by the sword, and every year it is getting worse. Think of the thousands of slaves who are murdered yearly. You are aware of how they do things down south. I suppose you know they worked their slaves on those big plantations hard enough to kill them. So you see there is thousands of them murdered yearly. Would you not think it best to do away with slavery in a year or two by losing a few thousands in war than to have thousands of them murdered yearly for God knows how many years? To think how many of them have been murdered before this. I am against war, except in self defense, and I am like Patrick Henry, when he said "give me Liberty or give me death." I think the time is a coming when it will be done. We will sacrificed all we have to the cause, but we are willing to give up life itself for the good of humanity."

Aaron Stevens to Henry E. Stevens, January 30, 1860: "I feel happier now than I ever did before in my life. I have a very pleasant room in the jail, and I am treated as well as I could wish. My trial will begin tomorrow, I do not expect any thing better than my comrade got, but still let us hope for the best, I am ready for any thing that comes."

Aaron Stevens to Henry E Stevens, February 23, 1860: "I have just read your kind letter of Feb. 15th and now sit down to write you one in return, and it may be the last, but I will try to write you one more. I do hope you will not worry in least about me, for I am cheerful and happy, and if I have to die now, it will only be going before you a few years, we have all got to die sooner or later, and death has no terrors for me. Still I have a desire to live yet awhile for I am young yet and have just learned how to live. I should like to see you and yours very much, but I must give up these wants."

Raider 2. Watson Brown

Source: *Life and Letters of John Brown*, ed. Sanborn (1885), pp. 542–543, at http://www.archive.org/stream/lifeandlettersof00sanbrich/lifeandlettersof00sanbrich_djvu.txt

A Historical Inquiry into John Brown and His Raiders

Watson Brown (1835–1859) was one of John Brown's younger sons, child of John Brown and his second wife Mary Ann Day Brown. Watson Brown had been the only Brown son to remain in the East—left behind to help take care of his mother and sisters—while Brown and sons fought in Kansas in the mid-1850s. In 1859 he fought at Harper's Ferry, where he was killed October 18, 1859. When he went to Harper's Ferry he left behind his wife Isabella and their young son Freddy.

Watson Brown to Belle Brown, September 8, 1859

DEAR ISABELLA,

You can guess how I long to see you only by knowing how you wish to see me. I think of you all day, and dream of you at night. I would gladly come home and stay with you always but for the cause of ending slavery which brought me here. I have a desire to do something for others, and not live for my own happiness. I am at home, five miles north of Harper's Ferry, in an old house on a farm, where we keep some things for war.

The reason I did not write sooner was that there are ten of us here, and all who know them think they are with my father, and have an idea what he is at. So you see if each and every one writes, then all his friends will know where we all are. We do not want father caught.

I have just received your letter of August 30, and you may as well think I am glad to hear from you. You may kiss the baby a great many times a day for me; I am thinking of you and him all the time.

We have only two black men with us now. One has a wife and seven children in slavery. I sometimes feel as though I could not make the sacrifice. But what would I want others to do were I a slave in their place? Oh, Bell, I do want to see you and the little fellow very much, but I must wait. I sometimes think perhaps we shall not meet again. If we should not, you have an object to live for, to be a mother to our little Fred. He is not quite a reality to me yet.

We leave here soon for the last time. You will probably hear about us very soon after getting this, if not before, because we will be successful. We are all eager and confident of success. There was another murder committed near our place the other day, making in all five murders of slaves.

Give my regards to all the friends, and keep up good courage: there is a better day coming. If I should never see you again, believe me forever in love.

Your husband,

WATSON BROWN.

Raider 3. Oliver Brown

Source: (typescript copy), folder 12, box 1, series III, Brown-Gee Collection, Hudson Library and Historical Society, Hudson, OH.

Oliver Brown (1839–1859) was one of John Brown's younger sons, child of John Brown and his second wife Mary Ann Day Brown. Oliver Brown had fought alongside his father and brothers in Kansas, and in 1859 he fought and died at Harper's Ferry. He had married Martha Brewster Brown in 1858. She served with Annie Brown as housekeeper at the Kennedy farmhouse in Maryland prior to Brown's raid, and she was sent home in late September, pregnant with the couple's first child.

Oliver Brown to Martha Brown, October 9, 1859

MY DEAR MARTHA:

Having opportunity to write you once more is the greatest pleasure to myself. I hope of pleasing you. I arrived here two days sooner than father and Watson. They have gone back one more. We are all well at present. You can hardly think how I want to see you, or how lonesome I was the day I left you. That day I shall never forget. I made some good resolutions and I mean to live up to them.

Nothing else could strengthen me to do the right so much as the thought of you. It is when I look at your picture that I am wholly ashamed of my every meanness, weakness, and folly. I would not part with that picture of you for anything on earth except for you. I have made a case for your picture, and carry it close around my body. I am more and more determined every day to live a more unselfish life.

Now, Martha, you can hardly imagine my great anxiety about you in your present situation, and you will certainly allow me to suggest some ideas to you for your own good. Let me ask you to try to keep up good, cheerful spirits. Take plenty of sleep and rest; plenty of out-door exercise. Bathe often. And finally, do read good books, such as the pastor's sermons. These books will do much to keep you from being lonesome.

Finally, Martha, do try to enjoy yourself. Make the most of everything.

Please remember your affectionate husband,

OLIVER BROWN

Raider 4. John Copeland

Source: Electronic Oberlin Documents, http://www.oberlin.edu/external/EOG/Copeland/copeland_letters.htm

John Anthony Copeland Jr. (1834–1859) was a free African American who had been born in North Carolina. His parents moved to Ohio when he was young, and he attended Oberlin College, an institution known for its antebellum admission of women and African Americans. His uncle Lewis Leary recruited him to participate in Brown's raid, and the two traveled to Maryland in 1859. Copeland was captured, arrested, and put on trial in the aftermath of the raid. He was executed December 16, 1859, and he wrote this letter to his family in the week before his death.

John Copeland to His Family, December 10, 1859

MY DEAR BROTHER:

I now take my pen to write you a few lines to let you know how I am. Dear Brother, I am jailed, it is true. At present, I scarcely to know how to begin. Not that my mind is filled with fear as I sit in view of my near death. Not that I am terrified by the gallows from which I will be hung. I see the gallows and death staring me in the face, and I shall soon stand and suffer death for doing what George Washington did. George Washington, the so-called father of his great but slavery-cursed country, was made a hero for fighting evil while he lived and when dead his name was immortalized. Parents teach children his great and noble deeds on behalf of freedom. And now, brother, I fought with a General no less brave than Washington. I fought for an honorable and glorious cause. I am to suffer death. Washington fought for the freedom of the American people—not for the white men alone, but for both black and white. Nor were they only white men alone who fought for the freedom of this country. The blood of black men flowed as freely as that of white men. Yes, the very first blood that was spilt was that of a black man. It was the blood of that heroic man, Crispus Attucks, killed in the Boston Massacre in 1770.

It was evil wrongs made the noble Captain Brown attempt to give freedom to slaves who are now controlled by cruel laws and owned by cruel and unjust men. God created them and gave them freedom, justice, and humanity. They should have the enjoyment of it. And how dear brother, could I die in a more noble cause? I imagine that I hear you all, say—"No there is not a better cause for which we could see you die." Believe me when I tell you that though I am shut up in prison and under sentence of death, I have spent some very happy hours here. Dear brother, I want you and all to meet me in Heaven. Prepare your soul for death. Be ready to meet your God at any moment, and then, though we meet no more on earth, we shall meet in Heaven where parting is no more. Tell my nephews to be good boys, mind your mother and father, love and honor them, grow up to be good men, and fear the Lord your God. Give my love to all my family, and now my dear brothers, one and all, I pray to God we may meet in Heaven. Good bye.

I am now, and shall remain, your affectionate brother,

JOHN COPELAND

Raider 5. Jeremiah Anderson

Source: box 1, James William Eldridge Collection, 1797–1902, Huntington Library, San Marino, CA

Jeremiah Anderson (1833–1859) was the grandson of slaveholders. He grew up in Indiana, Illinois, and Iowa before emigrating to Kansas in 1857, where he met John Brown. He participated in Brown's raid into Missouri to free slaves in 1858 and then participated in the Harper's Ferry raid. He was killed at Harper's Ferry by one of the marines sent to put down the revolt. These excerpts are from letters to his brother.

Jeremiah Anderson to "dear brother," June 17, 1859: "Dear Brother, you need not be uneasy about us stealing slaves for that is not your business; but be patient and in due time you will learn of our business and how we succeed. Our approach is new, but undoubtedly good, and perfectly safe and simple, but I judge when we put it in practice it will astonish the world and mankind in general. We met with Frederick Douglass—the escaped slave—again and he encourages our party."

Jeremiah Anderson to "dear brother," September 28, 1859: "I expect to leave here soon. Our cooks are going to start back to N.Y. in the morning; they are our Captain's daughter and daughter in law. Our Captain has gone to Philadelphia for a few more helpers, and will be back in a few days, and then we will begin digging for precious metal, some time next week without doubt. Our mining company will consist of between 25 or 30 well equipped miners with tools. At present I do all that is honorable and will continue in the same way as we did in Kansas."

Millions of our fellow human beings require it of us, their cries for help go to the universe daily and hourly. Whose duty is it to help them? Is it yours, is it mine? It is every mans! But how few there are to help. There are a few who do dare to answer the calls of freedom and answer the call of freedom in a manner that will shake this land of Liberty and Equality. If my life is sacrificed it can't be lost in a better cause. Our motto is, We go into win no matter what the hazards. So if you should hear of a failure, it will be after a desperate struggle. But that is the least of our thoughts. Every thing seems to work and victory surely will be ours. Our Captain has had this operation in view for twenty years.

When I start again traveling, I expect to go through the state of Virginia, and on south just as circumstances are required. I'll be mining and prospecting and carrying the ore along with us. You can imagine what we are doing, and see it in your newspaper. Great excitement about new gold discoveries in Virginia.

I intend to be as careful of the scalp on my head as I would of my wife. Tell Mother not to worry herself because she thinks she may not see me again on earth, for we all must die sooner or latter. Farewell till you hear from me and hope for the best.

Yours for Liberty & Equality

J.G. ANDERSON

A Historical Inquiry into John Brown and His Raiders

Raider 6. Osborne Anderson

Source: folder 1, box 46, John Brown Collection, Chicago Historical Society, Chicago, IL

Osborne Anderson (1830–1872) was one of Brown's African American raiders. He had been born free in Pennsylvania, and he met John Brown in Canada in 1858. He was one of the few raiders to escape from Harper's Ferry, and he returned to Canada in its aftermath. In 1861 he published A Voice from Harper's Ferry, *the only raider account of the events. It is available online at www.wvculture.org/history/jbexhibit/voicefromhf.html. He enlisted in the army during the Civil War, and died in Washington, D.C., in 1872. Below is an excerpt from a letter he wrote to Mary Brown, John Brown's widow, in the months after the raid.*

Osborne Anderson to Mary Brown, January 23, 1860

Dear Madam:

It is with the deepest feelings of my soul that I now embrace this long hoped for opportunity of writing you a few lines in your sad condition, and those of your family circle. How sad must your moments be now as a wife without a husband.

While writing this, I think back to our raid which was planned and guided by the greatest man that has lived since the days of the Apostles, Capt. John Brown. Capt. Brown was guided by the divine inspiration of God to try to save four million slaves. The second of December, when he was killed, Capt. John Brown is now slumbering in a tomb. He has taught the slave the true lesson of Freedom starting on the 17th of October—when the raid began—will date the new era.

The Bible guided our dear old Hero's soul to establish peace on earth and good will to men. Capt. Brown could not stop the fight so help him God. And thus he was caught by the government hounds. Capt. Brown is fighting Pharaoh and he is our Moses. I thank God that I was one of the raiders of that sainted Old Hero. I cherish his name with my life. The first lessons he taught me was to seek those that were lost in slavery in order that they might be saved.

And now dear madam, you are at this time separated from one you cherished most in this life. Your separation is short and you will meet again to part no more in Heaven.

John Brown died a Christian martyr. When he was hanged, his soul swayed on the gentle wings of angels. His soul went up away from Earth and received an Everlasting blessing from God.

Your Friend

ANDERSON

Appendix D: Abridged Sources for Supporting Question Three

Newspaper Accounts of John Brown's raid at Pottawatomie (Kansas) Massacre (1856)

"It seems that this Brown is a power in the Kansas Territory—neither the Territory nor General Government having been able so far to stop his pillages and destructions. He is fast taking control and unless something is done to put a stop to his career, volunteer forces will be necessary to put him down."—The Kansas City Enterprise (1856)

"... there is no one the Kansans dread more than Captain [John] Brown. They hate him as they would a snake, but their hatred is composed of fear .... He is a strange, stubborn, vile, iron-willed, unstoppable old man."—The *New-York Tribune* (1856)

First Person Accounts of the Pottawatomie (Kansas) Massacre (1856)

Testimony of Mrs. Doyle: We were all in bed, when we heard some persons come into the yard, and rap at the door, and call for Mr. Doyle, my husband. ... several men came into the house, and said they were from the army. My husband was a pro-slavery man. They told my husband that he and the boys must surrender; they were then prisoners. I asked them, in tears, to spare him. In short time afterwards I heard the report of pistols; I heard two reports ... then moaning ... then I heard a wild whoop. My husband and two boys, my sons, did not come back any more. I went out the next morning and found [them] lying dead in the road about 200 yards from the house.

Testimony of Mrs. Wilkinson: We were disturbed by the barking dog .... I was sick with the measles and woke up Mr. Wilkinson and asked him if he heard the noise. "Are you a Northern armist?" He answered, "I am." I understood the answer to mean that my husband was opposed to the Northern or Free-Soil Party. My husband was a pro-slavery man, and was a member of the Territorial Legislature held at the Shawnee Mission. "You are my prisoner; do you surrender?" He said, "Gentlemen, I do." They said, "Open the door." They searched for arms ... then took my husband away. The next morning, Mr. Wilkinson was found about 150 yards from the house, in some dead brush. My husband was a quiet man, and was not engaged in arresting or disturbing anyone.

John Brown, in a letter to his wife, while watching Osawatomie burn (1856): God sees it; I only have a short time to live—only one death to die, fighting for this cause. There will be no more peace in this land until slavery is done for. I will give them something else to do than to extend slave territory. I will carry the war into the South.

Appendix E: Visual Depictions of John Brown

Image 4.1: John Steuart Curry (ca. 1938). Tragic Prelude. United Missouri Bank of Kansas City. https://commons.wikimedia.org/wiki/File:THUMBNAIL001L.jpg Bank

Image 4.2: John Brown (ca. 1899) [Photograph]. Retrieved from the Library of Congress, https://www.loc.gov/item/93500813/

Image 4.3: Black & Batchelder, Copyright Claimant, Black, J. W., & Lawrence, M. M. [Photographer]. (ca. 1859, December 12). *John Brown* [Photograph]. Retrieved from the Library of Congress, https://www.loc.gov/item/2009633569/

Image 4.4: Currier & Ives. (ca. 1863). *John Brown. Meeting the slave-mother and her child on the steps of Charlestown jail on his way to execution* [Photograph]. New York: Published by Currier & Ives, 152 Nassau St., New York. Retrieved from the Library of Congress, https://www.loc.gov/item/2003674588/

A Historical Inquiry into John Brown and His Raiders

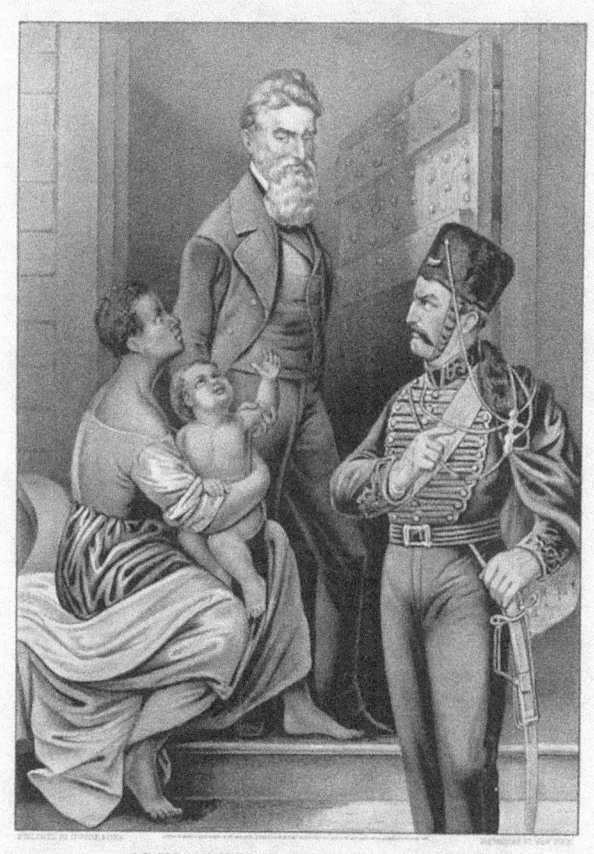

Image 4.5: Currier & Ives. (ca. 1870). *John Brown—the martyr* [Photograph]. New York: Published by N. Currier. Retrieved from the Library of Congress, https://www.loc.gov/item/2002707674/

Image 4.6: Querner, G. (1865). *John Brown exhibiting his hangman* [Photograph]. Retrieved from the Library of Congress, https://www.loc.gov/item/2008661690/

A Historical Inquiry into John Brown and His Raiders

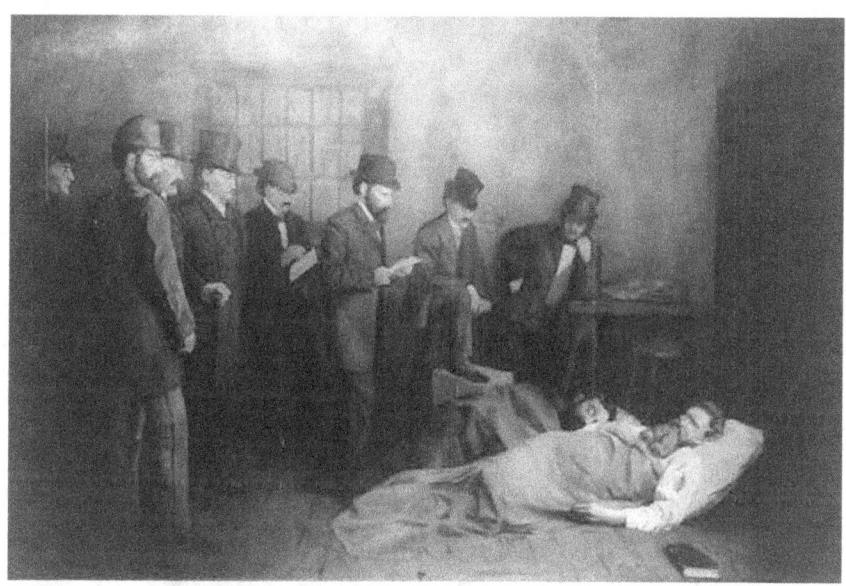

Image 4.7: (ca. 1906). *[Death warrant of John Brown]* [Photograph]. Retrieved from the Library of Congress, https://www.loc.gov/item/2005688486/

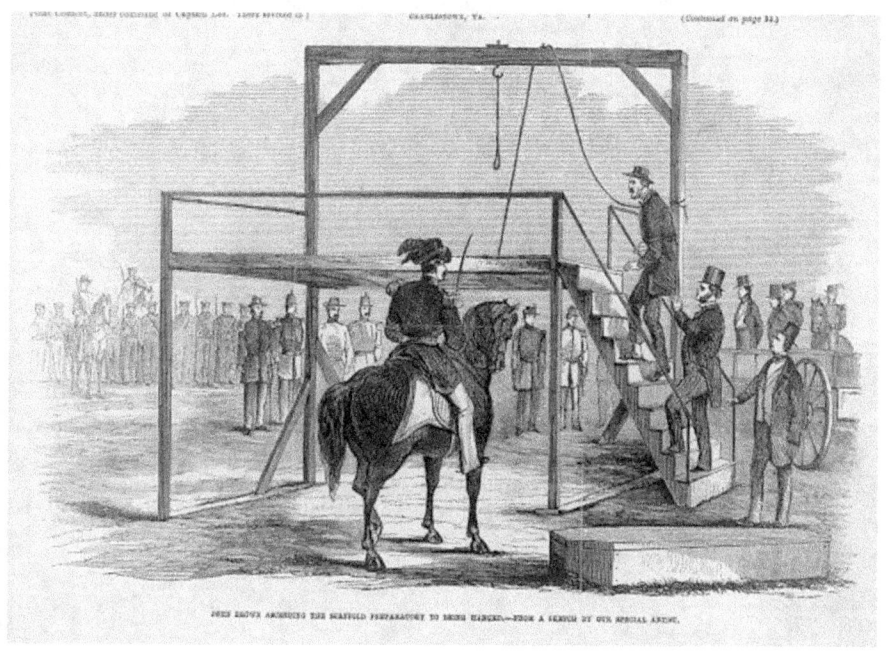

Image 4.8: (1859). *John Brown ascending the scaffold preparatory to being hanged/from a sketch by our special artist* [Photograph]. Charleston, WV. Retrieved from the Library of Congress, https://www.loc.gov/item/2002735876/

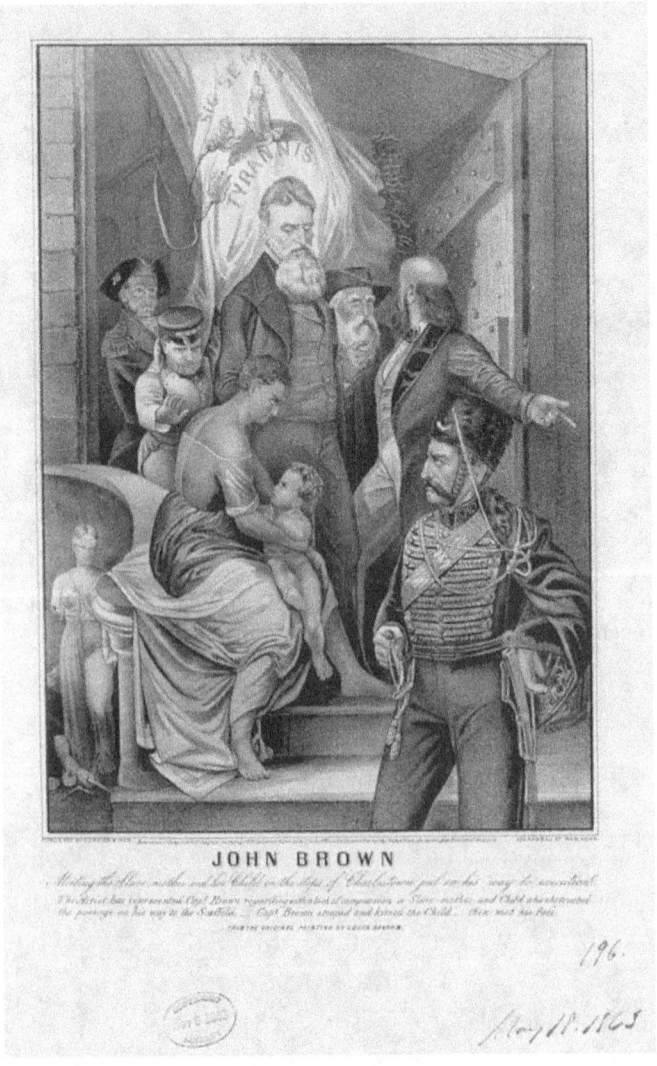

Image 4.9: Hovenden, T., & Gebbie, G. (ca. 1885, August 12). *The last moments of John Brown leaving the jail on the morning of his execution/Hovenden N.A., painter & etcher* [Photograph]. Philadelphia: Geo. Gebbie publisher. Retrieved from the Library of Congress, https://www.loc.gov/item/2012648890/

Image 4.10: (1859). *John Brown riding on his coffin to the place of execution [Charlestown, W. Va.]* [Photograph]. Retrieved from the Library of Congress, https://www.loc.gov/item/99614097/

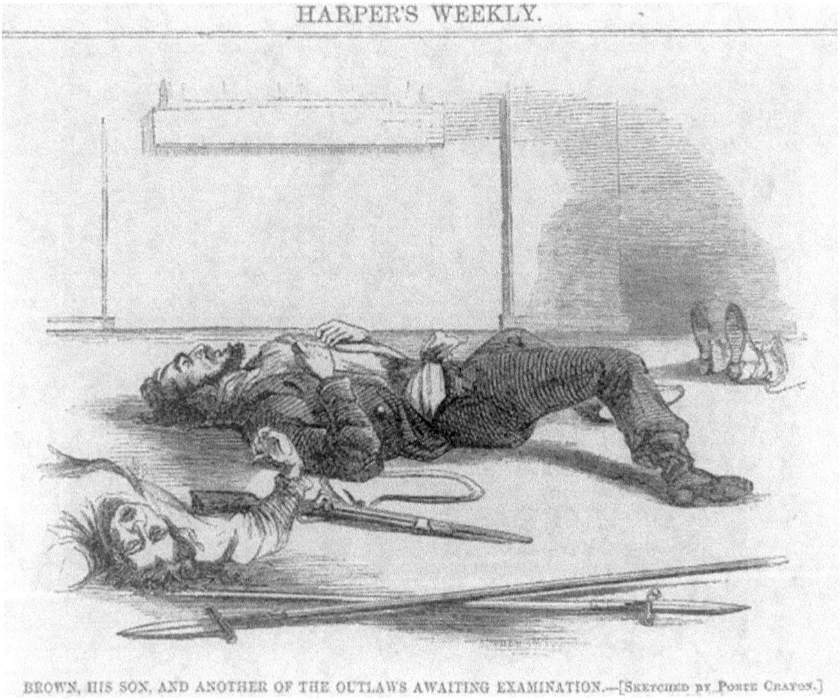

Image 4.11: (1859). *[John Brown,—1859, full-length portrait, lying wounded on floor beside his son]* [Photograph]. Retrieved from the Library of Congress, https://www.loc.gov/item/2005687548/

A Historical Inquiry into John Brown and His Raiders

Image 4.12: (1859). *En route for Harper's Ferry* [Photograph]. Retrieved from the Library of Congress, https://www.loc.gov/item/2006677988/

References

Anderson, L., & Krathwohl, D. (Eds.). (2001). *A taxonomy for learning, teaching, and assessing: A revision of Bloom's taxonomy of educational objectives.* New York, NY: Longman.

Appleby, J., Brinkley, A., Broussard, A., McPherson, J., & Ritchie, D. (2014). *Discovering our past: A history of the United States.* New York, NY: McGraw-Hill.

Benassi, V., Overson, C., & Hakala, C. (Eds.). (2014). *Applying science of learning in education: Infusing psychological science into the curriculum.* Washington, DC: American Psychological Association.

Berger, D. (2006). *Outlaws of America: The weather underground and the politics of solidarity.* Chico, CA: AK Press.

Berson, M. J., Howard, T. C., & Salinas, C. (2009). *The United States: Making a new nation.* Orlando, FL: Harcourt.

Bickford, J. (2010a). Complicating students' historical thinking through primary source reinvention. *Social Studies Research and Practice, 5*(2), 47–60.

Bickford, J. (2010b). *Un*complicated technologies and erstwhile aids: How PowerPoint, the Internet, and political cartoons can elicit engagement and challenge thinking in new ways. *The History Teacher, 44*(1), 51–66.

Bickford, J. (2016). Integrating creative, critical, and historical thinking through close reading, document-based writing, and original political cartooning. *The Councilor: A Journal of the Social Studies, 77*(1), 1–9.

Bickford, J., & Rich, C. (2014). Examining the representations of slavery within children's literature. *Social Studies Research and Practice, 9*(1), 66–94.

Bickford, J., & Schuette, L. (2016). Trade books' historical representation of the Black Freedom Movement, slavery through civil rights. *Journal of Children's Literature, 41*(1), 20–43.

Carton, E. (2002). *Patriotic treason: John Brown and the soul of America*. New York, NY: Free Press.

Chowder, K. (2000). The Father of American terrorism. *American Heritage, 51*(1). Retrieved from https://www.americanheritage.com/content/father-american-terrorism

Connolly, P. (2013). *Slavery in American children's literature, 1790–2010*. Iowa City: University of Iowa Press.

Davis, J. (1859, December 8). Speech to the U.S. Senate. Retrieved from http://www.digitalhistory.uh.edu/active_learning/explorations/brown/public_davis.cfm

Davis, K. C. (2011). *Don't know much about history: Everything you need to know about American history*. New York, NY: HarperCollins.

DeCaro, L., Jr. (2002). *"Fire from the midst of you": A religious life of John Brown*. New York: New York University Press.

Finkelman, P. (Ed.). (1995). *His soul goes marching on: Responses to John Brown and the Harper's ferry raid*. Charlottesville: University Press of Virginia.

Foner, E. (2017). *Give me liberty! An American history*. New York, NY: W.W. Norton.

Garcia, J., Ogle, D., Risinger, C. F., & Stevos, J. (2005). *Creating America: A history of the United States*. Evanston, IL: McDougal Littell.

Gilpin, R. B. (2011). *John Brown still lives! America's long reckoning with violence, equality, and change*. Chapel Hill: University of North Carolina Press.

Horwitz, T. (2011). *Midnight rising: John Brown and the raid that sparked the Civil War*. New York, NY: Henry Holt.

Isenberg, N. (2016). *White trash: The 400-year untold history of class in America*. New York, NY: Viking.

Jay, B., & Lyerly, C. L. (2016). *Understanding and teaching American slavery*. Madison: University of Wisconsin Press.

Laughlin-Schultz, B. (2013). *The tie that bound us: The women of John Brown's family and the legacy of radical abolitionism*. Ithaca, NY: Cornell University Press.

Lesh, B. A. (2010). *Why won't you just tell us the answer? Teaching historical thinking in grades 7–12*. Portsmouth, NH: Stenhouse.

Loewen, J. (2007). *Lies my teacher told me: Everything your American history textbook got wrong*. New York, NY: Simon and Schuster. (Originally published in 1995)

Lubet, S. (2015). *The "colored hero" of Harper's ferry: John Anthony Copeland and the war against slavery*. Cambridge: Cambridge University Press.

McCurry, S. (1995). *Masters of small worlds: Yeoman households, gender relations, and the political culture of the antebellum South Carolina low country*. New York, NY: Oxford University Press.

McGlone, R. (2009). *John Brown's war against slavery*. Cambridge: Cambridge University Press.

Middendorf, J., Mickute, J., Saunders, T., Najar, J., Clark-Huckstep, A., Pace, D., . . . Miller, D. (2016). Creating a reflective classroom community. *Learn+teach+share: the Facing History community of southern California*. Retrieved from http://lanetwork.facinghistory.org/docmiller

McGrath, N. (2015). What's feeling got to do with it? Decoding emotional bottlenecks in the history classroom. *Arts & Humanities in Higher Education, 14*(2), 166–180.

Monte-Sano, C., De La Paz, S., & Felton, M. (2014). *Reading, thinking, and writing about history: Teaching argument writing to diverse learners in the common core classroom, grades 6–12*. New York, NY: Teachers College Press.

National Council for the Social Studies. (2013). *College, career, and civic life (C3) framework for social studies state standards: Guidance for enhancing the rigor of k–12 civics, economics, geography, and history*. Silver Spring, MD: Author.

National Governors Association Center for Best Practices & Council of Chief State School Officers. (2010). *Common core state standards for English language arts and literacy in history/social studies, science, and technical subjects*. Washington, DC: Author.

Nokes, J. (2011). Recognizing and addressing the barriers to adolescents' "reading like historians". *The History Teacher, 44*(3), 379–404.

Nokes, J. (2013). *Building students' historical literacies: Learning to read and reason with historical texts and evidence*. New York, NY: Routledge.

Nudelman, F. (2004) *John Brown's body: Slavery, violence, and the culture of war*. Chapel Hill: University of North Carolina Press.

Oates, S. (1970). *To purge this land with blood: A biography of John Brown*. Amherst: University of Massachusetts Press.

Peterson, M. D. (2002). *John Brown, the legend revisited*. Charlottesville: The University of Virginia Press.

Reynolds, D. (2005). *John Brown, abolitionist: The man who killed slavery, sparked the Civil War, and seeded civil rights*. New York, NY: Alfred A. Knopf.

Russo, P., & Finkelman, P. (Eds.). (2005). *Terrible swift sword: The legacy of John Brown*. Athens: Ohio University Press.

Roberts, S. (2015). A review of social studies textbook content since 2002. *Social Studies Research and Practice, 9*(3), 51–65.

Schoen, J. (2015). *Abortion after Roe*. Chapel Hill: University of North Carolina Press.

Sheppard, S. (2010). Creating a caring classroom in which to teach difficult histories. *The History Teacher, 43*(3), 411–426.

Shuster, K., Jay, B., & Lyerly, C. (2017). *Teaching hard history: A framework for teaching American slavery.* Teaching Tolerance: A Project of the Southern Poverty Law Center. Retrieved from https://www.tolerance.org/sites/default/files/2018-02/TT-Teaching-Hard-History-Framework-Feb2018.pdf

Seixas, P., & Morton, T. (2012). *The big six historical thinking concepts.* Toronto, ON: Nelson College Indigenous.

Stauffer, J. (2001). *The black hearts of men: Radical abolitionists and the transformation of race.* Cambridge, MA: Harvard University Press.

Swan, K., Lee, J., & Grant, S. G. (2015). The New York State toolkit and the Inquiry Design Model: Anatomy of an inquiry. *Social Education, 79*(5), 316–322.

Swan, K., Lee, J., & Grant, S. G. (2018). *Teaching hard history: Teaching American slavery through inquiry.* Retrieved from https://www.tolerance.org/sites/default/files/2018-02/TT-Teaching-Hard-History-C3-Report-WEB-February2018.pdf

Taylor, A., & Herrington, E. (Eds.). (2005). *The afterlife of John Brown.* New York, NY: Palgrave Macmillan.

Teaching Tolerance. (n.d.). *Let's talk! Discussing race, racism, and other difficult topics with students.* Retrieved from https://www.tolerance.org/magazine/publications/lets-talk

Thoreau, H. D. (1859, October 30). A plea for Captain John Brown. Retrieved from http://avalon.law.yale.edu/19th_century/thoreau_001.asp

VanSledright, B. (2014). *Assessing historical thinking and understanding: Innovative designs for new standards.* New York, NY: Routledge.

Watt, C. S. (2017, July 11). "Redneck Revolt: The armed left-wing group that wants to stamp out fascism," *The Guardian.* Retrieved November 4, 2018, from https://www.theguardian.com/us-news/2017/jul/11/redneck-revolt-guns-anti-racism-fascism-far-left

Wineburg, S., Martin, D., & Monte-Sano, C. (2011). *Reading like a historian: Teaching literacy in middle and high school classrooms.* New York, NY: Teachers College Press.

5. 1860: The Election That Started the War

Elizabeth Barrow

Other chapters in this book have spoken to the long-term causes of the Civil War—the tension following the Compromise of 1850, Bleeding Kansas, the *Dred Scott* case, and John Brown's raid. The goal of this chapter is to challenge misconceptions regarding the election of 1860 and complicate the discussion of how this election contributed to a temporary separation of the Union. Race figured prominently in public discourse and political maneuvering by candidates in 1860. Calls for protection of states' rights were really calls to protect the institution of slavery and maintain white superiority (Huston, 2003) while calls to keep the Union together were seen as a threat to the Southern livelihood. This chapter will: (1) challenge the inevitability of Lincoln's nomination as the Republican candidate; (2) focus on what the four candidates reveal about the complexity of the election; and (3) challenge misconceptions about the role race and slavery played in the election. The chapter concludes by offering some lesson ideas connected to the C3 Framework and National Council for the Social Studies (NCSS) themes (National Council for the Social Studies (NCSS), 2013).

Teaching about the election of 1860 and the causes of the Civil War can be especially difficult in the South where remnants of the Civil War remain visible. Confederate statues still stand guard on town squares and college campuses. Confederate battle flags (the Saint Andrews Cross) still fly in the yards of private residences, on the side of highways, and above some federal buildings (Kennedy, 2017). The Civil War and the confederacy have been immortalized. Yes, the war is part of our collective history; however, many are either ignorant of, or choose to ignore, the causes of the war. History teachers in the South face the challenge of teaching the election of 1860 when place-based identities (Jennings, Swidler, & Koliba, 2005) may contribute to the sustained legacy of the Confederate States of America. The lessons associated with this chapter offer two examples of how teachers can challenge students to think more critically about the causes of the Civil War within the context of political, social, and economic history.

Four Candidates, Two Races, One Main Issue

The election of 1860 was a particularly interesting one in American history. Four candidates vying for president of the United States ran in what was essentially two separate elections: Lincoln (Republican) and Douglas (Northern Democrat) in the North and Breckinridge (Southern Democrat) and Bell (Constitutional Unionist) in the South. Popular history contends that the two races were completely separate; however, this is inaccurate. The Constitutional Union party did try to tarnish both the Republican and Northern Democrat campaigns while both sides of the Democratic party concentrated on attacking each other (Holt, 2017). Slavery was not the only issue contested in the election of 1860 but it did largely dominate conversations. In order to understand the complexity of the election of 1860 and how it was a cause of the Civil War I will briefly introduce the four parties and explain their position on slavery in the territories.

The election of 1860 marks only the second presidential election for the Republican party. Although he did not win, John C. Frémont's success in 1856 insured that the Republican party would be considered a mainstream party, unlike the waning Know-Nothing party. Since its inception, the Republican party "intensified partisan debate about freedom" (Neely, 1991, p. xiii). Republicans' stance on slavery was not for the abolition of the institution in areas where it already existed; instead, they were against the extension of slavery into territories. While "opposition to slavery and its extension" was considered a "critically important facet of [the Republican's] electoral appeal" the Republican party also focused on corruption within the previous administration under President Buchanan (Holt, 2017, p. 163). The next section of this chapter will focus more on the nomination and subsequent election of Abraham Lincoln as the 16th president of the United States.

When the Democratic national convention convened in Charleston, South Carolina, on April 23, 1860 the party was ripe for a split. For years, party tension had increased between supporters of the *Dred Scott* decision and supporters of popular sovereignty. Any movement towards Stephen Douglas as the nominee and a platform promoting popular sovereignty would likely result in Southern Democrats seceding from their own party (Huston, 2003). And this is exactly what happened. Douglas was identified as the potential

Democratic candidate; however, infighting over the platform resulted in a stalemate and anti-Douglas supporters withdrawing from the convention. Now unable to garner the majority votes needed, the Democratic convention voted on a recess until June (Holt, 2017). When the party reconvened in Baltimore, Maryland, on June 18 Northern Democrats nominated Douglas as their candidate and maintained the position of popular sovereignty in the territories, a position that fire-eaters in the South saw as too weak. Southern Democrats wanted someone to champion for not only the survival of slavery, but its extension into other states and territories. A position of popular sovereignty allowed for the *possibility* that slavery could be denied in the territories and this was unacceptable for pro-slavery advocates.

Southern Democratic Senators, rallying behind Jefferson Davis, were more concerned by the possibility that slavery might be denied access to the territories due to popular sovereignty and therefore pushed for a series of "slave codes," insisting that their

> slaves be considered as property, that southerners could take their property into the territories, that territorial government had no sovereignty to disapprove of slavery, [and] that the federal government must intervene in a territory's affairs if slavery could not be protected by local authorities. (Huston, 2003, p. 227)

In a separate convention of Southern Democrats, held across Baltimore from the Northern Democrat convention, John C. Breckinridge was nominated as their candidate running on a pro-slavery platform. The essence of the Breckinridge platform was "the absolute necessity of preserving the equal rights of all states" (Holt, 2017, p. 130). To Southern Democrats, equality meant taking slaves to all territories. This idea of equality and the goodness of slavery surpassed concerns raised by leaders about splitting the party (Holt, 2017). Therefore, the Democratic party split over the idea of slaves as property and an individual's ability to travel with property into any territory.

The Constitutional Union party's sole agenda in 1860 was to focus on issues other than slavery. As Holt (2017) posited, the Constitutional Union party intended to "bury the slavery issue" (p. 75). Supporters of this party were against both the Republicans and Democrats, alleging that conversations around the territorial extension of slavery, including popular sovereignty, had completely dominated the country and incited fear as the leaders of the mainstream parties pitted their supporters against their rivals in a battle for control of the Union (Holt, 2017). The Constitutional Union party hoped to gain supporters by highlighting how Republicans and Democrats aggravated sectional ideologies in the United States. Therefore, when the Constitutional Union party met in Baltimore in May the adopted platform highlighted the principles of the Constitution as it was written and advocated for the protection of our national government. Most gentlemen considered for the presidential nomination were quite a bit older than their counterparts in other political parties. John Bell of Tennessee was selected as the Constitutional Union's presidential candidate and Edward Everett of Massachusetts as the vice presidential candidate. They were former Whigs running on a platform of nationalism; Bell, however, had little to no chance to win the election. Supporters of the Constitutional Union party proselytized that the purpose of Bell's entrance into the 1860 presidential contest was to prevent a majority vote in the Electoral College and therefore send the election to the House of Representatives where they hoped Bell would meet a more favorable audience (Holt, 2017).

In 1860 the country was primed for conflict. Tensions over slavery and its extension had been boiling for over a decade. Yet, as Holt (2017) illuminated, both mainstream political parties and individual citizens were "delusional" regarding the extent to which the division between Republican and Democrat and anti-slavery and pro-slavery (and variations within) would manifest if Abraham Lincoln won the presidential election of 1860.

The Rise of Lincoln and the Role of Race

In November 1860 Abraham Lincoln, the Republican candidate for president, won the Electoral College vote despite running against three other candidates. In the wake of his election seven southern states seceded from the union, proving that the political, social, and economic tension over slavery in the United States had reached a point whereby the election of an anti-slavery president meant the severing of the Union. The election of 1860 brought to the forefront just how divided the United States was over slavery and, by extension, the role of race in determining state and national politics. But it was not a forgone conclusion that Lincoln would be the nominee.

In 1858 Lincoln ran for Senator in Illinois against incumbent Stephen Douglas. When Lincoln accepted the nomination, he gave the now famous *House Divided Speech*.

> A house divided against itself cannot stand. I believe this government cannot endure, permanently half *slave* and half *free*. I do not expect the Union to be *dissolved*—I do not expect the house to *fall*—but I do expect it will cease to be divided. It will become *all* one thing or *all* the other. Either the *opponents* of slavery, will arrest the further spread of it, and place it where the public mind shall rest in the belief that it is in the course of ultimate extinction; or its *advocates*

will push it forward, till it shall become alike lawful in *all* the Sates, *old* as well as *new*—*North* as well as *South*. (Oates, 1994, p. 143; italics in original)

Lincoln goes on in this speech to advocate for the end of slavery, a very radical position in 1858 (Oates, 1994). His position was that the institution of slavery was *wrong* and that the Democrats, and by default Stephen Douglas, did not view slavery as such (Potter, 1976, p. 339). Lincoln viewed slavery as a moral wrong, but even more important, he viewed slaves as humans who deserved to be considered citizens and to be able to reap the benefit of the sweat of their own brow (Potter, 1976).

Lincoln lost the 1858 Illinois senate race but ultimately gained the 1860 presidential nomination. In 1858 he caught the attention of Republican party members in Illinois who saw in him an "available" candidate for president in 1860.[1] During Lincoln's first major speech leading up to the 1860 Republican National Convention, the Cooper Union speech, he was a relative unknown. Many saw a scrappy man in a dusty suit with a squeaky voice and laughed at his chances to be president (Hayes, 1960; Holzer, 2004). However, Lincoln's performance at the convention in New York not only provided an opportunity to showcase his stance on slavery, but also proved he could be the candidate for all Republicans, including the sophisticated elite of the east. But Lincoln had to backpedal on his views regarding race or risk losing more moderate Republicans. Accused of promoting racial egalitarianism Lincoln amended his position to state that whites would remain superior to blacks, even if they were no longer enslaved. Lincoln's embrace of white superiority is often overlooked because of his role in the abolishment of slavery. His position, however, was always one whereby slavery was wrong and should not be allowed to spread (Potter, 1976). As educators it is important to address this misconception about Lincoln and to complicate students' narrative about his views.

Three months after Lincoln gave the Cooper Union Address in New York he won the Republican presidential nomination. Lincoln owes his nomination to his supporters on the ground in Chicago, Illinois, during the nomination convention. He would run on a platform that opposed the extension of slavery into the territories even if it did not explicitly outline a "Congressional

---

1. Mainstream Republican party members wanted William Seward to be the 1860 presidential nominee; however, Seward had amassed many enemies throughout his political career whereas Lincoln did not have any political skeletons that could potentially derail his campaign (Hayes, 1960; Neely, 1991).

law against slavery expansion" (Oates, 1994, p. 180). The 1860 platform did include planks related to topics other than slavery; however, Lincoln maintained, as he did in 1858, that slavery was a moral wrong and should not be allowed to extend.

Lincoln focused on natural rights and freedom of mankind, frequently reciting the Declaration of Independence (Neely, 1991). Even as a man of the law, Lincoln's rhetoric against slavery favored the "moralistic anti-slavery sentiment" over the Constitutional (Neely, 1991, pp. 215–216). Lincoln was making the slavery issue a moral one while Southerners were making it about states' rights and Constitutional Unionists were more concerned with Constitutional precedent (Holt, 2017). Lincoln was trying to humanize the issue and this was seen as a threat.

The Republican party, and Lincoln in particular, represented to the Southern Democrats a threat to their very livelihood. Financially, white southern slaveholders relied on free slave labor and the abolition of slavery would drastically reduce their profits. Radical pro-slavery advocates feared Lincoln's election would mean the end of slavery and they threatened to secede if he was elected (Oates, 1994).

While public opinion of the election of 1860 has focused on state's rights versus a strong federal government, the reality is that Southern Democrats saw the attack on slavery as an attack on their ability to hold property, which was subsequently an attack on their financial stability (Huston, 2003). Republicans believed slavery was wrong and wanted to stop its extension. Northern Democrats did not believe slavery was wrong; they simply wanted popular sovereignty to decide if slavery could extend into a territory or not. Southern Democrats believed that "slavery was good" and they wanted the institution to extend for this reason (Holt, 2017, p. 93). Secondarily, Southerners in power feared that a Republican victory would mean the "rules" regarding slavery would change without their input and this would lead to a loss of "fortunes, social achievement, and political preferment" (Huston, 2003, p. 232). Lincoln's personal views on slavery evolved over time (another issue in this complex narrative that should be interrogated), but in 1860 he maintained the position that slavery was wrong.

It is unclear if Lincoln would have won had the Democratic party not split; most involved in the election knew the decision would come down to the votes in the North (Holt, 2017). Lincoln's name did not appear on Southern ballots yet he was able to gain a majority in the Electoral College and 40% of the popular vote as well (see Figure 5.1). Slaveholding Southern Democrats' worst nightmare had come true.

1860: The Election That Started the War

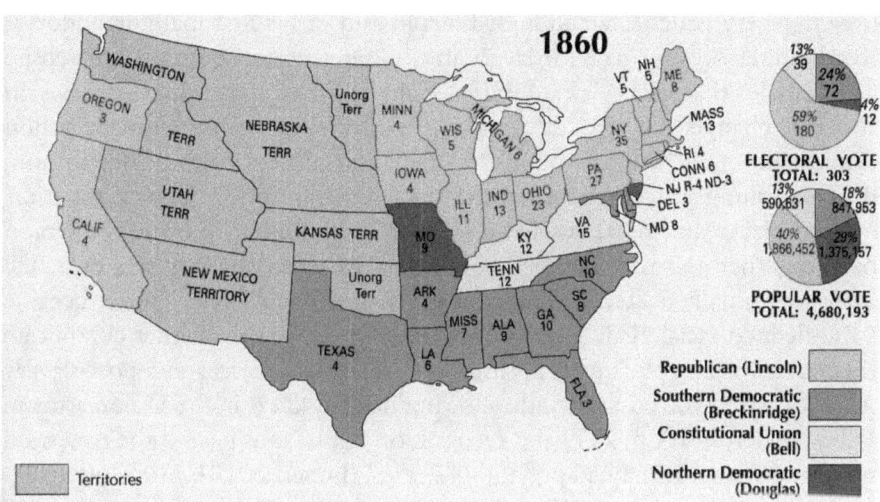

Image 5.1: 1860 Electoral and Popular Vote Map (https://commons.wikimedia.org/wiki/File:1860_Electoral_Map.png)

Legacy

In the events leading up to the election, Southern Democrats claimed that the election of a Republican president, with anti-slavery views, would mean the end of the Union. After the Electoral College met on December 20, 1860 (Image 5.1) making Lincoln's presidency official, South Carolina seceded from the Union. This break was followed by the secession of Mississippi, Florida, Alabama, Georgia, Louisiana, and Texas. Seven states left the Union just because a Republican president was elected. Seven states left the Union because the president of the United States held anti-slavery views. The remaining four states that eventually joined the Confederacy (Virginia, Arkansas, Tennessee, and North Carolina) were waiting for an "overt" act to secede. This came when fighting broke out at Fort Sumter, South Carolina on April 12, 1861. Vitriolic rhetoric about a divided nation was no longer hypothetical. The result was a bloody four-year war that ended in Union victory, the 13th amendment, and a long process to rebuild the Union. Lincoln lived to see the abolishment of slavery throughout the Union but unfortunately the Compromise of 1877 paved the way for Jim Crow laws and a civil rights fight that still continues to this day.

It is indisputable that slavery was a major cause of the American Civil War. Abraham Lincoln's election resulted in a temporary separation of the Union over this very issue. Even though Lincoln said in his first inaugural address that he did not want to end slavery in the states where it already existed he was adamant that slavery's extension should be halted. Over time his views on abolition changed. As a result of the war, Lincoln put forth the Emancipation Proclamation and worked to pass the 13th amendment to the Constitution, thus abolishing slavery in the United States Lincoln spoke of white superiority over blacks, but he knew that a war had to be fought to bring the Union back together and that slavery could not exist when the war was over. He may have initially fixated on "all men are created equal" yet he never became a full-fledged racial egalitarian (Foner, 2010, p. xviii). To further complicate the narrative, Lincoln's own position on "the role of blacks in a post-slavery America" had evolved to include allowing black soldiers in the Union army in 1863 (Foner, 2010, p. 249) and recognition of blacks as part of the American population, a status he had previously denied (Foner, 2010). Lincoln's evolving position is an often under-represented theme within the election of 1860 and the aftermath of the election.[2]

Helping students understand the complex role of race in the election of 1860—and throughout our history—is vital. In this case, it important to ensure students do not conflate Lincoln's anti-slavery position with a commitment to racial equality. Race relations in the mid-19th century, like today, were much more complicated and nuanced. Teaching about the election of 1860 provides an opportunity for teachers to investigate this complexity with their students. Lincoln's ideas for Reconstruction were very different from radical Republicans who wanted the South to "pay" for the war. We will never know how the United States might have progressed with regard to racial tension and rights had Lincoln not been assassinated, but I wonder what he might think of the "debate" over Confederate statues and the Confederate flag continuing in the 21st century.

Bringing in the Social

As educators, one of the most difficult things we do is to bridge the past and present. With regards to race and racism, teachers may be reluctant to engage in lessons or dialog with their students for fear of these controversial topics. Yet connecting the past and present, especially race and racial tensions, is critical to instruction. One way to do so is to get comfortable teaching the social history of the Civil War and not just the military and political history. If we

---

2. For more information on Lincoln's changing positions on slavery and race see *The Fiery Trial: Abraham Lincoln and American Slavery* by Eric Foner.

engage students in topics about the social history of a given era then we offer students the opportunity to learn about narratives that can "counter balance the 'Great Man' theories of history and [allow] a broader range of students to see people more like themselves in the historical record" (Bair & Ackerman, 2014, p. 223). In their article, "Not Your Father's Civil War: Engaging Students through Social History," Bair and Ackerman (2014) argue that it is time to look at the American Civil War from a different perspective; and to teach students about "topics that reflect experiences they themselves are more likely to have" (p. 223). By focusing on the social as much as the political and economic students can gain an understanding of how race played a role in the election of Lincoln and the war. Bair and Ackerman (2014) offer new ways to look at gender, race, and civilians during the Civil War through individuals' social history. In this vein, I offer a lesson that focuses on a social approach to teaching the causes of the Civil War, and specifically the election of 1860. This lesson can be found in the third section of this book.

The purpose of this lesson is to "investigate" individuals who did or did not vote for Lincoln in the 1860 election. In Barrow, Anderson, and Horner (2017) the authors use the Humans of New York (HONY; www.humansofnewyork.com) photoblog concept to modify a traditional lesson on the history of the Civil War into one that incorporates more of the social history of the war era. The lesson, as presented by Barrow, Anderson, and Horner (2017), includes research, interviewing, digital presentations, and teacher/student debriefs, and it addresses all four dimensions of the C3 Framework. In this lesson, students take on the role of an individual from the Civil War representing military and civilian individuals, males and females, free and slave and they create a photoblog identifying the "Humans of the Civil War." The purpose of this assignment is to provide students with multiple perspectives of what caused the war and what life must have been like during the war. To modify this lesson, teachers can have students research individuals who did and did not vote for Lincoln in 1860 and have their students "interview" each other. *Rethinking Schools* published a role-play activity on the Election of 1860, which can be used to supplement the research component of the "Humans of the Civil War" lesson. Bigelow (n.d.) challenges students to address the misconceptions they might have regarding the election and the "electoral alliance [Lincoln] had to assemble to win the presidency" (p. 2).

The *Rethinking Schools* lesson pulls together the social and the political by asking students to step into the shoes of different groups from the 1860s (Lincoln, Western farmers, Northern factory owners and merchants, Southern plantation owners, and Northern workers). Students are asked to answer the compelling question "Why did some people vote for Lincoln and not others?" By evaluating why some people would vote for Lincoln and not others, students may gain a greater understanding of the complexity of the election. After completing the research, students can "interview" each other using mobile devices and create a "Humans of the Civil War" blog page to showcase what they have learned. See Barrow, Anderson, and Horner (2017) for more details. This lesson utilizes technology and 21st century skills while covering the NCSS Themes of: (1) Culture; (4) Individual development and identity; (5) Individuals, groups, and institutions; (10) Civic ideals and practices.

Teaching the Election of 1860

The complexity of the election of 1860 makes it perfect to engage students in historical inquiry. Key to learning about the importance of the election of 1860 is to understand the context in which each of the four candidates came to run for office. I offer a second lesson idea (see Section 3) that stems from the National Park Service's (2016) lesson plan "1860: The Election that Led to War." This lesson plan walks students through the election of 1860 using primary sources to analyze the election results and includes a mix of the political and social context of the election. Through this lesson students may gain a greater understanding of Lincoln's rocky road to becoming the president-elect and the role race and slavery played in the election. This lesson connects to the following NCSS themes: (2) Time, Continuity, and Change; (5) Individuals, Groups, and Institutions; (6) Power, Authority, and Governance; and (10) Civic Ideals and Practices. Students will also be exposed to all four dimensions of the C3 Framework.

The purpose of this second lesson is for students to answer the compelling question, "Why did Lincoln win the Electoral College vote in 1860 but not the popular vote?" This lesson can stand alone, however, students may offer a more rich discussion and analysis of the complexity that was 1860 if they have already completed lesson one.

In four groups, students will investigate the presidential candidates of 1860 and provide a graphic illustration of how each came to be nominated for president. Students develop questions and plan how they want to investigate their candidate. Next they do the work of a historian to analyze primary sources and other resources to apply what they know towards a claim about the similarities and differences between the presidential candidates and their platforms. Finally, students will analyze the *1860 Electoral and Popular vote* map before presenting their arguments as to why Lincoln won the election of 1860 but not the popular vote.

For an extension, students can compare and contrast the results of the 1860 election with other elections in which the candidate-elect won the Electoral College but not the popular vote. Students can investigate the following elections: 1824 (John Q. Adams), 1876 (Rutherford B. Hayes), 1888 (Benjamin Harrison), 2000 (George W. Bush), and 2016 (Donald J. Trump).

Conclusion

The Civil War cannot be taught without teaching the election of 1860 and how the election of a Republican president was the final cause of the war. Instead of glossing over the election, educators may want to provide students the opportunity to investigate the ways in which race drove the election and subsequent separation of the Union. In both lessons associated with the election of 1860 students (and teachers) must grapple with complex historical themes and issues. It is our job as educators to complicate the discussion of the election by focusing conversations on how Lincoln won his party's nomination and the presidential election amid heightened tensions over the institution of slavery and racial equality. By examining the role race played in the division of the Democratic party coupled with the Republican stance of anti-slavery extension and the Constitutional Union's exclusion of the topic in conversations we can see how the election of a Republican president in 1860 was the final impetus for a divided Union that resulted in the American Civil War.

References

Bair, S. D., & Ackerman, K. (2014). Not your father's Civil War: Engaging students through social history. *The Social Studies, 105*, 222–229.

Barrow, E., Anderson, J., & Horner, M. (2017). The role of photoblogs in Social Studies classroom: Learning about the people of the Civil War. *Contemporary Issues in Technology and Teacher Education, 17*(4), 504–521. Retrieved from https://citejournal.s3.amazonaws.com/wp-content/uploads/v17i4SocialStudies1.pdf

Bigelow, B. (n.d.) The election of 1860 role play. *Rethinking Schools*, 1–12. Retrieved from https://1.cdn.edl.io/JLNKpej8enqsqac8iQI3ahL8f9tWLWyVpISovGemOBhN6eOv.pdf

Foner, E. (2010). *The fiery trial: Abraham Lincoln and American slavery*. New York, NY: W.W. Norton.

Hayes, M. L. (1960). *Mr. Lincoln runs for president: The complete story of the presidential campaign of 1860 from nominating convention to the White House*. New York, NY: The Citadel Press.

Holt, M. F. (2017). *The election of 1860: "A campaign fraught with consequences."* Lawrence: University Press of Kansas.

Holzer, H. (2004). *Lincoln at Cooper Union: The speech that made Abraham Lincoln president.* New York, NY: Simon & Schuster.

Hurston, J. L. (2003). *Calculating the value of the Union: Slavery, property Rights, and the economic origins of the Civil War.* Chapel Hill: The University of North Carolina Press.

Jennings, N., Swidler, S., & Koliba, C. (2005). Placed-based education in the standards-based reform era: Conflict or complement? *American Journal of Education, 112*(1), 44–65.

National Council for the Social Studies (NCSS). (2013). *The college, career, and civic life (C3) framework for social studies state standards: Guidance for enhancing the rigor of K–12 civics, economics, geography, and history.* Silver Spring, MD: Author.

National Park Services. (2016). 1860: The election that led to War. Retrieved from https://www.nps.gov/teachers/classrooms/1860-the-election-that-led-to-war.htm

Neeley M. E., Jr. (1991). *The fate of liberty: Abraham Lincoln and Civil liberties.* New York, NY: Oxford University Press.

Oates, S. B. (1994). *With malice toward none: A life of Abraham Lincoln.* New York, NY: HarperPerennial.

Potter, D. M. (1976). *The impending crisis: 1848–1861.* New York, NY: Harper Torchbooks.

Section 2: Pedagogical Challenges

6. Facing Hard History: Confronting the Disconnect in Student Understanding of the Causes of the Civil War

BONNIE LAUGHLIN-SCHULTZ

I open with a confession: the 1850s have long been my favorite era to teach. As a preservice teacher I designed my first unit plan on the coming of the Civil War, and I love now as much as I did then tracing the emerging divide over slavery, a division firmly cemented with Lincoln's election and the onset of war. Change over time, context, causality, contingency, complexity—all the great elements of historical thinking that Flannery Burke and Thomas Andrews (2007) have identified—are present in the study and student exploration of the 1850s. The historical content is rich, and the essential questions are meaningful. How did some white Americans come to believe that slavery—present at the foundational moments of British North America—was a sin that needed stamping out? How did free and enslaved African Americans alike fight to end the institution and achieve personal freedom? How and why did white Southerners, slaveholder and non-slaveholder alike, become more committed than ever to defending the "peculiar institution"—ultimately by moving to dissolve the Union?

Students in the American history survey course apply historical thinking skills, examining change-over-time, continuity, and cause and effect as they answer these questions, carefully tracing how pivotal events such as the Mexican-American War, the introduction of the Wilmot Proviso, and the mayhem induced by the introduction of popular sovereignty in territorial Kansas led to sectional polarization over the future of slavery in the nation. Students dissect newspaper editorials from the time, marveling at the divergent opinions expressed about Southern Congressman Preston Brooks' beating of Massachusetts anti-slavery Senator Charles Sumner in 1856. Students ably contrast the Charleston *Mercury*'s characterization of Brooks as a chivalric hero with the New York *Tribune*'s claim that Sumner "has been savagely and brutally assaulted" by a Ruffian on the floor of the Senate (May 23, 1856), noting how both newspapers read much (if divergent) meaning into a beating. "We are either to have Liberty or Slavery," the *Tribune* declared, while the *Mercury* feared the influence of "a coarse and malignant" abolitionist influence. Moving forward from Bleeding Kansas and the Sumner-Brooks debacle, students identify and explain sectional reception to the Dred Scott decision in 1857 and John Brown's raid two years later. The stage is thus set for southern secession in response to the Republican Lincoln's 1860 election.

It all adds up: mounting division over slavery, a rising pro-slavery defense in the South, increasing support of abolitionism in the North, and the emergence of a sectional party with a platform that included the non-extension of slavery. The Civil War and slavery are thus linked in 1861, and students answer essay prompts explaining the growing divide with reference to such events outlined above. Class moves on and the Civil War is fought, complete with the destruction of slavery and Lee's surrender at Appomattox. The demise of slavery allows for some nuance, complexity, and contingency as we talk about African American agency in bringing about the end of slavery and Lincoln's gradual evolution to embrace emancipation as a war aim (Foner, 2010; Oakes, 2014).

And then something perplexing happens. Some of the same students who could once trace a linear development from the Compromise of 1850 through the secession of South Carolina a decade later somehow stop believing that the Civil War came about because of slavery. A 2015 McClatchy-Marist Poll found that 41% of Americans nationally (and 49% of Southerners) believed slavery was not the "main reason" for the war (Murphy, 2018). Clearly, some of this disconnect may be because the surveyed nonbelievers were not taught the trajectory of the 1850s that I just presented. James Loewen, author of the popular *Lies My Teacher Told Me*, has written about the persistent myths that endure about the Civil War. In "Getting the Civil War Right" (2011), he notes that even among teachers, erroneous beliefs remain. Such beliefs can be even worse than an erroneous understanding of the war's origins, but a wholesale Lost Cause version of the past that not only denies slavery as a root but idealizes both the Confederate cause and experience of slavery.

But these beliefs do not persist only in those students taught faulty history. I see them in my own high school and university students: the same students who carefully trace sectional divide over slavery later look skeptical when the very same slavery is cited as the cause of the Civil War. If the topic comes up, others look uncomfortable or avert their eyes, and a few clearly believe I am offering up liberal lies—despite direct evidence to the contrary. Some of this stems no doubt from the fact that the existence of slavery is a hard truth of American history. Talking about slavery, race, and racism in the United States impacts students emotionally, creating what Joan Middendorf and Leah Shopkow (2018) label as "bottlenecks" to learning. As Joan Middendorf et al. (2015) describe, "When history students feel that they or their family are implicated in events of the past, that their beliefs are being impugned, or that their basic assumptions are being challenged, it is often because *their* preconceptions are causing them to feel uncomfortable with the historical content" (p. 171).

In my own classroom, I have adopted three practices in response to this disconnect in student's transferable understanding of the causes of the Civil War. Perhaps offered together they may encourage student understanding in a manner that will cement understanding of the particular sequence that led to the Civil War and even move outward from the walls of our classroom, transforming student engagement with historical thinking, the nature of history, and the long history of racist belief in America.

Practice 1. Focus on Memory, and with That, the Nature of History, Long Before the War Ends

I very pointedly teach students about historical memory, not as its own separate thing but alongside the actuality of the events of 1860–1861. "In recent years," Civil War scholar Eric Foner (2001) writes, "the study of historical memory has become something of a scholarly cottage industry." Memory, he notes, is neither straightforward nor unproblematic. Instead, "it is 'constructed,' battled over and in many ways political" (para. 2) But memory does not serve us in the classroom because it is fashionable. Rather, teaching about historical memory unpacks the very nature of history for our students, teaching them that history, like the memory-making done in its name, is constructed. Many students are drawn towards a belief that history is objective—a narrative based entirely on facts—but we want them to know that history is instead an argument offered about the past, one situated in the present-day context of the historian.

In the case of the American Civil War, history (and memory) was constructed repeatedly in the decades after Lee's surrender at Appomattox. But it has not served me well to reference historical memory only when the Lost Cause emerges in full force in the Jim Crow era, or when *Birth of a Nation* painted a distorted history of Reconstruction through mockery of African American intellect and glorification of the post-war Klan. Instead,

I have found the need to make memory-making part of my content even before 1861, flashing forward to show various distortions and myth-making of events as they emerged in real time. Through this concerted attention to memory, I hope that students will be more comfortable defying the persistent myths and distortions of Civil War history that remain.

Teaching Scenarios

John Brown

One easy place to discuss historical memory and the nature of history comes when we reach 1859, the year of John Brown's raid. I try to showcase the ways in which Brown was remembered as a hero by African Americans and a villain by white Southerners. We examine his casting as a craven, murdering abolitionist in the Warner Brothers film *Santa Fe Trail* (1940). As historian Merrill Peterson (2002) notes, the film was "a pseudo western that shamelessly distorted his life and purpose," adding, "If it was possible for a motion picture or any theatrical production to libel the dead, *Santa Fe Trail* libeled John Brown." The beauty of the film is that students' viewing of a wild-eyed Raymond Massey as John Brown makes accessible a complicated historiography—the infamous early 20th century Dunning school and others that asserted that fanatical abolitionists had brought on a needless civil war, one that harmed blacks and whites alike through a misguided era of Reconstruction. (Smith & Lowery, 2013) It was nearly this same year that Brown was shown as a selfless martyr by African American painter Jacob Lawrence in his series of 22 paintings. In "The Legend of John Brown," Lawrence offered what historian Blake Gilpin (2011) has called an "alternate narrative of America's past," one meant to "inspire the on-going pursuit of freedom, justice, and equality" (p. 158) The co-existence of such diverse portrayals of the same man helps students explore the contested nature of history, and the way that memory of the past serves the present moment.

Frederick Douglass

In addition, I highlight Frederick Douglass' post-war activism—his insistence that the war had been to end slavery, and that the United States must live up to the 14th Amendment's declaration of citizenship and equal protection under the laws—at the same time as we discuss Douglass' powerful 1852 speech "What to the Slave is the Fourth of July." In it Douglass proclaimed, "Your high independence only reveals the immeasurable distance between us. The blessings in which you, this day, rejoice, are not enjoyed in common ... This Fourth [of] July is *yours*, not *mine*." Douglass continued until his death in 1895 to insist that his nation live up to the ideals of the Declaration. I gesture in this antebellum moment to Douglass' poignant commemoration of John Brown at Storer College in Harpers Ferry in 1881 and to Douglass' continued activism on behalf of an emancipationist memory of the Civil War, again showcasing the fierce contest over narratives of the American past (Blight, 1991, chaps. 9–10).

Practice 2. Let the Creators of the Lost Cause Show Themselves as "Creators"

Teaching Historical Analysis

I also try to allow those actors who created the confusion students still hold over the war's origins story to expose themselves in the act of creating the mythical version of the Civil War in the post-war United States. To do this, I showcase their early ideas and writings alongside their later (contrarian) assertions. Rather than telling students how memory changed over time, I try to facilitate their own discovery (and thus, deeper understanding) of the phenomenon as it played out in real time. Pivotal actors from 1861—Robert E. Lee, Jefferson Davis, Alexander Stephens, Frederick Douglass, Abraham Lincoln—offered their interpretation of the causes of the conflict in that moment, and they continued to do so in the years after the war.

Regional Interests

At the outset of war Abraham Lincoln's late-war (1865) assertion that both North and South knew that the "peculiar and powerful interest" constituted by American slaves were "somehow the cause of the war" was obvious in Confederate documents. The South Carolina Declaration of Secession (1860), for one, carefully identified the "increasing hostility on the part of the non-slaveholding States to the institution of slavery" that had culminated "in the election of a man to the high office of the President of the United States, whose opinions and purposes are hostile to slavery," putting it undoubtedly on the path of "ultimate extinction." Mississippi (1861), too, noted "no choice left us but submission to the mandates of abolition, or a dissolution of the Union" (p. 127). And Texas (1861) complained that northerners had proclaimed not just anti-slavery fervor but "the debasing doctrine of the equality of all men, irrespective of race or color" (p. 142).

South Carolina Declaration

To this mounting evidence, I am adding a second documentary set. In past years I have shown the South Carolina Declaration (1860) on a PowerPoint slide, highlighting the centrality of slavery to the onset of war. To this, I now approach the story from a second tangential angle, letting those agents who we can find again speaking after the war to tell their story of origins and aftermath. The worst offenders—and best case studies—are Jefferson Davis and Alexander Stephens, President and Vice President of the Confederacy, who lived decades past the onset of war. Both, according to Charles Dew (2001), abandoned their early understanding of the war's origins to instead adopt "a passionate insistence that states' rights, and states' rights alone, lay at the root of the recent conflict" (p. 15). Rather than telling students about Dew's assertion, I instead allow Davis and Stephens to reveal themselves creating a distorted history.

Diverse Perspectives

In the week that John Brown was executed in December 1859, Jefferson Davis gave a speech on the floor of Congress. In it, he equated the militant abolitionist Brown with the emerging Republican party. Both, he announced, posed an equal threat to slavery. "When the Government gets into the hands of the Republican party, the arm of the General Government, we are told, will not be raised for the protection of our slave property. … Then John Brown, and a thousand John Browns, can invade us, and the Government will not protect us," he thundered. Given this danger, he declared the South had the right to be released from their allegiance to the Union, as they would be unable to protect slavery within it. This speech offers a highly useful way to teach responses to John Brown's raid—one can read this, show the electoral map of 1860, and suddenly Southern secession is explained.

But Jefferson Davis changed *his own* origins after Southern defeat. In 1881, Jefferson Davis published a long memoir in which he told an entirely different history of the onset of the war, denying the role of slavery. "The sectional hostility was not the consequence of any difference on the abstract question of slavery," he wrote, adding, "It would have manifested itself just as certainly if slavery had existed in all the States, or if there had not been a negro in America" (p. 461).

Students can also discover the shift—*this post-war creation of a new memory*—in the writings of Alexander Stephens. Stephens had famously declared that protection of slavery was at the crux of his new nation. Appalling to modern ears, in 1861 he proudly declared, "Our new government is founded upon exactly the opposite idea; its foundations are laid, its cornerstone rests, upon the great truth that the negro is not equal to the white man; that slavery subordination to the superior race is his natural and normal condition." But as early as 1868, he, like Davis, began to claim a different origins story of the war. The war "had its origin in *opposing principles* ... It was a strife between the principles of Federation, on the one side, and Centralism, or Consolidation, on the other," with slavery "but *the question*" on which the principles came into conflict (pp. 459–460). In other words, looking at these (or longer) passages from Davis and Stephen's own words, students come to see that the states'-rights-not-slavery notion of the war's origins was born only *after* the last shots were fired.

In contrast stand Ulysses S. Grant, Frederick Douglass, and a host of Union veterans and African Americans who continued to put slavery at the center of the war's origins story (Blight, 2018; Gannon, 2011; Jordan, 2011; Varon, 2013). Students might be struck by the declaration of Ulysses S. Grant (1885), composing his memoirs as he died of cancer in 1884, that slavery remained the "cause of the great War of the Rebellion against the United States." Elizabeth Varon (2013) has shown the diverging stories of Appomattox told and spun by Grant and Lee even in the year after 1865, as Lee looked to ignore brutality against the formerly enslaved and to uphold what he thought of as Confederate honor. Perhaps in future semesters I will let them battle over war memory, too.

Standards and Curriculum Alignment

Both of these approaches—teaching historical memory writ large and its happenings in contrast to words offered in 1860–1861—fall nicely within the social studies standards that guide teachers. The *Common Core State Standards* (2010) on History/Social Studies outline various standards that the primary source analysis work described above fulfills. Students comparing accounts by Jefferson Davis and Alexander Stephens and denoting change over time in the origins story of the war would be both "determin[ing] the central ideas or information of a primary ... source" and "attending to such features as the date and origin of the information." (See Table 6.1 for the full text and references for the aligned Common Core standards.) Students comparing Grant and Davis memoirs would align with other CCSS standards, such as that which asks students to "compare the point of view of two or more authors for how they treat the same or similar topics, including which details they include and emphasize in their respective accounts."

Table 6.1: Standards Implicated in Teaching Civil War Memory

Common Core State Standards (2010)	College, Career, & Civic Life C3 Framework for Social Studies State Standards (2013)
CCSS.ELA-Literacy.RH.11–12.2 Determine the central ideas or information of a primary or secondary source; provide an accurate summary that makes clear the relationships among the key details and ideas.	**D2.His.6.9–12** Analyze the ways in which the perspectives of those writing history shaped the history that they produced.
CCSS.ELA-Literacy.RH.9–10.1 Cite specific textual evidence to support analysis of primary and secondary sources, attending to such features as the date and origin of the information.	**D2.His.7.9–12** Explain how the perspectives of people in the present shape interpretations of the past.
CCSS.ELA-Literacy.RH.9–10.6 Compare the point of view of two or more authors for how they treat the same or similar topics, including which details they include and emphasize in their respective accounts.	**D2.His.17.9–12** Critique the central arguments in secondary works of history on related topics in multiple media in terms of their historical accuracy.

Similar strands appear in the *College, Career, & Civic Life C3 Framework for Social Studies State Standards* (2013) produced by the National Council for the Social Studies (NCSS), particularly in its discussion of the disciplinary tools of history. A particularly compelling standard is the one that asks students to think about links between historical context and perspective, both in actual experience and in the creation of history itself. The C3 also asks "students to think about causes and complexity in the writing of history, inviting them to be agents able to identify distortions in how we remember and think about the past." Finally, teachers might prompt students to examine some of the recent textbook controversies with the standard that compels students to "critique the central arguments in secondary works of history on related topics in multiple media in terms of their historical accuracy."

The above standards offer a vision for what NCSS has termed "powerful" social studies, where both historical content and thinking skills are at work. The NCSS Task Force describes study of the past as not unpredictably tied to analysis of the "causes and consequences of events." But the charge offered in its *National Curriculum Standards for Social Studies* (2010) goes further, to the very nature of history: "Knowing how to read, reconstruct and interpret the past allows us to answer questions such as: How do we learn about the past? How can we evaluate the usefulness and degree of reliability of different historical sources?" (para. 7) The stakes for this work are high, particularly when it comes to the Civil War origins story.

Practice 3. Attend to the Distinction Between Slavery and Racism in 1861

It is not enough to attend only to historical memory and the shaping of the false Lost Cause narrative. Instead, I have grown much more careful in my discussions of slavery and racism, emphasizing to students how the Civil War uprooted one and not the other. Divide over slavery was not part and parcel with beliefs in equality. In some rare cases of abolitionists like John Brown it may have been one and the same, but for the bulk of the white northern population, even once the war for Union became a war for emancipation it was not one waged in the name of equality of the races. And in some ways, this is hardly surprising: belief in racial hierarchies showcased in antebellum pro-slavery defenses had been carefully built on 250 years of racist ideas that Ibram Kendi has outlined in his recent *Stamped from the Beginning: The Definitive History of Racist Ideas in America* (2016). It is not coincidence that Kendi draws the title of his work from another Jefferson Davis Senate speech. In that speech, Davis proclaimed government for white men only; the inequality of the races, he declared, had been "stamped from the beginning." The Civil War upended the system of slavery, but it did not uproot such racist ideas.

A mythical origins story of the war, as David Blight (2001) has powerfully shown, was directly tied to these racist ideas and beliefs. Distortion of the Civil War as fought for states' rights separate from slavery, denial that the Confederacy was founded to protect white supremacy, and the Dunning school histories of Reconstruction were predicated on "the denigration of black dignity and the attempted erasure of emancipation from the national narrative of what the war had been about" (p. 5). "Deflections and evasions" about slavery and race, Blight notes, most often served the cause of Jim Crow (p. 5). As David Von Drehle (2011) explains, "History is not just about the past. It also reveals the present. And for generations of Americans after the Civil War, the present did not have room for that radical idea laid bare by the conflict: that all people really are created equal. That was a big bite to chew" (para. 9).

A big bite indeed, and one that Jefferson Davis, Alexander Stephens, and a host of ordinary Americans could neither bite nor chew in the decades after the Civil War. To confront the racist beliefs that enabled slavery and continued after its demise is extraordinarily difficult, but it is the right and moral thing to do. And it means I have to be comfortable with their discomfort and try to overcome the "emotional bottlenecks" that presenting and discussing the slavery-based origins of the Civil War—and the racism that remained. According to Ibram Kendi (2018), "We paint over racist reality to make a beautiful delusion of self, of society. We defend this beautiful self and society from our racist reality with the weapons of denial" (para. 23). Our students' desire to look away from the origins story of the Civil War is rooted in denial. I must work harder to directly confront it in the classroom and to do all I can to overcome it. If the methods outlined here don't yield payoff, I must continue to search for methods that will help me accomplish this goal.

"History that comes to us as nostalgia and fable does more harm than good," Southern historian Edward Ayers (2005) has written. "Honest history," he adds, "answers our questions only by asking something of us in return" (p. 17). For teachers of history, what is asked in return is to correct the flaws perpetuated by not just ordinary Americans but by historians of the early twentieth century and to move towards better, harder, honest history that trains students in both historical rigor and thinking while making honest reckoning with origins of the War and abuses of the origins story.

References

Primary Sources

Davis, J. (1859, December 8). Speech to the U.S. Senate. Retrieved from http://www.digitalhistory.uh.edu/active_learning/explorations/brown/public_davis.cfm

Davis, J. (1881/2008). Excerpts from *The rise and fall of the Confederate government*. In J. Fowler (Ed.), *The Confederate experience reader: Selected documents and essays* (pp. 460–462, esp. 461). New York, NY: Routledge.

Declaration of the immediate causes which induce and justify the secession of South Carolina from the federal union. (1860, December 24). Retrieved from http://avalon.law.yale.edu/19th_century/csa_scarsec.asp

Declaration of the immediate causes which induce and justify the secession of Mississippi from the federal union. (1861, January 26/2010). In J. Loewen & E. Sebasta (Eds.), *The confederate and neo-confederate reader: The 'Great Truth' about the 'Lost Cause'* (pp. 127–129, esp. 127). Jackson: University Press of Mississippi.

Declaration of the causes which impel the state of Texas to secede from the federal union. (1861, February 2/2010). In J. Loewen & E. Sebasta (Eds.), *The confederate and neo-confederate reader: The 'Great Truth' about the 'Lost Cause'* (pp. 140–144, esp. 142). Jackson: University Press of Mississippi.

Douglass, F. (1852). What to the slave is the 4th of July? Retrieved from http://teachingamericanhistory.org/library/document/what-to-the-slave-is-the-fourth-of-july/

Grant, U. (1885). *Personal Memoirs of U.S. Grant*. 2 vols. New York, NY: Charles L. Webster. Retrieved from https://www.gutenberg.org/files/4367/4367-h/4367-h.htm

Lincoln, A. (1865, March 4). Second inaugural address. Retrieved from http://avalon.law.yale.edu/19th_century/lincoln2.asp

Stephens, A. (1861/2008). Cornerstone speech. In J. Fowler (Ed.), *The confederate experience reader: Selected documents and essays* (pp. 151–154, esp. 151). New York, NY: Routledge.
Stephens, A. (1868/2008). Excerpts from *A constitutional view of the late war between the states*, In J. Fowler (Ed.), *The confederate experience reader: Selected documents and essays* (pp. 459–460). New York, NY: Routledge.
Untitled Editorial. (1856, May 28). Charleston *Mercury*. In L. Benson (Ed.), *Secession era editorial project*. Furman University. Retrieved from http://history.furman.edu/benson/docs/sccmsu56528a.htm
Untitled Editorial. (1856, May 23). New York *Tribune*. In L. Benson (Ed.), *Secession era editorial project*, Furman University. Retrieved from http://history.furman.edu/benson/docs/nytrsu56524a.htm

Secondary Sources

Andrews, T., & Burke, F. (2007). What does it mean to think historically? *Perspectives on History*, 45(1). Retrieved from https://www.historians.org/publications-and-directories/perspectives-on-history/january-2007/what-does-it-mean-to-think-historically
Ayers, E. (2005). What caused the Civil War? *North & South*, 8(5), 12–18.
Blight, D. (1991). *Frederick Douglass's Civil War: Keeping faith in jubilee*. Baton Rouge, LA: LSU Press.
Blight, D. (2001). *Race and Reunion: The Civil War in American Memory*. Cambridge: Belknap Press.
Blight, D. (2018). *Frederick Douglass: Prophet of freedom*. New York, NY: Simon & Schuster.
Colaiaco, J. (2006). *Frederick Douglass and the fourth of July*. New York, NY: Palgrave Macmillan.
Common core state standards for English language arts & literacy in history/social studies, science, and technical subjects. (2010). Common Core State Standards Initiative. Retrieved from http://www.corestandards.org/wp-content/uploads/ELA_Standards1.pdf
Dew, C. (2001). *Apostles of Disunion: Southern Secession Commissioners and the Causes of the Civil War*. Charlottesville: The University of Virginia.
Foner, E. (2001, March 4). Selective Memory. Review of *Race and Reunion* by David Blight. *New York Times*. Retrieved from http://www.nytimes.com/books/01/03/04/reviews/010304.04fonert.html
Foner, E. (2010). *The fiery trial: Abraham Lincoln and American slavery*. New York, NY: W.W. Norton.
Gallagher, G., & Nolan, A. (Eds.). (2000). *The myth of the Lost Cause and Civil War history*. Bloomington: Indiana University Press.
Gannon, B. (2011). *The won cause: Black and white comradeship in the Grand Army of the Republic*. Chapel Hill: University of North Carolina Press

Gilpin, R. (2002). *John Brown lives! America's long reckoning with violence, equality, and change* (esp. 158 and Chap. 9). Chapel Hill: University of North Carolina Press.

Horwitz, T. (2011). *Midnight rising: John Brown and the raid that sparked the Civil War.* New York, NY: Henry Holt.

Janney, C. (2013). *Remembering the Civil War: Reunion and the limits of reconciliation.* Chapel Hill: University of North Carolina Press.

Jordan, B. (2011). Living monuments: Union veteran amputees and the embodied memory of the Civil War. *Civil War History, 57*(2), 121–152

Kendi, I. (2016). *Stamped from the beginning: The definitive history of racist ideas in America.* New York, NY: Nation Books.

Kendi, I. (2018, January 13). The heartbeat of racism is denial. *New York Times.* Retrieved from https://www.nytimes.com/2018/01/13/opinion/sunday/heartbeat-of-racism-denial.html

Laughlin-Schultz, B. (2013). *The tie that bound us: The women of John Brown's family and the legacy of radical abolitionism.* Ithaca, NY: Cornell University Press.

Loewen, J. (2011). Getting the Civil War right. *Teaching Tolerance, 40.* Retrieved from https://www.tolerance.org/magazine/fall-2011/getting-the-civil-war-right

McPherson, J. (2004). Long-legged Yankee lies: The southern textbook crusade. In A. Fahs & J. Waugh (Eds.), *The memory of the Civil War in American culture* (pp. 64–78). Chapel Hill: University of North Carolina Press.

Middendorf, J., Mickutè, J., Saunders, T., Najar, J., Clark-Huckstep, D., & Pace, D. (2015) What's feeling got to do with it? Decoding emotional bottlenecks in the history classroom. *Arts & Humanities in Higher Education, 14*(2), 166–180, esp. 171

Middendorf, J., & Shopkow, L. (2018). *Overcoming student learning bottlenecks: Decode the critical thinking of your discipline.* Sterling, VA: Stylus Publishing.

Miller, D. (2015, August 5). 8 components of a reflective classroom. *Facing Today Blog.* Brookline, MA: Facing History and Ourselves. Retrieved from http://facingtoday.facinghistory.org/8-components-of-a-reflective-classroom

Murphy, T. (2018). States' rights and 'historical malpractice.' *Teaching Tolerance, 58,* 27–29.

National Council for the Social Studies. (2010). *National curriculum standards for social studies: A framework for teaching, learning, and assessment.* Retrieved from https://www.socialstudies.org/standards/strands

National Council for the Social Studies. (2013). *College, career, & civic life C3 framework for social studies state standards.* Retrieved from http://www.socialstudies.org/system/files/c3/C3-Framework-for-Social-Studies.pdf

Oakes, J. (2014). *Freedom national: The destruction of slavery in the United States, 1861–1865.* New York, NY: W.W. Norton.

Peterson, M. (2002). *John Brown, the legend revisited* (esp. 113–114). Charlottesville: University of Virginia Press.

Sigward, D. (Ed.). (2015). *The Reconstruction era and the fragility of democracy.* Facing History and Ourselves Foundation.

Smith, J., & Lowery, J. (Eds.). (2013). *The Dunning school: Historians, race, and the meaning of reconstruction.* Lexington: University Press of Kentucky.
Teaching Tolerance. (2018). *Teaching hard history: A framework for teaching American slavery.* Montgomery, AL: Southern Poverty Law Center. Retrieved from https://www.tolerance.org/frameworks/teaching-hard-history/american-slavery
Varon, E. (2013). *Appomattox: Victory, defeat, and freedom at the end of the Civil War.* New York, NY: Oxford University Press.
Von Drehle, D. (2011, April 7). 150 years after Fort Sumter: Why we're still fighting the Civil War. *Time Magazine.* Retrieved from http://content.time.com/time/magazine/article/0,9171,2063869,00.html

7. Why Did the South Secede?: Using Inquiry to Confront Contentious History

CARLY MUETTERTIES AND RYAN A. LEWIS

Debate over the prominence of Confederate symbols, monuments, and the overall racial legacy of America's slavery past, has kept historical interpretation of the Civil War in public discourse. Many communities have subsequently begun to grapple with how the Confederacy and Civil War should be remembered. A Pew Research Poll (2011) found that 48% of respondents believed the main cause of the Civil War was states' rights, while 38% believed it to be slavery. In a more recent McClatchy-Marist Poll (2015), 53% of respondents believed slavery led to the Civil War, while 41% disagreed. Though presenting different results, both polls illustrate public division on an issue generally agreed upon by scholars. "No matter what we do or the overwhelming consensus among historians," says David Blight, a prominent Civil War historian, "out in the public mind, there is still this need to deny that slavery was the cause of the war" (quoted in Von Drehle, 2011). Such denial of slavery's role in Civil War history is perpetuated within and outside the classroom.

Aside from visible public symbols, such as the Confederate flag and statues of Confederate military leaders, a sanitized version of the Civil War and Confederacy also manifests in state curriculum. The ahistorical presentation of content became particularly evident in Texas, when the state adopted revised standards in 2010. Board member Pat Hardy stated slavery's role in the Civil War was a "side issue" to states' rights. The Texas standards' mandatory readings reinforce this perspective, as required primary sources focus on state sovereignty, while excluding influential documents emphasizing slavery as the conflict's cornerstone (Brown, 2015).

These issues, coupled with many years as social studies teachers, informed our work as fellows for the Southern Poverty Law Center's *Teaching Tolerance* educational initiative for teaching American slavery in 2017. For this fellowship, we created materials to help teachers tackle important, but often difficult, content related to American slavery. Tasked with creating curricular materials grounded in primary sources from the *Library of Congress*, we chose southern secession as a topic for an inquiry unit as the intersection between historical and public discourse revolving around the Civil War make it an ideal means for students to engage in rigorous historical practices.

What follows is a discussion of the context informing the writing of the inquiry, with a description of the inquiry using the Inquiry Design Model (IDM), wherein we explain our curricular choices. We hope that our process of curriculum building provides guidance for those wishing to teach this material, as well as offer perspective on the process of inquiry writing.[1]

Grounding Inquiry in the Classroom Context

As teachers of young learners, the selection of *what we teach* is as important as *how we teach*. This is all the more important when approaching the contentious discussion of the reasoning behind southern secession. Though particularly notable in Civil War scholarship, students may not recognize history as a field built on controversy and debates. In our respective classrooms, positioning students at the center of learning means challenging such preconceived ideas of both content and the nature of historical study.

Before writing the inquiry, we considered how we have previously asked students to explore the Civil War's causes. As James Loewen (2011) advocates, our curricular decisions focused on directing students' attention to primary documents from Southern states providing reasons for secession. Various sources highlight perspectives of southern politicians and policymakers, including South Carolina's 1860 secession declaration. Given that much of the Civil War's controversy centers around the role of slavery, author Ryan Lewis challenged his students with the following question: "Was slavery the primary reason for the secession of South Carolina?" Using the voices of southern lawmakers as evidence, students either affirmed or refuted slavery as the war's central cause. Lewis found many students easily created arguments

---

1. The inquiry unit is available through the Southern Poverty Law Center's curricular resources, found here: https://www.tolerance.org/frameworks/teaching-hard-history/american-slavery

based on the South Carolina declaration, as it repeatedly discusses both slavery and the concept of states' rights.

However, at the end of their discussion, students' responses led to more questions: Are there *more* possibilities for the cause of the Civil War? Is it simply a choice between slavery and the doctrine of states' rights? Should students be made to choose between these two ends of the historical continuum? Do students even understand the meaning of states' rights? Do our modern definitions of states' rights comport with the Antebellum understanding? Would a southerner in 1860 have made a realistic distinction between the rights of states and the right to own slaves?

It was at this point, we began our fellowship with the Southern Poverty Law Center (SPLC), providing an opportunity for us to grapple with these questions in much the same way as our students. SPLC's *Teaching Hard History* revolves around a "Framework for Teaching American Slavery," wherein teaching materials were developed to help teachers tackle content critical to fostering student understanding of slavery's historical significance (Shuster, Jay, & Lyerly, 2018). Particularly, the *College, Career, & Civic Life (C3) Framework for Social Studies State Standards* (2013) and corresponding Inquiry Design Model (IDM) provide the structure to engage students in the process of historical inquiry. Interpretation of the past allows better understanding of present circumstances, where the Civil War's legacy continues to permeate public discourse (Swan, Lee, & Grant, 2018). Our fellowship team created curriculum materials using primary documents in order to address SPLC's key concepts and objectives, including this inquiry.

Using Inquiry to Study the Civil War

The causes of southern secession was chosen for an inquiry unit, as its contentious nature makes it a topic particularly apt for developing students' historical disciplinary skills. Though our views are consistent with modern scholarship—the South's desire to expand and preserve slavery being *the* basis for Southern hostilities—we recognized the importance of introducing students to many different perspectives to provide a complex understanding of the Civil War's causes, as well as empower them to apply disciplinary literacies in a meaningful way, with relevancy outside the classroom.

Using inquiry-based approaches to historical interpretation provides teachers the structure to have students *do* history, similar to skills used by academic experts (Levstik & Barton, 2015). Per the *C3 Framework* Indicators, interpreting, critiquing, and assessing sources requires students consider the relationship between the source and broader historical context, while also laying the foundation to form claim-based arguments (NCSS, 2013). Using the Inquiry Design Model (IDM) provides the necessary framework and scaffolding to allow students to systematically examine evidence, make claims, and eventually create an original argument (Grant, Lee, & Swan, 2015). Revolving around a compelling question, the IDM structure consists of a series of supporting questions and formative tasks to support the historical inquiry process. By progressing through a structured historical inquiry, students develop the skills and content knowledge needed to create evidence-based arguments addressing the compelling question. As this topic particularly illustrates the role of historiography in historical study, we hoped an inquiry-based approach would propel further exploration by students into how history is written, remembered, and acted upon.

Compelling Question: Broadening Questions for an Inquiry

In order to appropriately address the causes of southern secession using the IDM, our original question needed broadening to provide students space to investigate the complexities impacting southern secession, rather than presenting it as a binary choice. After consulting with our fellowship colleagues, we chose the compelling question: "Why did the South Secede?" The compelling question was designed to be both student-friendly and intellectually rigorous, in that it holds significance for young people, is clear, reflects an enduring historical issue, and has implications beyond the classroom (Grant, 2013). By investigating the compelling question, students explore conflicting perspectives, challenging simplistic or uncomplicated views of secession, and come to their own conclusions.

Staging the Inquiry

To stage the inquiry, we wanted to determine a baseline of students' current understandings of southern secession. Three statements were chosen, reflecting the two main discourses revolving around the topic: (1) states have the right to leave/secede from the rest of the United States; (2) slavery was the reason for the secession of the South; and (3) the protection of state sovereignty was the reason for the secession of the South. Students consider the extent to which they agree or disagree with those statements, ultimately being required to explain why they hold this viewpoint. The staging exercise allows students to see how their classmates understand the issue, emphasizing this historical topic's potential contentiousness, even among their peers. This portion of the inquiry was also included to validate students' ability to think historically. Even though, as teachers, we hold particular perspectives, the staging provides a means to model a respectful discussion of differences.

Supporting Question 1: In What Ways Did States Attempt to Compromise?

In order to prepare students for understanding events during the secession movement of 1860–1861, they need to consider the various compromises and legislation that that were passed during the antebellum era. Collectively, these sources illustrate the various actions taken by federal and state governments to address issues of slavery and state sovereignty, particularly in the context of territorial expansion. The featured sources include: the Missouri Compromise of 1820, which defines slavery's northern boundary; Henry Clay's Resolutions for the Compromise of 1850, addressing the slavery question for newly annexed territories; an excerpt from the Compromise of 1850's Fugitive Slave Act, which prevented those who had escaped slavery from testifying in their own defense; a portion of the Kansas-Nebraska Act, wherein popular sovereignty would determine slavery in territories; and the *Scott v. Sandford* Supreme Court decision, which denied enslaved people their citizenship based on race.

Sources chosen reflect the long progression of compromises. However, we recognize that our list could not be complete as it did not include such events as the U.S. Constitution's compromises, the entire Compromise of 1850, nor other land acquisitions from Mexico (e.g., the Treaty of Guadalupe Hidalgo, Gadsden Purchase). Though we would encourage teachers to include additional events when approaching this supporting question, the sources included were chosen to highlight the enduring nature of these issues—the central arguments in 1820 continuing into the secession crisis with compromise being a bandage on maintaining national unity rather than contributing to a lasting solution.

As chronological progression is at the heart of this supporting question, the chosen formative performance task is an annotated timeline. A timeline allows students to visualize how the slavery question endured for nearly a century in the United States, thereby establishing foundational content for subsequent supporting questions.

Supporting Question 2: In What Ways Did the Election of 1860 Divide the Nation?

After first considering how compromise maintained national unity, but illustrating the nation's increasing fracturing, the next step of the inquiry addresses the Presidential Election of 1860. This supporting question has students consider the extent to which the 1860 election divided the nation, and therefore was a cause for secession, or if the election was the final straw of division. Sources chosen illustrate the existing ideological, geographical, and political divisions, thereby connecting content with the previous supporting question, while also highlighting how the election piqued tension throughout the country. Sources also address how slavery's territorial expansion, preservation of southern political power, and issues of federal and national power all intermingled as sources of division. As the supporting question addresses the election, sources reflect various types of information integral to understanding elections. The ways in which they relate to one another also provides a means to create a synthesis in the formative task, rather than analyzing each source in isolation. The featured sources include: an editorial cartoon illustrating the divisiveness of the election; an electoral map of the election results; descriptions of the four parties' platforms; and a *Charleston Mercury* broadside, announcing South Carolina's secession from the Union. The ways in which these sources relate to one another lends itself to writing a summary paragraph, however teachers may use other types of classroom exercises. Most importantly, they build on the previous inquiry's material, while also presenting the complexities of assessing evidence about secession.

Supporting Question 3: What did Southerners Say About Secession?

Pivotal to understanding southern secession is choosing sources that provide viewpoints of Antebellum Southerners, as reflected in this supporting question. Southern perspectives of secession or slavery are not monolithic, therefore we recognize these sources are not exhaustive. However, the chosen sources emphasize southern discourse prior to and during the Secession Crisis, thereby presenting a challenge to the historiographical record's revisionist versions. The sources are all considered to be historically significant in that they were prominent perspectives influential in encouraging other states to secede.

Though this supporting question and accompanying sources are particularly valuable in addressing the compelling question, rhetoric concerning slavery and maintaining the institution often use highly racialized language, which many students might find shocking or triggering. Though cognizant of this fact, we did not want to present a softened version of slavery, as that would ultimately present an ahistorical version of the past. Instead, these materials present teachers with an opportunity to engage students in a discussion about the ways in which racism permeated and shaped society.

Why Did the South Secede?   111

The featured sources include:

- South Carolina's secession declaration, which forcefully addresses the reasons for which they chose to leave the Union, centered on the perpetuation and expansion of slavery.
- An excerpt from a speech by future Vice President of the Confederacy, Alexander Stephens, wherein he indicates compromise with northern states is unattainable.
- A senator's speech from 1850, encouraging southern secession, rather than continued compromises.
- The "Thanksgiving Sermon" from New Orleans Reverend B.M. Palmer, offering a religious justification for slavery, often credited for being pivotal in Louisiana's decision to secede.
- Stephens' famous *Cornerstone Speech*, wherein he identifies slavery as the cornerstone of the South.

The formative performance task for this question is a Venn diagram summarizing arguments concerning secession. This particular exercise was chosen as it has students assess both variances and similarities among stated reasons for secession. Putting this question and task after previous supporting questions addressing the compromises and the 1860 election helps students consider how the previous rhetoric of Southern leaders culminated into the arguments put forth in the chosen sources. This also provides students the means to begin constructing evidence-based arguments reflecting nuanced understandings of the issue at hand.

Supporting Question 4: What Did Northerners Say About Secession?

Balancing the previous supporting question, which focuses on prominent Southerners, the final supporting question presents Northern viewpoints about why the South seceded. Using non-Southern voices provides a necessary perspective, showing how southern secession was perceived throughout the Union. For this question, there were many different ways to present students with Northern voices. Though letters to President Lincoln are included, one notably absent voice is Abraham Lincoln, himself. Certainly there are many available pieces on which we, or other teachers, could have drawn to show students Lincoln's perceptions. However, the sources that accompany the supporting question instead reflect voices more ambivalent to the issue, further creating a complicated picture of secession throughout the country.

The featured sources for this supporting question include two political cartoons satirizing the seceded states' actions, as well as emphasizing their destruction of the country being antithetical to the South's espoused beliefs. The remaining featured sources are letters to President Lincoln from Horace Greeley of the *New-York Tribune* and the New York Republicans. Whereas Greeley believes war is preferable to "another nasty compromise," the Republicans urge Lincoln to consider compromise and avoid war. The fourth formative tasks builds off the third task, as students add additional information to their Venn diagram and create a more complete picture as to why the South seceded. Importantly, it shows a balance of how Americans at the time, North and South, would have interpreted current events. Just as perspectives on issues do not all align today, this task brings together sometimes conflicting opinions to create a more comprehensive historical perspective with which students can address the compelling question.

Summative Assessment: Why Did the South Secede?

Through the course of this inquiry unit, students studied various aspects of southern secession in order to foster more nuanced understandings, complicating dominant narratives of the Civil War. Critical to the IDM structure is "argument stems." These argument stems are the several potential arguments students could develop by inquiry's end, stemming from the original compelling question. Though students' answers may not reflect all of the possible responses, this component of the IDM is perhaps one of the most important considerations in inquiry-building, as it prompted us to consider several possible nuanced perspectives, rather than predetermining a single answer we want our students to find. As previously noted, teachers have their own perspectives on the causes of the Civil War, but recognize engaging students in history means allowing them time to practice wading through historical sources, weighing evidence, and coming to their own conclusions, rather than repeating what we deem as "correct." Possible argument stems for this inquiry are:

- Southern states seceded for a variety of reasons, but the main factor was the protection and continuation of the institution of slavery, the influence of which was woven throughout Southern society.
- Western expansion disrupted the national equilibrium regarding slavery, leading the South to fear they would lose federal power.
- While the protection of slavery was an important factor, the primary motivation for secession was fear of having lost control over the federal government when Lincoln was elected.

- Slavery and control of the federal government were woven together in many Americans' minds, North and South, leading to the South's decision to secede.

The possible arguments each address the compelling question and reflect the skills and content fostered through the process of completing the inquiry. It is important to note that teachers would not give these arguments to students; but rather teachers can anticipate some variation of the stems to appear in students' responses based on the tasks and sources.

One of the key purposes of historical study is to connect content to modern circumstances, making the material relevant to students' civic lives (Barton & Levstik, 2008). Correspondingly, the two final components of this inquiry were designed to bridge the content and summative task to current democratic processes. The chosen extension exercise has students participate in a Structured Academic Controversy activity, based on the National History Education Clearinghouse's guidelines.[2] Similarly to the inquiry's staging exercise, this style of discussion provides a framework to foster productive classroom dialog, promoting argumentation skills without devolving into a competitive debate.

Considering the prominence of Civil War history in modern American culture, there are many different ways we considered for students to apply the content and skills learned for the final component of the IDM, the *Taking Informed Action* (TIA) piece. In Kentucky, where both authors live, Confederate statues generated much public debate, leading to the relocation of two statues in 2017 from Lexington's Cheapside Park, a former slave auction site. Considering how the Civil War is remembered in textbooks and in public memorials would certainly have been a meaningful way to apply the inquiry's content. However, we decided to instead focus on the tension between state sovereignty and federal power—not because we believe it is more important or relevant, but rather it would be more applicable to students in states outside of those who participated in the Civil War.

Disputes between state and federal governments concerning topics including environmental regulation, civil rights, immigration, and energy conservation share similarities with debates concerning state sovereignty, slavery, and slavery's expansion. However, we caution teachers to not frame these disputes as merely about state and federal power. Teachers should also emphasize the content of said disputes. For example, assessment of "states'

---

2. Information pertaining to Structured Academic Controversies (SAC) can be found here: http://teachinghistory.org/teaching-materials/teaching-guides/21731

rights" arguments should not exclude the "rights" to which they referred: to protect and continue slavery. Likewise, subsequent "states' rights" debates have centered on limiting civil rights of marginalized groups. Applying this inquiry in an *informed* civic action requires students consider the context and content of state and national power disputes.

To take informed action, students research a topic of interest to them concerning state versus federal power, then draft a letter to a state or federal representative presenting an evidence-based position paper concerning the issue, thereby engaging students in active citizenship. Teachers may cue students to assess particular political leaders to compare on what issues they seek more state versus federal control.

Conclusion

The process of writing this inquiry highlighted several sets of difficulties in creating meaningful curriculum on the topic of southern secession. Students may be aware of the issues surrounding secession, but their understandings can often be incomplete, informed by modern controversies, and not based on the wealth of historical scholarship on the Civil War. Therefore, it is imperative that students engage in historical inquiry by completing a series of historical sources, questions, and tasks. Teachers should craft and adapt inquiries to be responsive to students' abilities, existing knowledge, and interests. In this regard, the goal of inquiry is not to make history so oblique that it is unattainable, but to provide foundational historical questions for students.

Another difficulty for teaching the Civil War relates to the role of the teacher as instructional gatekeeper (Thornton, 2005). This inquiry represents an admittedly incomplete picture of the origins of the Civil War. However, the primary sources selected do offer broad and nuanced perspectives. As facilitators, it is imperative that teachers allow students to conduct inquiries in order to come to their own conclusions. As teachers, this can be difficult, particularly about a topic about which many feel strongly. However, this inquiry was designed to remain true to the skills of historical study—meaning, we do not tell students *what* to think about historical events and interpretation, but rather provide space to teach them *how* to think.

References

Barton, K. C. & Levstik, L. S. (2008). History. In J. Arthur, I. Davies, & C. Hahn (Eds.), The Sage Handbook of Education for Citizenship and Democracy (pp. 355–366). Sage.

Brown, E. (2015, July 5). Texas officials: Schools should teach that slavery was 'side issue' to Civil War. *The Washington Post.* Accessed from https://www.washingtonpost.com/local/education/150-years-later-schools-are-still-a-battlefield-for-interpreting-civil-war/2015/07/05/e8fbd57e-2001-11e5-bf41-c23f5d3face1_story.html?utm_term=.dc96730a973e

Civil War at 150: Still Relevant, Still Divisive (2011, April 8). The Pew Research Center. Accessed from http://www.people-press.org/2011/04/08/civil-war-at-150-still-relevant-still-divisive/

Grant, S. G. (2013). From inquiry arc to instructional practice: The potential of the C3 framework. *Social Education, 77*(6), 322–326, 351.

Grant, S. G., Lee, J., & Swan, K. (2015). The inquiry design model. Retrieved from www.C3teachers.org/IDM

Levstik, L. S., & Barton, K. C. (2015). *Doing history: Investigating with children in elementary and middle school.* New York, NY: Routledge.

Loewen, J. W. (2011). Using confederate documents to teach about secession, slavery, and the origins of the Civil War. *OAH Magazine of History, 25*(2), 35–44.

McClatchy-Marist Poll. (2015, August 6). A nation still divided: The confederate flag. *Marist College Institute for Public Opinion.* Accessed from http://maristpoll.marist.edu/86-a-nation-still-divided-the-confederate-flag/

National Council for the Social Studies (NCSS). (2013). *The college, career, and civic life (C3) framework for social studies state standards: Guidance for enhancing the rigor of K–12 civics, economics, geography, and history.* Silver Spring, MD: Author.

Shuster, K., Jay, B., & Lyerly, C. L. (2018). *Teaching hard history: A framework for teaching American slavery.* Southern Poverty Law Center: Teaching Tolerance.

Swan, K., Lee, J., & Grant, S. G. (2018). Teaching American slavery through inquiry. Southern Poverty Law Center: Teaching Hard History. Retrieved from https://www.tolerance.org/magazine/publications/teaching-american-slavery-through-inquiry

Thornton, S. J. (2005). *Teaching social studies that matters: Curriculum for active learning.* New York, NY: Teachers College Press.

Von Drehle, D. (2011, April 7). 150 years after Fort Sumter: Why we're still fighting the Civil War. *Time Magazine.* Accessed from http://content.time.com/time/magazine/article/0,9171,2063869,00.html

8. Civil War Memories: Untangling the Long and Difficult History of the Causes of the Civil War

Kevin Caprice, Ricky Dale Mullins and David Hicks

> Some history can be difficult because it is traumatic; because it is difficult for most people in the present to fathom; or because it raises issues of identity, marginalization, and oppression that are more easily ignored than addressed for many students and teachers. (Stoddard, Marcus, & Hicks, 2016, p. 4)

Sentiments and discussions surrounding the Civil War are not typically "civil." Teaching about the Civil War can be difficult; and in many ways the above quote effectively captures the reasons why teaching about the causes and history surrounding the Civil War is hard/difficult history to teach and learn. The Civil War is pedagogically challenging because it is both *affectively* and *conceptually* difficult. Affectively difficult history is "when events dealing with conflict, violence, death, identity loss, and personal social trauma are perceived by some students as too personal, sensitive, unfair, disturbing, uncomfortable, shameful, emotive, or culturally controversial" (Walsh, Hicks, & van Hover, 2016, p. 18). Conceptually difficult history is difficult because history as a discipline is a "dynamic, fluid discipline: complex, conceptually challenging, contested, counter intuitive, and academically controversial" (Walsh et al., 2016, p. 19). To teach such histories requires focusing on the goals of educating students for historical literacy through an evidence-based and carefully structured approach (Walsh et al., 2016). The C3 Framework (NCSS, 2013), as well as scholarship within the social studies (see Grant, Lee, & Swan, 2014; Grant, Swan, & Lee, 2016; Lee & Swan, 2013; Levinson & Levine, 2013; Swan, Lee, & Grant, 2015; VanSledright, 2013) similarly stresses the importance of teaching and learning social studies as systematic and sophisticated disciplinary literacy, that moves students through the Inquiry Arc.

We also see this importance, and therefore, in this chapter we build on the historical analysis chapter entitled "Struggling to 'Remember' the Causes of the American Civil War" and introduce ways in which teachers can take the content and analysis from that chapter and make it pedagogically ready for classroom use. Specifically, this chapter is structured to support teachers and students as they begin to navigate through the challenging terrain of how the causes of the American Civil War were initially articulated on the eve of war and subsequently remembered and re-purposed over time and space in the decades following the end of the Civil War. Guided by the compelling question: "If history relies on facts and dates, why is there so much controversy around the causes of the American Civil War over time and space?," this chapter seeks to help teachers and students carefully investigate both the conceptually and affectively difficult history of the causes of the American Civil War through a disciplined and structured analysis of contextually sensitive historical sources that when brought together can serve to support evidence-based claims, not just around the causes of the Civil War, but the role of ideology in shaping how and why how we remember the Civil War as so difficult and different.

In this chapter we will provide different approaches for starting this lesson, provide and describe primary and secondary historical sources, suggest a scaffold for analyzing these sources, identify how we would approach a discussion centered around these documents, and provide follow-up activities a teacher can choose from to reinforce the material presented in this chapter. In setting up this lesson, we pull from guidelines recommended in a Structured Academic Controversy (SAC) (see http://teachinghistory.org/teaching-materials/teaching-guides/21731), but we also provide different scaffolds, strategies, and insights throughout to further aid the teacher in teaching the difficult topic of the American Civil War specifically, and could serve as a framework for teaching other difficult histories moving forward.

Suggested Options for Beginning the Lesson

The teacher should start class by introducing the compelling question: "If history relies on facts and dates, why is there so much controversy around the causes of the American Civil War over time and space?" After introducing the question, there are several options for beginning the lesson (see Table 8.1). Option one is showing a clip entitled "Calhoun's Prophecy" from the film Amistad filmed in 1997 where South Carolina senator John C. Calhoun speaks of his prediction for the unfolding of the Civil War. Option two is a clip from *the Simpsons* where Apu attempts to expand on the complexity of

Table 8.1: Description of Options for Beginning the Lesson

Option 1: Examine the clip on Calhoun's Prophecy http://funtvkids.com/videokids-Calhoun-39-s-Prophecy-wmv_foWXsb4mfqVo.html
Option 2: Watch a clip from *The Simpsons*, "Apu Explains the Civil War's Causes" https://www.youtube.com/watch?v=SFwHQYDqf6c
Option 3: Read the article from the *Washington Post* entitled, "The debate over John Kelly and Ken Burns's 'The Civil War' is making us stupider" https://www.washingtonpost.com/news/act-four/wp/2017/11/01/the-debate-over-john-kelly-and-ken-burnss-the-civil-war-is-making-us-stupider/?utm_term=.e9cd3f4dff88
Option 4: Read the article from CNN entitled, "John Kelly get Civil War history wrong" https://www.cnn.com/2017/10/31/politics/john-kelly-historians-civil-war-race/index.html
Option 5: Examine Ken Burn's Twitter feed about the Civil War https://twitter.com/KenBurns/status/925471048975429632?ref_src=twsrc%5Etfw

the war, but is told to just answer "slavery." Option three is an article from the *Washington Post* examining the Twitter debate between John Kelly and Ken Burns over the cause of the Civil War. Option four is a similar article from CNN looking at the debate between John Kelly and Ken Burns over the cause of the Civil War. Option five is Ken Burn's actual Twitter feed, which provides students with the option to examine the Twitter feed themselves instead of relying solely on the articles. Option one and two work well together because they provide both a serious and humorous introduction to the cause(s) of the Civil War. Options three, four, and five work well together, because they are all centered around a conversation between John Kelly and Ken Burns. However, a teacher can pair the options in many different ways, depending on the context of their class, though we imagine certain combinations working best together.

Introducing the Sources

After using one of the recommended starting options, the teacher should look to provide the class with a range of pre/post-Civil War sources that inform the students on the effects of memory on Civil War history; what follows is a description of the sources, but we also provide the actual sources in the appendices of this chapter (also see Table 8.2 for a short description of sources). In a letter from Stephen F. Hale to the Governor of Kentucky from 1860 during the Secession Winter, Hale, a consultant on secession from Alabama, explained his fears that Lincoln and the Republican Party would destroy slavery. South Carolina's Declaration of Secession, also from 1860,

Table 8.2: Features Sources Pre-Civil War, Features Sources Post-Civil War

Featured Sources Pre-Civil War	Featured Sources Post-Civil War
Source A (South Pre-War)-Letter from Stephen F. Hale to Governor of Kentucky Beriah Magoffin, December 27, 1860. http://teachingamericanhistory.org/library/document/stephen-f-hale-to-governor-beriah-magoffin/	Source E (South Post-War)—Davis, Jefferson. (1881). *The Rise and Fall of the Confederate Government* (Vol. I) New York: D. Appleton and Company. (pp. 77–78).
Source B (South Pre-War)-Confederate States of America—Declaration of the Immediate Causes Which Induce and Justify the Secession of South Carolina from the Federal Union, December 24, 1860. http://avalon.law.yale.edu/19th_century/csa_scarsec.asp	Source F (South Post-War)—Dr. R.C. Cave, inscribed on the Confederate Monument in St. Louis, December 5, 1914
Source C (North Pre-War) President Lincoln's First Inaugural Address, 1861. http://teachingamericanhistory.org/library/document/first-inaugural-address-2/	Source G (North Post-War) Charles W. Eliot, inscribed on the Memorial to Robert Gould Shaw and the Massachusetts Fifty-Fourth Regiment, May 31, 1897.
Source D (North Pre-War) A proposed Thirteenth Amendment to prevent secession, 1861. https://www.gilderlehrman.org/content/proposed-thirteenth-amendment-prevent-secession-1861	Source H (North Post-War) Shaara, Michael. (2003). *The Killer Angels*. (pp. 29–30) New York: Ballantine Books. Source I (Post-War) Ellis, E.S. (1899). *The eclectic primary history of the United* States. Second Edition. (pp. 189–190) New York, Cincinnati, Chicago: American Book Company. Source J (Post-War) Simkins, F.B., Hunnicut, S. Poole, S.P. (1957). *Virginia: History, government, geography*. (pp. 404–406). New York: Charles Scribner's Sons. Source K (Post-War) Davidson, J.W. & Batchelor J.E. (1991). *The American nation*. (pp. 386–388). Englewood Cliffs, New Jersey: Prentice Hall. Source L (Post-War) Your Own Teacher's Classroom Textbook

Civil War Memories 121

deems the fear that Northern powers will destroy slavery to be the reason they are seceding. President Lincoln's first inaugural address, from 1861, makes explicit his sole desire to preserve the Union, and his intention not to touch slavery. The proposed Thirteenth Amendment, passed in the Spring of 1861, would have protected slavery from federal interference, an attempt to calm the fears of southern states. In an excerpt written by Jefferson Davis' history of the Confederacy, written and published over a decade following the Civil War, he remembers that slavery was not the cause of the Civil War. The inscription on a Confederate monument in St. Louis, Missouri, dedicated in 1914, provides an example of how slavery can be obscured when describing why the South went to war. The inscription of a memorial to Robert Gould Shaw and the Massachusetts Fifty-Fourth Regiment, a northern monument dedicated in 1897, shows that the North has memory issues of its own, praising black troops for fighting for the Union, when they would have been among the few troops who went to war primarily for emancipation. Also provided is an excerpt from *The Killer Angels* by Michael Shaara, originally published in 1974; this fictional book about the Battle of Gettysburg has Union officer Joshua Chamberlain proclaim that the North is fighting for emancipation, when most men were fighting to preserve the Union. An excerpt from a history book entitled *The Eclectic Primary History of the United States* written in 1899 identifies "states' rights" as the southern cause of the Civil War, and is silent on slavery. An excerpt from a Virginia history textbook *Virginia: History, Government, Geography*, written in 1957, also exemplifies "states' rights" rather than slavery, as the southern cause of the war. An excerpt from an American history textbook *The American Nation* written in 1991 has a more balanced approach, but serves to show students how the war was remembered and represented in textbooks has changed over time. We also encourage teachers to use their own textbook as a source. After students thoroughly analyze the sources, they will then be able to have an informed discussion around issues relating to the Civil War.

Analyzing the Sources

After providing the sources, the teacher should look to break the students into groups; there may be many groups within the class, but each group should look at either the pre-war sources or the post-war sources. The teacher will then model how to use the SCIM-C Scaffold for the students (Hicks, & Doolittle, 2008; Hicks, Doolittle, & Ewing, 2004: Hicks et al., 2016). The

SCIM-C Scaffold is a scaffold developed for analyzing historical sources in which students Summarize, Contextualize, Monitor, and then Corroborate historical sources (also see http://www.historicalinquiry.com/#part2; the SCIM-C scaffold is provided in the appendices). By having students read sources using this scaffold, the teacher can help avoid bringing outside emotion into the discussion. Students will Corroborate the sources using the questions, provided by the SCIM-C Scaffold, as a guide. As they Corroborate the sources, the students should look to develop a timeline of the sources and note changes in ideas about the cause of the Civil War based on time, location, and context. After Corroborating, the students will use the evidence they have gathered from the SCIM-C to craft a response to the compelling question given at the beginning of the lesson, "If history relies on facts and dates, why is there so much controversy around the causes of the American Civil War over time and space?" The teacher can also provide supporting questions to further guide the students in crafting a response, such as:

1. What do the sources tell you about why the South and North entered the Civil War?
2. How are the causes of the Civil War remembered and represented in the late 19th and 20th century?
3. What was/is slavery?
4. What exactly were white southern slaveholders upholding?
5. There was a lived reality of slavery as it shaped the social, political, and economic life of the Southern States. What would happen to those states if slavery disappeared, collapsed, or was demolished?

Structuring a Discussion

After students spend time crafting responses, the next step is structuring a discussion; we recommend following the guidelines of a SAC, which we will describe below. A SAC provides a structured approach for deliberating controversial issues in the classroom and helps students to realize that some topics are complex and nuanced, and there is therefore much to consider before reaching a conclusion (teachinghistory.org, n.d.). Based on their readings and analysis, students should now choose a position; the teacher may also decide to assign positions based on the make-up of the class. The two positions we recommend for this discussion are: (a) Slavery was the cause of the American Civil War; (b) Slavery was not the cause of the American Civil War. Students should spend some time formulating their position. Below is an example of a

Civil War Memories

Table 8.3: Position A: Slavery was the cause of the American Civil War; Position B: Slavery was NOT the cause of the American Civil War

Position A: Slavery was the cause of the American Civil War	**Position B:** Slavery was NOT the cause of the American Civil War
Evidence 1:	Evidence 1:
Evidence 2:	Evidence 2:
Evidence 3	Evidence 3:
Evidence 4:	Evidence 4:

handout, adapted from teachinghistory.org, that a teacher could use to support students in formulating a position (see Table 8.3; also see teachinghistory.org, n.d. for other handout examples).

In beginning the discussion, each group will present their side of the argument. After the presenters provide their point of view, the listeners are to repeat back what they understood from the presentation; the goal of the listeners is not to debate the presenters about their point of view. When the presenters are content with what they have heard from the listeners, the next group will follow using the same guidelines. After all groups have presented, the class will attempt to reach an agreement. If the class cannot reach an agreement, then the class should identify the differences in their thoughts.

Suggested Follow-Up Activities

In Table 8.4 we provide several options for follow-up activities for this lesson. Like before, we imagine certain combinations and options working better together. Option one has students look at their own textbooks and recommend improvements in the Civil War chapter(s) of their text; this option helps students think about the material around them critically. Option two allows

Table 8.4: Description of Options for Follow-Up Activities

Option 1: Students could look at their own textbooks after reading the sources and identify improvements they would make.
Option 2: Students could create newspaper headlines representing each perspective about the cause of the Civil War.
Option 3: Students could create a graffiti wall identifying each perspective.
Option 4: Students could write 25-word summaries of each perspective.

students to create newspaper headlines about each perspective and would be a nice way to decompress after a particularly tense discussion. Options three and four ask students to create a graffiti wall and write 25-word summaries about each perspective, respectively. Options three and four work particularly well together, in that the class could process the material in groups and then have individual assignments where they reflect on the material.

Conclusion

Historical content such as the Civil War, "breaks through the separation of 'thought from feeling' (Rosaldo, 1994, p. 406)" (Stoddard et al., 2016, p. 14). Additionally, Rosaldo (1994) notes:

> [t]eachers can use such feelings as starting points for analysis and intellectual discussion ... matters that arouse strong feelings often concern students deeply and can lead to more search analyses than other issues ... The result is that classrooms become less comfortable than they were before. Instead of seeking maximum comfort, teachers should strive for tolerable discomfort. (pp. 406–407)

The goal of this chapter was to push the conversation in the classroom and have students engage in hard discussions around difficult issues. Students are going to talk about such contested issues outside of the classroom, therefore, it is of utmost importance that we give them a space and opportunity to have informed discussions around difficult histories to further foster historical inquiry and deliberation. It is therefore of necessity that teachers have the pedagogical supports to approach such difficult histories in the classroom.

References

Grant, S. G., Lee, J., & Swan, K. (2014). The inquiry design model. *C3 Teachers*.
Grant, S. G., Swan, K., & Lee, J. (2016). How do we shape our environment? An Inquiry from the New York State social studies toolkit. *Social Studies and the Young Learner, 28*(3), 31–32.
Hicks, D., & Doolittle, P. (2008). Fostering analysis in historical inquiry through multimedia embedded scaffolding. *Theory and Research in Social Education, 36*(3), 206–232.
Hicks, D., Doolittle, P., & Ewing, E. T. (2004). The SCIM-C strategy: Expert historians, historical inquiry, and multimedia. *Social Education, 68*(3), 221–225.
Hicks, D., Johnson, A., van Hover, S., Lisanti, M., McPherson, K., & Zuckerwar, S. (2016). Teaching with primary sources: Junior detectives as a bridge to disciplinary literacy. *Social Studies and the Young Learner, 29*(1), 9–15.
Lee, J., &Swan, K. (2013). Is the common core good for social studies? Yes, but .... *Social Education, 77*(6), 327–330.

Levinson, M., & Levine, P. (2013). Taking informed action to engage students in civic life. *Social Education, 77*(6), 339–341.

National Council for the Social Studies. (2013), *The college, career, and civic life (C3) framework for social studies state standards: Guidance for enhancing the rigor of K–12 civics, economics, geography, and history.* Silver Spring, MD: Author.

Rosaldo, R. (1994). Cultural citizenship and educational democracy. *Cultural Anthropology, 9*(3), 402–411.

Stoddard, J., Marcus, A., & Hicks, D. (2016). Using film to teach difficult histories. In J. Stoddard, A. Marcus, & D. Hicks (Eds.), *Teaching difficult history through film* (pp. 3–16). New York, NY/London, England: Routledge.

Swan, K., Lee, J., & Grant, S. G. (2015). The New York State toolkit and the inquiry design model: Anatomy of an inquiry. *Social Education, 79*(6), 316–322.

Teachinghistory.org. (n.d.). Structured academic controversy (SAC). Retrieved from http://teachinghistory.org/teaching-materials/teaching-guides/21731

VanSledright, B. (2013). Can assessment improve learning? Thoughts on the C3 framework. *Social Education, 77*(6), 334–338.

Walsh, B., Hicks, D., & van Hover, S. (2016). Using film to reveal the perspective of "the other" in difficult history topics. In J. Stoddard, A. Marcus, & D. Hicks (Eds.), *Teaching difficult history through film* (pp. 17–36). New York, NY/London, England: Routledge.

9. Collective Memory of Secession: On Outbreaks and Moral Arcs

GABRIEL A. REICH, MELANIE L. BUFFINGTON AND WILLIAM R. MUTH

Anyone who grew up with a sibling or is a classroom teacher is familiar with the centrality of assigning blame in a narrative description of a fight. "Who started it?" is *the* essential question in such disputes. Similarly, history is a moral argument in narrative form (Ahonen, 2018; Rüsen, 2005). Through patterns of selection, omission, significance, and perhaps, most importantly assigning blame for the origins of a historical phenomenon, people communicate a moral argument about who was in the right or wrong. Such arguments can become an article of faith that draws people together, supports a shared identity, and defines who is in and out of a group.

The technical term for such identity affirming narratives is *collective memory* (others use heritage and myth, e.g., Lowenthal, 1996). Whereas academic historians generally focus on interpretation of sources, and constructing nuanced, accurate, and multi-faceted historical narratives, collective memories present a useable past with narratives that are simple, easily remembered, and emotionally charged (Wertsch, 1998). The narrative tropes and historical content that make up collective memories are resources members of society draw on to explain the world and to mobilize others for political ends (Nordgren, 2016). In this chapter, we describe four collective-memory narratives that have come to define the origins of the Civil War in the collective memories of many Americans. If the ultimate aim of history education is the preparation of democratic citizens, then teachers should help students to recognize when and how collective memory is employed in the public sphere to achieve political and social ends (Nordgren, 2016).

The beginnings of the American Civil War offer an excellent case study of how central figures in the conflict managed the perception that one side or the other started it. Southern Articles of Secession explained their reasons for leaving the Union. Those documents borrow heavily from the moral argumentation style that Thomas Jefferson used in the "Declaration of Independence," which names English policies as the catalyst for Independence. The first such document, ratified in South Carolina (South Carolina Convention on Secession, 1860), begins with the following:

> The people of the State of South Carolina, in Convention assembled, on the 26th day of April, A.D., 1852, declared that the frequent violations of the Constitution of the United States, by the Federal Government, and its encroachments upon the reserved rights of the States, fully justified this State in then withdrawing from the Federal Union; but in deference to the opinions and wishes of the other slaveholding States, she forbore at that time to exercise this right. Since that time, these encroachments have continued to increase, and further forbearance ceases to be a virtue. (para. 1)

The message of that Secession document is borne out by its structure. It begins by offering a grievance against actions taken by the U.S. federal government, which it characterizes as "encroachments upon the reserved rights of the States." Thus, the story the conventioneers convey framed Secession as a just reaction to the United States for restricting the rights of enslavers to expand enslavement. Not to be outdone, Abraham Lincoln maneuvered another precipitating event, the firing on Fort Sumter in Charleston Harbor, with clear understanding that if South Carolina fired the first shot he would win an important propaganda victory (McPherson, 2003/1988).

Claiming a particular event as the act that precipitated the Civil War, becomes *the* pivotal point upon which historical narratives of the war construct a moral universe. That was true for the political players in 1860–1861, for those who framed the conflict in histories after the war, and often for people today. There are four major collective memory traditions identified by historians (Blight, 2001; Gallagher, 2008): the Lost Cause, Unionist, Emancipationist, and Reconciliationist narratives. Each of those narratives handles the war's origins differently, creating a unique moral argument. We will describe each in the findings sections along with supporting data from the study.

Data and Analysis

To better understand contemporary views of young adults, we collected data from 54 undergraduates at a diverse public university located in the American South in 2011 (see Reich, Buffington, & Muth, 2015 for a fuller account of the method). Respondents were enrolled in an introductory course on educational development and completed a short survey instrument. Participants self-identified their race and the state in which they attended high school, but not gender. Each responded to a questionnaire that asked: "Please explain why the Southern states elected to leave the United States and form a new country called the Confederacy." In addition, respondents were given a list of eight Civil War figures—four Confederates and four Unionists/abolitionists—and asked to rate them in order of heroism and provide a definition of heroism. We have included excerpts from the responses below verbatim, without editing them or indicating inconsistent or incorrect grammar or historical content.

The responses were analyzed using Wertsch's (1998; cf., Burke, 1969) method of narrative analysis, which focuses on five elements of a story: act, agent, agency, scene, and purpose. The act, Secession, and the agent exercising agency, the seceding Southern states, were provided in the question itself. We asked participants to provide the scene and purpose that contextualize the other three elements. The scene refers to the historical context of an event that informs the purpose of the action taken. Participants were also free to disrupt the prompt as given by shifting agency away from the Southern states to Northern ones. We made judgments about the moral arguments presented by looking at when the story begins and what details are included or omitted, and by associating that response with one of the four collective memory traditions described below. The terms used for the four Civil War memory traditions in this chapter differ from the terms we used in our article upon which this chapter is based (Reich, Buffington, & Muth, 2015). We are using Gallagher's taxonomy here in order to illustrate continuity with a collective memory tradition. The reader should understand, however, that collective memories change over time and that individuals typically borrow, mix and match elements of historical narratives with typically little awareness of, or attention paid to, those narrative forms that are of interest to scholars.

Findings

Lost Cause

Lost Cause responses ranked Confederates in the top three hero positions and included elements of the traditional Lost Cause narrative (Blight, 2001; Gallagher, 2008), such as mentions of states' rights, a focus on Northern or federal power (e.g., Northern economic and/or military superiority), the threat to southern livelihood, and a minimization of enslavement. Thirteen out of 54 responses were coded as Lost Cause, and those responses indicated a clear continuity with that narrative's historical manifestations. For example, a 21-year-old Asian respondent who attended high school in Virginia wrote the following in response to our prompt:

> Most states believed that the North was trying diminish Southern states rights as well as diminish their revenue from plantations. Slavery was another factor. With the North believing that the South should not be able to own slaves, that were essential to Southern capital. It was like the North was trying to take away their livelihood.

In that response, the responsibility for Secession is placed on the North for trying to destroy "Southern capital." Similarly, the following response from a 21-year-old white respondent who attended high school in Virginia also places agency in the hands of the North:

> The Southern states elected to leave the United States and form the Confederacy for many reasons. Some of the reason that I can remember were that the southern states were being exploited for their plantations and for their laborers. The states that were big into farming and producing crops were stuck in a position where they had to sell their crops to the northern states because that was their only option. Also the southern states had more land and less population density so they were under-represented in congress. Some more reasons were that the South wanted to self-govern because they thought that they could do a better job of being fair for themselves.

The second answer goes beyond the first, describing the political and economic relations between North and South in colonial terms, and Secession as a justifiable act of rebellion against oppression. That the narrative is built upon a serious distortion of the historical record is important, but may be beside the point. Collective memory, as Wertsch (2002) describes is about "how events can be emplotted in the service of creating a valuable past" (p. 95). In this case, value is that which justifies the moral righteousness of Secession.

Unionist

The responses we are calling Unionist differ from Gallagher's (2008) description of that narrative as it existed in the late 19th century. In our data, Unionist narratives focused on the Civil War as a pivotal event in the expansion of freedom that pitted a progressive North against a reactionary South. Evidence for that narrative included the defense of slavery as the main reason for Secession, and the selection of Union leaders in the top 2–3 choices of most heroic figures. Of the 54 total responses, 12 were coded as Union. The following response by a 24-year-old black respondent was typical:

They [Southern states] did not want to be associated with what the Northern states chose to believe in. The Northern States wanted to provide freedom to its citizens as well as a democracy to have all states be independent. The Northern States also wanted to have civil liberty and have justice. The Confederacy did not want to end slavery.

Unionist responses employ the Civil War in ways that reaffirm U.S. nationalism, in which the nation united ensures the expansion of freedom.

Emancipationist

In the Emancipationist narrative, the Civil War was a war of liberation that forced an end to enslavement. Seven of the 54 responses were coded Emancipationist because they went beyond presenting the origins of the war in U.S. nationalist terms, and included a critique of enslavers as leading Secession for narrow self-interest rather than to uphold a set of political ideals (Gallagher, 2008). Some Emancipationist responses discussed slavery as a human rights or freedom issue, and others cast it as an economic institution, but all mentioned enslavement as a cause of Secession. The following response written by a white 19-year-old Virginian provides a good illustration:

> One of the biggest reasons the southern states decided to secede from the Union was over the issue of slavery. The 'Union' believed it to be wrong, while the 'Confederacy' wasn't as concerned with the morals as the[y] were with the free labor they needed to run their businesses, especially agriculture. Rather than lose their business, they decided they didn't want to be part of a country that believed slavery was wrong.

Similar to responses coded Unionist, the participants framed Secession as a difference over the institution of slavery. Unlike the Unionist responses, however, a more cynical take is evident regarding the centrality of enslavement as a business interest that leads to moral corruption. Although the focus on the cynicism of the Secession movement is consistent with a tradition of Emancipationist narratives, these responses focused less on the enslaved than on the enslavers. That may be because the prompt asked respondents to focus on Secession. Had it asked a more general question about the Civil War, we would expect responses coded Emancipationist to focus more centrally on freedom from enslavement.

Reconciliationist

We call the final group Reconciliationist because the narratives did not present a singular, consistent moral stand on the issue of Secession. The

Reconciliationist narrative paints the Civil War as a tragic misunderstanding, a setback in the inevitable march of progress. Historically, it ignored enslavement, and other facts that might assign blame on one side or another and instead focused on the tragedy of (White) brothers fighting each other (Blight, 2001; Gallagher, 2008). Fourteen out of the 54 total responses were considered Reconciliationist because they consisted of juxtaposed elements from different traditions in response to the first question, or because they included very different responses to the Secession question and the question about heroism. The following response was typical in that it first attempts to explain Secession from a pro-Secession perspective, judges that perspective as morally wrong and points to its disastrous consequences. A white, 26-year-old Virginian explained that,

> The first few [southern] states that left the union did so for the same reason the colonists left Europe. They felt that their rights were being infringed on, and instead of dealing with it, they decided to fight. Their [Southerners] ideals and morals were not necessarily 'right' however, in this country we should all be able to practice our beliefs. Slavery was a large issue, but it was not the only one. The southern states acted very radically, and violent to get their points across. Abraham Lincoln was a President with strong morals, and ideals. He believed that we were all created equal, and that nobody's ideals should interfere with another. He was a much different president then Jefferson Davis was. In my personal opinion I believe the southern states get a poor reputation for their role in the war. In our modern day texts they are seen as a bunch of rednecks with low education and standards. However, they were men just like our union soldiers, they were just fighting for what they believed in.

That response begins with a moral justification for Secession, then undermines that position with a moral opposition to enslavement, and then endorses Americans' right to "practice our beliefs" including, presumably, enslaving others. Then the participant writes in support of Lincoln as a moral leader, superior to Confederate President Davis, but then is critical of how the South is treated in textbooks and ending with the ultimate Reconciliationist trope that all soldiers "were just fighting for what they believed in." In other words, what ultimately signifies reconciliation is either a suspense of, or a "both sides" approach to moral judgment.

Implications for Teachers

This research is valuable for teachers for several reasons. It illustrates the broad outlines of four collective memory traditions that persist in the popular culture, and points out some differences between these living memories and the ways that historians discuss them. We suggest that teachers ask their students a similar question about Secession when commencing a unit on the Civil War. Student responses will reveal the collective memory traditions that they believe represent historical truth. Awareness of such prior beliefs can be a powerful formative assessment for teachers to gauge whether students consider different perspectives, or incorporate new content to create more nuanced historical narratives upon concluding a Civil War unit. It can also be useful for teachers to pinpoint the content they will focus on in order to engage students with counter-stories or to highlight points of controversy. Ultimately, however, knowledge of students' prior understandings can be used by teachers to help students recognize that such traditions exist, that they are distinct from historiography, and that they are drawn upon in political and popular culture. Self-awareness of the narrative beliefs we hold that are distinct from the historical record, is a first step towards gaining some critical distance from those narratives and gaining the analytical capacity to recognize them in ourselves, others, and in contemporary political discourse.

The most obvious example, and the one most in need of confronting, is the Lost Cause. Belief in the Lost Cause, or the adoption of Confederate symbols by whites as an identity symbol is *not* limited to the South, and is statistically associated with racial animus (Strother, Piston, & Ogorzalek, 2017). Tropes that emerge from that narrative, particularly the use of terms like "states' rights" have been used since the Civil Rights era to protect local elites, overwhelmingly white, from federal policies designed to promote equity. In the South, the resentment of the Civil War as an undoing of a golden age, of a colonization of the South by the North, has been conflated with the notion of a distinct Southern heritage (Cobb, 2005). Potentially, helping students gain self-awareness about the Civil War narratives that circulate in their communities, and recognizing how politicians tap into those tropes in order to garner support, may be a first step towards a more historically accurate understanding of the conflict. The lead up to the outbreak of the war is a key area to focus on when doing that work.

References

Ahonen, S. (2018). Sustainable history lessons for post-conflict society. In *Teaching and learning difficult histories in international contexts: A critical sociocultural approach* (pp. 17–30). New York, NY: Routledge.

Blight, D. W. (2001). *Race and reunion: The Civil War in American memory*. Cambridge, MA: Belknap Press of Harvard University Press.

Burke, K. (1969). *A grammar of motives*. Berkeley: University of California Press.

Cobb, J. C. (2005). *Away down South: A history of southern identity*. New York, NY: Oxford University Press.

Gallagher, G. W. (2008). *Causes won, lost, and forgotten: How Hollywood & popular art shape what we know about the Civil War*. Chapel Hill: University of North Carolina Press.

Lowenthal, D. (1996). *Possessed by the past: The heritage crusade and the spoils of history*. New York, NY: Free Press.

McPherson, J. M. (2003/1988). *Battle cry of freedom: The Civil War era* (2nd ed.). New York, NY: Oxford University Press.

Nordgren, K. (2016). How to do things with history: Use of history as a link between historical consciousness and historical culture. *Theory and Research in Social Education, 44*(4), 479–504.

Reich, G. A., Buffington, M., & Muth, W. R. (2015). (Dis)Union at 150: Collective memories of secession. *Theory & Research in Social Education, 43*(4), 499–527.

Rüsen, J. (2005). *History: Narration, interpretation, orientation*. New York, NY: Berghahn Books.

South Carolina Convention on Secession. (1860). Declaration of the immediate causes which induce and justify the Secession of South Carolina from the Federal Union. Retrieved from http://avalon.law.yale.edu/19th_century/csa_scarsec.asp

Strother, L., Piston, S., & Ogorzalek, T. (2017). Pride or prejudice? Racial prejudice, Southern heritage, and White support for the Confederate battle flag. *Du Bois Review, 14*(1), 295–323. doi:10.1017/S1742058X17000017

VanSledright, B. A. (2008). Narratives of nation-state: Historical knowledge and school history education. *Review of Research in Education, 32*, 109–146.

Wertsch, J. V. (1998). *Mind as action*. New York, NY: Oxford University Press.

Wertsch, J. V. (2002). *Voices of collective remembering*. New York, NY: Cambridge University Press.

10. The Civil War and the Inquiry Design Model

S.G. Grant, Kathy Swan and John Lee

Among the many topics students learn in U.S. history classrooms, perhaps none is as interesting as the Civil War. The human tragedy of slavery, the drama of brother fighting brother, the intriguing characters on both sides of the Mason-Dixon line—all combine to promote an engaging narrative.

Narrative history is important. But narrative is neither the only kind of history (White, 1994), nor is it the only means by which history can be taught (Bain, 2005; VanSledright & Brophy, 1992). In fact, narrative's greatest strength is also its greatest weakness. The power of narrative history comes through as a story well told. A story can be useful, but it is only a single story. History gains intellectual power when told from multiple points of view. History teachers who narrate a compelling story may keep their students' attention. In the end, however, they may only enable their students to mimic the story rather than think their ways into and around it.

With the typical heavy focus on content, state standards tend to reinforce a narrative view of history. Yet even more problematic than pushing a narrative view of history and teaching as telling is the fact that few standards documents even acknowledge the possibility of alternative narratives. Standards writers may offer a nod to multiple perspectives in introductory pages. That nod fades, however, as teachers read standards that seem to promote only a single vision of the history to be taught.

Inquiry-Based Practice and the IDM

An antidote to history as narrative and teaching as telling is inquiry-based practice. Here, the emphasis is on genuine questions, on sources that offer a range of perspectives, and on tasks that enable students to make evidence-based arguments. Such an approach does not deny the importance of narrative history; instead it promotes the value of multiple narratives. Similarly, inquiry does not deny the usefulness of lecturing; instead it supports the use of lecture as one of several instructional strategies.

These advantages have been long noted, but slow to develop as common classroom practice (Grant, Swan, & Lee, 2017). The reasons are several—inquiry-based practice demands considerable planning time, teachers worry that students will not succeed, and standardized assessments seem to promote traditional teaching approaches. These challenges notwithstanding, the research literature strongly supports inquiry-based practice as a powerful approach to teaching and learning (Grant, Swan, & Lee, 2017). Moreover, the benefits accrue to *all* students—elementary, secondary, and academically challenged as well as academically gifted (Grant, 2018).

These empirical findings will convince few teachers if inquiry-based practice seems more abstract than practical. Even teachers who wanted to pursue more ambitious instruction have been thwarted as there have simply not been effective models for them to employ.

The Inquiry Design Model (IDM) is intended to meet these several challenges. By offering a concise, practical approach to developing classroom inquiries, IDM offers teachers a way to see their way into inquiry-based practice. And with a bank of nearly 200 inquiries available (at C3Teachers.org), teachers can save considerable planning time.

The Inquiry Design Model is rooted in the *blueprint*, a one-page representation of the common elements of inquiry-based practice—questions, tasks, and sources. The blueprint offers a visual snapshot of an entire inquiry such that the individual components *and* the relationship among the components can all be seen at once. As such, they focus on the following elements necessary to support students as they address a compelling question using disciplinary sources in a thoughtful and informed fashion:

- Standards (anchor the content of the inquiry);
- Compelling questions (frame the inquiry);
- Staging the compelling question tasks (create interest in the inquiry)
- Supporting questions (develop the key content);
- Formative performance tasks (demonstrate emerging understandings);
- Featured sources (provide opportunities to generate curiosity, build knowledge, and construct arguments);
- Summative performance tasks (demonstrate evidence-based arguments);
- Summative extensions (offer assessment flexibility);
- Taking informed action exercises (promote opportunities for civic engagement).

The Civil War and the Inquiry Design Model 137

In the sections that follow, we unpack the defining elements of inquiry—questions, tasks and sources—relevant to an inquiry on the Civil War in general and the secession of southern states in particular. In doing so, we highlight the compelling and supporting *questions* that frame and organize this inquiry; the formative and summative assessment *tasks* that provide opportunities for students to demonstrate and apply their understandings; and, the disciplinary *sources* that allow students to practice disciplinary thinking and reasoning (see Table 10.1).

High School Inquiry on Southern Secession

Why Did the South Secede?

National Standards for Teaching American Slavery	8.3 Discuss the 1860 Presidential election of Abraham Lincoln as a Republican who ran on a platform of the non-expansion of slavery in the territories. 8.4 Examine the preservation of slavery as essential to the Southern decision to secede from the Union.
Staging the Question	Examine a map of America showing seceded states and analyze and respond to three (3) statements on the potential reasons for Southern secession.

Supporting Question 1	Supporting Question 2	Supporting Question 3	Supporting Question 4
In what ways did states attempt to compromise on the issues of slavery, state sovereignty, and territorial expansion?	In what ways did the Election of 1860 divide the nation?	What did Southerners say about Secession?	What did Northerners say about Secession?
Formative Performance Task	**Formative Performance Task**	**Formative Performance Task**	**Formative Performance Task**
Construct an annotated timeline detailing the compromises over issues of slavery, state sovereignty and territorial expansion.	Write a paragraph describing the ways in which the Election of 1860 divided the nation.	Complete a Venn diagram and construct an evidence-based claim that answers the supporting question.	Complete a Venn diagram and construct an evidence-based claim that answers the supporting question.
Featured Sources	**Featured Sources**	**Featured Sources**	**Featured Sources**
Source A: "Missouri Compromise, (1820)" Source B: "Compromise of 1850" Source C: "Fugitive Slave Act, (1850)" Source D: "Kansas-Nebraska Act, (1854)" Source E: "Dred Scott v Sanford (1857)"	Source A: "Dividing the National Map" Source B: "Election map of 1860" Source C: "Election of 1860 Party Platforms" Source D: "The Union is Dissolved!"	Source A: "Declaration of the Immediate Causes…" Source B: "Who is Responsible for this War?" Source C: "Nashville Convention Speech" Source D: "Thanksgiving Sermon" Source E: "Cornerstone Speech"	Source A: "DisUnited States" Source B: "South Carolina Topsey in a fix" Source C: "Horace Greely Letter to Lincoln" Source D: "New York Republicans Letter to Lincoln"

Summative Performance Task	ARGUMENT Why did the South Secede? Construct an argument (e.g., detailed outline, poster, essay) that addresses the compelling question using specific claims and relevant evidence from contemporary sources while acknowledging competing views.
	EXTENSION Participate in a Structured Academic Controversy by arguing a claim that answers the compelling question.
Taking Informed Action	UNDERSTAND Research an issue within your own state that created tension between Federal and state power (e.g. environmental regulation, energy conservation, civil rights investigations, border control, etc.)
	ASSESS Take a position on whether your state or the Federal government has the power to govern the direction of the issue you selected.
	ACT Draft a letter to your state or Federal representative stating your position on the selected issue, completed with claims and evidence to support your position.

Table 10.1: IDM Blueprint of an Inquiry about Southern Secession

The Importance of Questions

Questions form an integral part of any teacher's instructional practice; they are also key to inquiry-based curriculum design. In the Inquiry Design Model (IDM), questions come in two forms—compelling and supporting. Though different in form and function, these two kinds of questions work together to build academic rigor and student relevance into an inquiry.

A good compelling question hits both of those marks. Academically rigorous questions reflect an enduring issue, concern, or debate in history—an idea worth thinking through. For example, the compelling question "Why Did the South Secede?" asks students to wrestle with one of the central issues of the Civil War: What would impel nearly one-third of the states to choose to leave the Union rather than compromise? Understanding that choice has huge subject matter considerations that go well beyond a simple listing of causes and standard explanations—slavery, states' rights, territorial expansion—enabling students to explore these ideas on their own merits *and* in interaction with the others. Adding another layer of academic challenge is the fact that the divisions that resulted in war cut across geographic, political, economic, and social dimensions. Far from a tidy and conventional narrative, the beginnings of the Civil War continue to inspire debate.

And a debatable question is the first consideration in deciding whether a compelling question is relevant to students. With the "answer" to the compelling question still unresolved, the inquiry invites students into an active discussion. The compelling question also points to realities within students' daily lives—how do people, as individuals and groups, decide to break relations? As a content topic, the Civil War is of huge importance. But by connecting it to students' lived experiences, teachers magnify that importance.

Compelling questions set the broad frame for an inquiry; supporting questions help build out the content to fill that frame. To do so, supporting questions demonstrate a logical flow of ideas such that students generate content-based understandings that enable them, at the end of the inquiry, to construct an evidence-based argument.

In the *Secession* inquiry, the sequence of supporting questions demonstrates a contrasting perspectives logic where students have an opportunity to see how differing views emerged and flourished:

1. In what ways did states attempt to compromise on the issues of slavery, state sovereignty, and territorial expansion?
2. In what ways did the Election of 1860 divide the nation?
3. What did Southerners say about secession?
4. What did Northerners say about secession?

As a group, the supporting questions take students from the idea of compromise-seeking to the act of secession by highlighting a range of issues and a range of perspectives on those issues. Supporting question #1 asks students to consider the various actions (e.g., the Missouri Compromise) taken to resolve emerging tensions. The second supporting question posits Abraham Lincoln's election in 1860 as a kind of flash point for those tensions. The third and fourth supporting questions, then, push students to consider how the issues at hand played out along geographic boundaries.

We think this set of compelling and supporting questions are mutually intersecting—the compelling question framing the inquiry and the supporting questions giving it a coherent internal structure. Yet there is no right compelling question on secession nor is there a right set of supporting questions. We can imagine all kinds of alternatives and we invite teachers to play with them.

To that end, all IDM inquiries available on C3 Teachers (c3teachers.org) are available in both PDF and Word documents so that teachers can adapt and improve the inquiries for their particular classroom contexts.

The Function of Tasks

Compelling and supporting questions set the stage for learning; formative and summative tasks offer evidence that students are learning. Yet tasks serve instructional as well as evaluative purposes so the IDM features a range of performance tasks as well as extension activities and taking informed action opportunities that surface students' knowledge of the inquiry's compelling and supporting questions.

Because an IDM inquiry begins with a compelling question and ends with students constructing an evidence-based argument), students' summative products are *convergent*—that is, their investigations result in the construction of evidence-based arguments that address the compelling question. The formative performance tasks students complete in response to each supporting question can also be considered convergent tasks. An IDM inquiry also includes opportunities for *divergent* thinking through the extension activities and taking informed action exercises.

The heart of each inquiry, however, rests between two points—the compelling question and the summative argument. What comes in between (i.e., supporting questions, formative performance tasks, and sources) is designed to prepare students to move constructively between the compelling question and the summative task. Readers will note, however, that the summative performance task begins with the compelling question followed by the phrase, "construct an argument." The verb *construct* was purposefully chosen to indicate that not all arguments must be expressed in essay form.

In crafting an evidence-based argument, students must engage with content and skills throughout an inquiry. To support them, formative performance tasks function as content and skill *exercises* intended to scaffold students toward the goal of making and supporting their arguments. Although these tasks do not include all of what students might need to know and do, they do include the major content and skills that provide a foundation for their arguments.

In the *Secession* inquiry, the formative performance tasks follow directly from the supporting questions and provide students with opportunities to develop the knowledge (e.g., understanding the factors involved in the decision to secede) and practice the skills (e.g., reading sources and supporting claims with evidence). Following the contrasting perspectives logic of the supporting questions, the formative performance tasks ask students to:

1. Construct an annotated timeline detailing the compromises over the issues of slavery, state sovereignty, and territorial expansion.
2. Write a paragraph describing the ways in which the election of 1860 divided the nation.
3. Create a Venn diagram and construct and evidence-based claim that answers the supporting question.
4. Complete a Venn diagram and construct and evidence-based claim that answers the supporting question.

Rather than having students answering end-of-chapter questions, formative performance tasks enable students to more directly build the content knowledge and skills they will need to make and support their summative arguments.

Although they reflect the overall purpose of the inquiry in general and the students' arguments in particular, summative extensions offer students a chance to flex their creative muscles. Extension activities can take any number of graphic, textual, oral, and even performance forms. Key, however, is that the extension offers students a chance to reuse their initial arguments in a new form. In the *Secession* inquiry, the extension activity features a Structured Academic Controversy, an assessment in which teams of students research a range of perspectives on an issue and then communicate their findings in a defined format.

One last type of IDM task is taking informed action. These experiences offer students opportunities to engage the content of an inquiry in an active civic form in a variety of contexts both inside and outside of the classroom. Key to any action, however, is the idea that it is informed: In taking informed action activities, students build their knowledge and understanding of an issue before engaging in any type of social action. In the *understand* stage, students demonstrate that they can think about the issues behind the inquiry in a new setting or context. The *assess* stage asks students to consider alternative perspectives, scenarios, or options as they begin to define a possible set of actions. And the *act* stage is where students decide if and how they will put into effect the results of their planning. For the *Secession* inquiry, the taking informed action sequence is:

> **UNDERSTAND:** Research an issue within your own state that created tension between Federal and state power (e.g. environmental regulation, energy conservation, civil rights investigations, border control, etc.)
> **ASSESS:** Take a position on whether your state or the Federal government has the power to govern the direction of the issue you selected.
> **ACT:** Draft a letter to your state or Federal representative stating your position on the selected issue, completed with claims and evidence to support your position.

Following the taking informed action stages enables students to transfer their understandings from the inquiry directly to a contemporary issue and to make decisions about how they might use their voices to participate in public discourse around the matter.

The Work of Sources

Questions and tasks define key components of an inquiry; sources weave throughout by providing access to the substance and the content for an inquiry. Disciplinary sources require students to dig into the materials and to apply their analytical skills to move the inquiry forward.

Three purposes define source use in an inquiry: (1) to spark and sustain student curiosity in an inquiry; (2) to build students' disciplinary (content and conceptual) knowledge and skills; and (3) to enable students to construct arguments with evidence. Employed in this fashion, sources support each part of the IDM blueprint: staging the compelling question, formative performance tasks, summative performance tasks, and additional tasks (i.e., extensions and taking informed action exercises).

To spark students' curiosity, a source can be used in the staging activity. For example, in the *Secession* inquiry, students can look at a map of the United States after the southern states began seceding in 1861 and brainstorm responses to three claims:

- States have the right to leave/secede from the rest of the United States.
- Slavery was the reason for the secession of the South.
- The protection of state sovereignty was the reason for the secession of the South.

Teachers can then have students move to the respective sections of the classroom for those who agree or disagree with each statement and to express their reasoning for doing so. Such an activity alerts students to the competing views behind the inquiry and offers teachers valuable formative information about their students' knowledge of the topic.

Sources also play a central role in helping students' build their disciplinary knowledge and skills. Content and conceptual knowledge is important, but no more than disciplinary skills such as historical thinking and geographic reasoning. The long-standing debate between content and skills is over; students need both. And they can gain both through the use of sources to complete formative and summative tasks.

Within the *Secession* inquiry, students encounter a range of disciplinary sources—from legislation (Missouri and 1850 compromises) to judicial opinion (*Dred Scott v. Sanford*) to maps and political documents (related to the election of 1860) to speeches, sermons, newspaper accounts, and letters to the editor. No textbook summary can rival the intellectual engagement possible when students interact directly with traces of the past; no workbook exercise can compete with the intellectual challenge of building knowledge and understanding toward the goal of constructing one's own argument.

Yet, rarely will sources, as created, be perfectly suited for use in an inquiry. These sources were not created with the inquiry in mind or with high school students as the intended audience. More often than not, then, sources need to be adapted to suit the needs of students and the inquiry. Some sources—artwork, videos, and photographs, for example—may be used as is in an inquiry. Many others, however, require adaptation in order to meet students' disparate academic needs. Some of those needs can be attended to by scaffolds (e.g., SCIM-C); others can be supported by adapting the sources in any of three ways:

- Excerpting—involves using a portion of the source for the inquiry. Care should be taken to preserve information in the source that students may need to know about the creator and context of the source.
- Modifying—involves inserting definitions and/or changing the language of a text. Modifying texts increases students' accessibility to sources.

- Annotating—involves adding short descriptions or explanations in order to introduce a text or to explain a challenging concept. Annotations allow teachers to set a background context for sources.

For example, the text-heavy legislative and judicial documents can be effectively excerpted such that the key elements of the source related to the supporting question and formative performance task are highlighted. Teachers may also make the full texts available so that interested students can pursue their understandings.

It is true that some observers object to altering sources on that grounds that doing so invariably alters meaning. Although a valid concern, teachers should keep in mind the purpose of the source in the inquiry and ask themselves whether they are using the source for the source's sake or to accomplish their learning goal. Rarely will teachers use a source solely for the sake of using it in its original form.

Bringing It All Together

Research findings confirm what most teachers know: Students crave the intellectual challenge of engaging with genuine questions. There are many ways to engage students, but inquiry-based practice offers strong evidence that students of all ages and of all ability groups can profit (Grant, 2018). But inquiry-based practice requires attention to questions, tasks, and sources both individually and in interaction. With inquiry as its origin point, a compelling question serves to initiate an inquiry; a summative performance task, where students address that question, serves to pull the inquiry together. The beginning and end points are important, but no more so than the elements—supporting questions, formative performance tasks, and sources—that comprise the middle of the Inquiry Design Model.

Alert readers will notice that the IDM does not result in fully developed and comprehensive curriculum units or modules. The guidance within each inquiry around the key components of instructional design—questions, tasks, and sources—is considerable, but it is not exhaustive. Experience tells us that teachers teach best the material that they mold around their particular students' needs and the contexts in which they teach. Good teachers need no scripts and they ignore those who argue that teaching and learning are generic activities. IDM, therefore, encourages teachers to draw on the wealth of their teaching experiences as they add to and modify activities, lessons, sources, and tasks that transform the inquiries into their own, individual pedagogical plans.

Conclusion

In this chapter, we use the framework of the Inquiry Design Model to illustrate the possibilities of inquiry-based practice in general and of a more ambitious approach to teaching about the Southern state secession during the Civil War. The inquiry featured in this chapter is one of many teacher-created on the Civil War that are featured on C3 Teachers, illustrating both the capacity of IDM to represent content in lots of different ways and the importance of teachers in the instructional design process. We encourage readers to try out this and other inquiries on related topics available for free at www.C3Teachers.org.

References

Bain, R. (2005). "They thought the world was flat?" Applying the principles of *How Students Learn* in teaching high school history. In M. S. Donovan & J. D. Bransford (Eds.), *How students learn: History, mathematics, and science in the classroom* (pp. 179–213). Washington, DC: National Academies Press.

Grant, S. G. (2018). Teaching practices in history education. In S. Metzger & L. Harris (Eds.), *International handbook of history teaching and learning* (pp. 419–448). New York, NY: Wiley-Blackwell.

Grant, S. G., & Gradwell, J. M. (Eds.). (2010). *Teaching history with big ideas: Cases of ambitious teaching*. Lanham, MD: Rowman & Littlefield.

Grant, S. G., Swan, K., & Lee, J. (2017). *Inquiry-based practice in social studies education: The inquiry design model*. New York, NY: Routledge.

VanSledright, B., & Brophy, J. (1992). Storytelling, imagination, and fanciful elaboration in children's historical reconstructions. *American Educational Research Journal*, *29*(4), 837–859.

White, H. (1994). *Metahistory: The historical imagination in nineteenth-century Europe*. Baltimore, MD: Johns Hopkins University.

Section 3: Lesson Plans and Resources

Resources for Classroom Teachers

CAROLINE R. PRYOR, CHARLOTTE JOHNSON, WHITNEY
BLANKENSHIP AND AMY WILKINSON

This volume, *Teaching the Causes of the American Civil War 1850–1861*, begins with the proposition that defining (and codifying) U.S. civil rights is central to understanding the antecedents of the war and the depth of emotion these definitions engender. This chapter provides resources that can help readers make sense of these rights; the list is not exhaustive rather it is a synthesis of resources we have found user-friendly in developing lesson plans. Several of these resources are composed of a deep scaffolding of information. Thus, planning for lessons can involve, for example—viewing the main page of the Library of Congress (www.loc.gov) and searching within these pages for Teacher Materials or topical units. We have categorized the resources by genre—books, websites, standards, lesson plan information, videos and other materials.

Our goal in developing this resource chapter is to augment the topics of the volume as presented by the essay authors. We also provide these resources so teachers can extend the ideas suggested by the chapter subheadings typically found in classroom textbooks. Thus, while this chapter includes resources that regard historical events, we suggest the need for a range of complexity in how we use our teaching sources—so these challenge broad student and teacher perspective.

For example, we suggest here that the very act of resource selection might indeed foster and/or is dependent upon the belief that a primary source is, by the very nature of its authenticity—a representation of truth. A source might, at first glance—appear as Truth however when an evaluation of a source is layered with personal conceptions, opinions and experience—that is the "available light" (Geertz, 2000)—of personal belief, one might reevaluate the information portrayed by a source. Therefore, as we select a source, we must also recognize that we are bound by the emotional overtones and potential non-neutrality a selection engenders.

Herein in lies the potential for resources to become mythological—a belief framed and then constructed by self-interpretation (Haggerson, 1993). An example of how a teacher might demythologize, or reduce the potential to portray a resource as truth—can be seen in activities such as placing Levine's (2015) description of the black confederate soldier alongside the web-link to Texas' White-washing of Civil War history (2015). Teachers could then ask students to demythologize these two resources by asking: Did these resources convince you that their position is myth, or is there evidence that the resource provides often-overlooked truth?

Using Resources to Augment Textbooks

To extend students' learning about a topic requires a range of resources and activities. For example, Loewen and Sebesta's 2010 book *Confederate and Neo-confederate Reader: "The Great Truth" about the "Lost Cause"* noted here—can be used to develop questions or teaching prompts for the critical historical thinking suggested by Howard Zinn in his 2003 book: *A People's History of the United States*. Questions—such as the role of the black confederate soldier—are unanswerable (or should be unanswerable) using the singular monotone of textbook chapter questions. Rather, it is for several reasons that we suggest that teachers draw on a variety of resources in designing lessons. First, using a range of sources signals to students that a single source, particularly a secondary source, cannot provide a level of nuanced information necessary to respond to the complexity of historical questions. Second, a range of resources, if not culled of controversy, can encourage students to struggle to respond to complex questions (see Bilgelow on Zinn Education in this chapter). Without exploring such complexity, myth, by its very nature of commonly held belief—can be revised from mere supposition to fact.

It might be that in our quest to "cover" a wealth of historical information—we employ teaching approaches that center on students' factual responses, an approach that disallows allows gradation of thought. If however, as teachers, we began to coordinate several resources—such as "The meaning of July Fourth for the Negro"—an 1852 speech, and asked students to explain how this source portrays a vision of civil rights, we might begin a more nuanced conversation. If we then followed the use of this source by asking students to reflect on the *Washington Post*'s article entitled "Texas' White Washing of Civil War History," the causes of the Civil War might be cast in a complexity unanswerable by simple myth—a belief in singular response.

It is critical, therefore, that teachers examine resources such as those included in this chapter—and others found in our nation's libraries (see e.g., the Library of Congress, loc.gov)—and coordinate the perspectives embedded in these sources as part of lesson plan development. The resources in this chapter are useful for this type of source coordination. This non-exhaustive list of resources can be foundational to the C3 inquiry lessons suggested by Grant, Swan and Lee's *Understanding by Design*, as we seek to eliminate the textbook driven genre of fact hidden in a mythological guise of complexity.

References

Douglass, F. (1952, July 5). The meaning of the fourth of July for the Negro. Retrieved May 16, 2019, from https://www.historyisaweapon.com/defcon1/douglassjuly4.html

Editorial. (2015, July 6). How Texas is whitewashing Civil War history. Retrieved from https://www.washingtonpost.com/opinions/whitewashing-civil-war-history-for-young-minds/2015/07/06/1168226c-2415-11e5-b77f-eb13a215f593_story.html?utm_term=.092496218b49

Grant, S. G., Swan, K., & Lee, J. (2017). *Inquiry-based practices in social studies education: Understanding the inquiry design model*. New York, NY: Taylor & Francis.

Geertz, C. (2000). *Available light anthropological reflections on philosophical topics*. Princeton, NJ: Princeton University Press.

Haggerson, N. L. (1993). Education for human rights: Demythologizing dysfunctional qualities of myths. *International Journal of Educational Reform*, 2(1), 49–55. doi:10.1177/105678799300200107

Levine, K. (2015, August 8). The myth of the black confederate soldier. *The Daily Beast*. Retrieved from http://cwmemory.com/; https://www.thedailybeast.com/the-myth-of-the-black-confederate-soldier?fbclid=IwAR2iv7NhSEGd6Z5OFM-taQC1eKvGasc2kQLD93GnkBAcMW82bbS29At0VwPQ

Loewen, J. W., & Sebesta, E. H. (2010). The confederate and neo-confederate reader: The "Great Truth" about the "Lost Cause."

Library of Congress (www.loc.gov).

Zinn, H. (2003). *A people's history of the United States*. New York, NY: HarperCollins.

Resources for Teachers

Standards

NCSS Standards and C3 Framework

An abbreviated version of the standards is available for free on the website. Teachers can also purchase a copy of the standards that includes sample lessons and activities aligned with the NCSS standards. Two additional books on the C3 Framework are also available for purchase.

https://www.socialstudies.org/standards

C3 Teachers
C3 Teachers provides information on conducting inquiry and access to full lesson plans developed using the Inquiry Design Model (IDM). Teachers can use the IDM generator to modify existing lessons or create new ones. Although the site requires a log-in, all materials are free of charge.
http://www.c3teachers.org/
Understanding the Inquiry Design Model
Grant, S. G., Swan, K., & Lee, J. (2017). *Inquiry-based practices in social studies education: Understanding the inquiry design model.* New York, NY: Taylor & Francis.

Common Core State Standards
The Social Studies standards are a sub-topic within the English/Language Arts Standards.
http://www.corestandards.org/ELA-Literacy/

Articles
Brown, E. (2015, July 5). Texas officials: Schools should teach that slavery was 'side issue' to Civil War. *The Washington Post.*
Although specifically looking at the Texas social studies standards, other states have also attempted similar projects when updating standards. Includes links to additional articles and to the standards.
https://www.washingtonpost.com/opinions/whitewashing-civil-war-history-for-young-minds/2015/07/06/1168226c-2415-11e5-b77f-eb13a215f593_story.html?fbclid=IwAR0dR5_AbYrDtzP8rho5wuWIqB8VvG1qma_JX4blS8fANzDxoX7mpUb15xA&noredirect=on&utm_term=.38f4b68e7cce
Kelley, B. (2014, August 18). "From Dred Scott to Ferguson: Missouri at the heart of a national debate." *The Root.*
Kelley provides insight into the links between the historic Dred Scott case and the events surrounding the death of Michael Brown in Ferguson, Missouri.
Levine, K. (2015, August 8). "The myth of the black confederate soldier." *The Daily Beast*
This article is written by Kevin M. Levine, a historian and educator from Boston. The article gives a brief history of the myth of the black confederate soldier based on his research. Information on the book, additional op eds, and other materials collected by the author can be found at: http://cwmemory.com/
https://www.thedailybeast.com/the-myth-of-the-black-confederate-soldier?fbclid=IwAR2iv7NhSEGd6Z5OFMtaQC1eKvGasc2kQLD93GnkBAcMW82bbS29At-0VwPQ
Loewen, J. (2015, July 1). Why do people believe myths about the Confederacy? Because our textbooks and monuments are wrong. *The Washington Post.*
James Loewen addresses the understanding of the causes of the Civil War and how these misunderstandings have filtered into monuments and textbooks.

https://www.washingtonpost.com/posteverything/wp/2015/07/01/why-do-people-believe-myths-about-the-confederacy-because-our-textbooks-and-monuments-are-wrong/?utm_term=.3116ffc44e35

https://www.commondreams.org/views/2014/08/18/dred-scott-ferguson-missouri-heart-national-debate

Wolfe, B. (2018). United daughters of the Confederacy & White Supremacy. Encyclopedia Virginia.

Wolfe presents the objections of the UDC to an article on the UDC and race published in the Encyclopedia Virginia and the ensuing conversation between the author and the UDC. The article speaks to the current debates over commemoration of the Confederacy and Civil War on monuments throughout the U.S. and would make a nice companion piece to discussions on the causes of the Civil War as presented by organizations such as the United Daughters of the Confederacy and the Sons of Confederate Veterans. Includes link to the original encyclopedia article.

https://www.evblog.virginiahumanities.org/2018/08/united-daughters-of-the-confederacy-white-supremacy/?fbclid=IwAR01wLFZqQ6uz2lGrSLvAtMNjyPDFEk3x-0KreRoQLN7KPvcX13zasbMhAhw

"What Caused the Civil War: Slavery and More." (2019, April 5). *History on the Net*. 2000–2019. Salem Media.

Article provides a brief overview of the causes of the Civil War and the Myth of the Lost Cause.

https://www.historyonthenet.com/what-caused-the-civil-war

Lesson Activities

Zinn Education provides a wide variety of sources, activities, and essays centered on alternative narratives of U.S. history. Sources of particular interest to readers of this volume are listed below and include a direct link to each source.

Bigelow, B. "If there is no struggle": Teaching a people's history of the abolition movement." *Zinn Education Project*

Bigelow presents a role playing exercise in which students become members of the American Anti-Slavery Society. A full lesson plan is available for download.

https://www.zinnedproject.org/materials/if-there-is-no-struggle-abolition-movement-history/

Olsen-Rymer, G. "Slavery and defiance." *Zinn Education Project*.

This teachers' guide provides ideas and critical thinking questions for teaching the history of resistance prior to the Civil War.

https://www.zinnedproject.org/materials/slavery-and-defiance/

Bigelow, B. "The draft riot mystery" *Zinn Education*.

Lesson plan for teaching draft riots of July 1863 with a focus on the complexity of the causes of the riots and the issues of anti-black, anti-rich, and anti-Republican sentiments.

https://www.zinnedproject.org/materials/draft-riot-mystery/

Bigelow, B. "Election of 1860 role play" *Zinn Education.*
The role play addresses the complexities of the 1860 election and seeks to move students away from simplistic narratives of the causes of the Civil War.
https://www.zinnedproject.org/materials/election-of-1860/
Singer, A. (2006). "Reclaiming a hidden history: Students create a slavery walking tour in New York." *Zinn Education Project.*
The teaching activity is centered on expanding students understanding of slavery as it existed in the North. It follows the work of students in New York in their quest to shine a light on the origins and practice of slavery outside of the South.
https://www.zinnedproject.org/materials/reclaiming-hidden-history/
Smith, N. "Reconstructing race: A teacher introduces his students to the slippery concept of race." *Zinn Education Project.*
Smith describes a series of lessons explaining the social construction of race.
https://www.zinnedproject.org/materials/reconstructing-race/
Bigelow, B. "A war to free the enslaved?" *Zinn Education Project.*
This lesson uses excerpts from Lincoln's first inaugural address, the 13th Amendment and the Emancipation Proclamation as a means to disrupt myths about the Civil War.
https://www.zinnedproject.org/materials/war-to-free-the-slaves
Bigelow, B. "Timeline on the Civil War and abolition"
Timeline to hand out to students as a resource for other lessons on abolition, the Civil War, and the end of slavery.
https://www.zinnedproject.org/materials/who-freed-the-slaves/

Books

Loewen, J. W., & Sebesta, E. H. (2010). *The confederate and neo-confederate reader: The "Great Truth" about the "Lost Cause."* Teacher resource containing primary documents on the causes of the Civil War.

Williams, D. (2006). A people's history of the Civil War: Struggles for the meaning of freedom. Teacher resource. Uses primary sources to tell the story of the Civil War through the eyes of everyday people.

Zinn, H. (2003). *A people's history of the United States.* New York, NY: HarperCollins.
Teacher resource providing a counter-narrative to traditional textbook accounts of U.S. history.

Curtis, C. P. (2018). *The journey of little Charlie.* New York, NY: Scholastic Press.
YA novel highlighting the impact of the Fugitive Slave Law.

Placco, P. (1994). *Pink and say.* New York, NY: Philomel Books.
Picture book for upper elementary telling the story of two both who meet and help each other during the Civil War.

Meltzer, M. (2006). *Underground man.* New York, NY: Vintage Crime/Black Lizard.
YA novel designed for middle school readers centered on the abolitionist movement and the Underground Railroad.

Resources for Classroom Teachers 153

Collison, Gary (1998). Shadrach Minkins: From Fugitive Slave to Citizen. Boston, MA: Harvard University Press.
Teacher resource relating the story of the first runaway to be arrested and prosecuted in New England under the Fugitive Slave Law.

Meyer, E. L. (2018). *Five for freedom: The African American soldiers in John Brown's army*. Chicago, IL: Chicago Review Press.
Teacher resource. The focus of this book is on the role of five African Americans who participated in the raid on Harper's Ferry. The story moves away from the traditional focus on John Brown to highlight the experiences of the African Americans who joined Brown's cause.

Sinha, M. (2016). *The slave's cause: A history of abolition*. New Haven: Yale University Press.
Teacher Resource. Historian Manisha Sinha from the University of Massachusetts-Amherst presents a comprehensive history of the abolitionist movement. It includes biographical information on a wide variety of individuals and groups that were part of the movement from its earliest years through the Civil War.

Video/Film

Frederick Douglass (1852, July 5). "The Meaning of July Fourth for the Negro."
Actor Danny Glover reads Douglass' 1852 speech. This resource offers an alternative to reading the text which can be especially helpful for English Language Learners.
https://youtu.be/mb_sqh577Zw

Brown, J. (1859 November 2). "History is a Weapon: John Brown's Last Speech."
Clip of Actor Josh Brolin reading Brown's last speech delivered November 2, 1859. Includes closed captioning.
https://youtu.be/oohWYWJJif4

Truth, Sojourner (1851). "Ain't I a Woman."
Actress Cicely Tyson reads the iconic speech of abolitionist and former slave Sojourner Truth given at the Women's Convention in Akron, Ohio, 1851.
https://youtu.be/-0YR1eiG0us

"Was the American Civil War a War over Slavery? (2012)." *Choices*. Brown University.
Film from the digital resources section of Brown University Choices Program. Features historian Michael Vorenberg narrating along with digital images.
http://www.choices.edu/video/was-the-american-civil-war-a-war-over-slavery/

Podcasts

Stuff You Missed in History Class offers engaging podcasts hosted by Tracy V. Wilson and Holly Frey. Episodes of interested to readers of this volume include:
"Frederick Douglass"
https://www.missedinhistory.com/podcasts/frederick-douglass.htm
"John Brown's Raid on Harpers Ferry"
https://www.missedinhistory.com/podcasts/john-browns-raid-on-harpers-ferry.htm
"Preliminary Emancipation Proclamation"

This episode includes commentary from Secretary of Education, Dr. John B. King, Jr. on what happened before the Emancipation Proclamation of 1863.
https://www.missedinhistory.com/podcasts/preliminary-emancipation-proclamation.htm

"The Incredible Escape of Robert Smalls" (first fugitive slave to be arrested under Fugitive Slave Act)
https://www.missedinhistory.com/podcasts/the-incredible-escape-of-robert-smalls.htm

Other Podcasts
"Both Sides Oversimplify the Civil War." (2010, April 12). NPR *Talk of the Nation*. (includes transcript)
https://www.npr.org/templates/story/story.php?storyId=125859203

"The Civil War and Reconstruction. 1845–1877"
Teacher resource from Yale Open Courses featuring Professor David Blight. Episodes 4 and 6–11 will be of particular interest to readers of this volume as they cover topics specific to the causes of the war.
https://itunes.apple.com/us/podcast/the-civil-war-and-reconstruction-era-1845-1877-audio/id341650730?mt=2

Primary Sources

Library of Congress (https://www.loc.gov/)

Abolition, Anti-Slavery Movements, and the Rise of the Sectional Controversy is an exhibition that showcases African American collections of the Library of Congress including books, government documents, manuscripts, maps, musical scores, plays, films, and recordings. The exhibit offers three sections of curated sources leading up to the Civil War: Slavery—The Peculiar Institution, Free Blacks in the Antebellum Period, and Abolition, Anti-Slavery Movements, and the Rise of the Sectional Controversy.
https://www.loc.gov/exhibits/african-american-odyssey/abolition.html

Abraham Lincoln Resource Guide provides links to several collections highlighting a variety of sources including artifacts, letters, speeches, acts, proclamations, treaties, newspaper articles, and photographs/prints all related to Abraham Lincoln.
https://guides.loc.gov/abraham-lincoln-guide/digital

The African American Odyssey: A Quest for Full Citizenship is an online exhibit of items related to Abolition, Anti-Slavery Movements, and the Rise of the Sectional Controversy.
https://www.loc.gov/exhibits/african-american-odyssey/overview.html

American Cartoon Prints Collection is a collection of more than five hundred prints made in America during the eighteenth and nineteenth centuries. The prints in this collection meet two criteria: they were originally designed to express sentiments relating to civic life and government in the United States and they were individually issued prints. Political cartoons created between 1850–1859
https://www.loc.gov/collections/american-cartoon-prints/?dates=1850/1859

Political cartoons created in 1860
https://www.loc.gov/collections/american-cartoon-prints/?dates=1860
Political cartoons created in 1861
https://www.loc.gov/collections/american-cartoon-prints/?dates=1861

Anti-Slavery and Civil War Ephemera is a collection of short-lived documents called ephemera created for a specific purpose, and intended to be read and thrown away. The Printed Ephemera Collection at the Library of Congress includes primary sources relating to the key events of American history including anti-slavery and the civil war.
https://www.loc.gov/collections/broadsides-and-other-printed-ephemera/articles-and-essays/introduction-to-printed-ephemera-collection/anti-slavery-and-civil-war-ephemera/

The Civil War in America is an online exhibit with more than two hundred items assembled to commemorate the sesquicentennial of the United States' greatest military and political upheaval. The set of sources come from many collections and includes two specific sections of interest related to the cause of the Civil War, "Prologue" and "April 1861—April 1862."
https://www.loc.gov/exhibits/civil-war-in-america/prologue.html

The Civil War: The Nation Moves Towards War, 1850–61 is a Primary Source Set that includes a Teacher's Guide with background information, a timeline of events from 1850–1861, suggested teacher activities and prompts, and links to additional resources related to the study of the Civil War.
http://www.loc.gov/teachers/classroommaterials/primarysourcesets/civil-war-approach/

Music for the Nation: American Sheet Music, ca. 1820–1860 collection links to popular, published sheet music on the topics of abolitionism and sectionalism. http://www.loc.gov/teachers/classroommaterials/connections/sheet-music-1820/history4.html

Link to full collection: https://www.loc.gov/collections/american-sheet-music-1820-to-1860/about-this-collection/

Nullification Proclamation Resource Guide provides links to several collections highlighting a variety of sources including letters, ephemera/broadsides, Draft of Proclamation to the people of South Carolina, Tariff Act of 1828 and 1832, and Elliot's Debates.
https://www.loc.gov/rr/program/bib/ourdocs/nullification.html

Primary Documents in American History: National Expansion and Reform, 1815–1860 is a Web Guide including primary sources surrounding important documents such as the Missouri Compromise of 1820, Kansas-Nebraska Act, and the Supreme Court decision *Dred Scott v. Sandford*.
https://www.loc.gov/rr/program/bib/ourdocs/nationalexpanhome.html

Slavery Resource Guide provides links to several collections highlighting a variety of sources including photographs, speeches, narratives, proclamations, letters, sheet music, and broadsides/ephemera related to slavery.
https://www.loc.gov/rr/program/bib/slavery/memory.html

Teaching with Library of Congress Blog—Uncle Tom's Cabin and the Fugitive Slave Act written by Rebecca Newland includes background information about Harriet Beecher Stowe and her novel, Uncle Tom's Cabin. Newland highlights broadsides that review *Uncle Tom's Cabin*, both of which specifically references the Fugitive Slave Act and its relationship to Stowe's novel.

https://blogs.loc.gov/teachers/2014/06/uncle-toms-cabin-and-the-fugitive-slave-act/

National Archives https://www.archives.gov/

The National Archives and Records Administration (NARA) is the nation's "record keeper." They preserve 1–3% of documents and materials created in the course of business conducted by the United States Federal government that are important for legal or historical reasons. These valuable records are preserved and available for free to the public and for research use with no registration.

Docs Teach: Teaching with Civil War Documents is an educator resource from National Archives that offers primary sources and online teaching activities covering the topic of Civil War.

https://www.docsteach.org/topics/civil-war

Educator Resources: Letters, Telegrams, and Photographs Illustrating Factors that Affected the Civil War

"Prior to and during the Civil War, the North and South differed greatly in the resources that they could use. Documents held by the National Archives can aid in the understanding of the factors that influenced the eventual outcome of the War Between the States" (Citation: https://www.archives.gov/education/lessons/civil-war-docs).

Press Kit: Discovering the Civil War; Virginia Ordinance of Secession

Virginia initially refused to go along with the seven Deep South states that left after Lincoln's election, but by mid April 1861, Fort Sumter in Charleston, South Carolina had fallen, and President Lincoln had called for 75,000 troops to put down the rebellion. In response, the Virginia convention reversed course and passed this Ordinance of Secession on April 17, by a vote of 88 to 55. A state-wide vote held a month later confirmed its decision" (Citation: https://www.archives.gov/press/press-kits/civil-war/gallery-page2.html).

Primary Sources: Expansion and Reform (1801–1861) is a search portal that can be refined by choosing one of the following document types: Textual Document, Photograph, Artwork and Artifacts, Poster, Map, and/or Data.

https://www.docsteach.org/documents/documents?fe=czoxOiI0Ijs=&rt=ZP28w-pAzaQDE

Primary Sources: Civil War and Reconstruction (1850–1877) is a search portal that can be refined by choosing one of the following document types: Textual Document, Photograph, Artwork and Artifacts, Poster, Map, and/or Data.

https://www.docsteach.org/documents/documents?fe=czoxOiI1Ijs=&rt=MWzp4z-4VG9PL

Digital Public Library of America (https://dp.la/)

DPLA connects people to the riches held within America's libraries, archives, museums, and other cultural heritage institutions. All of the materials found through DPLA—photographs, books, maps, news footage, oral histories, personal letters, museum objects, artwork, government documents, and so much more—are free and immediately available in digital format.

American Civil War is a topic with eight collections of sources from libraries, archives and museums across the United States. Politics of the Union, Creating the Confederacy, and Battles are several collections linking to a variety of primary sources created prior to the start of the civil war.

https://dp.la/browse-by-topic/american-civil-war

Primary Source Sets are collections of sources with a teaching guide to help students explore topics in history, literature, and culture. The following sets offer primary sources in a variety of formats for research:

Cotton Gin and the Expansion of Slavery
https://dp.la/primary-source-sets/cotton-gin-and-the-expansion-of-slavery

Frederick Douglass and Abraham Lincoln
https://dp.la/primary-source-sets/frederick-douglass-and-abraham-lincoln

Incidents in the Life of a Slave Girl by Harriet Jacobs
https://dp.la/primary-source-sets/incidents-in-the-life-of-a-slave-girl-by-harriet-jacobs

John Brown's Raid on Harper's Ferry
https://dp.la/primary-source-sets/john-brown-s-raid-on-harper-s-ferry

Secession of the Southern States
https://dp.la/primary-source-sets/secession-of-the-southern-states

Uncle Tom's Cabin by Harriet Beecher Stowe
https://dp.la/primary-source-sets/uncle-tom-s-cabin-by-harriet-beecher-stowe

The Underground Railroad and the Fugitive Slave Act of 1850
https://dp.la/primary-source-sets/the-underground-railroad-and-the-fugitive-slave-act-of-1850

Women of the Antebellum Reform Movement
https://dp.la/primary-source-sets/women-of-the-antebellum-reform-movement

Torn in Two: Mapping the American Civil War (Before the War-Rising Tensions) is an exhibit showcasing the geographic narrative of the civil war. The exhibit section, *Before the War-Rising Tensions*, explores the underlying causes of the war.

https://dp.la/exhibitions/mapping-american-civil-war/before-the-war-rising-tensions/sectionalism-and-westward-expa

Maps in American Culture (Depicting a Fractured Society: Civil War Maps) is an exhibit of maps that describe and define new confederacies or lost ground and population groups such as slaves or enemy combatants as depictions of a fractured society.

https://dp.la/exhibitions/maps-in-american-culture/civil-war-maps

O Say Can You See Project. Thomas III, William G., Kaci Nash, Laura Weakly, Karin Dalziel, and Jessica Dussault. (2015). *Early Washington, D.C., Law & Family.* University of Nebraska-Lincoln.

O Say Can You See is a digitized collection of freedom suits filed in early Washington D.C. between 1800–1862.
http://earlywashingtondc.org/

Books

Foner, R. (2010). *The fiery trial: Abraham Lincoln and American slavery.* New York, NY: W.W. Norton. A discussion of the intersection of Lincoln's character and the topics of slavery, race, opinion and politics.

Lawliss, C. (1991). *The Civil War sourcebook: A traveler's guide.* New York, NY: Harmony Books. A guidebook containing information and photographs of essential civil war elements, including biographies of leaders.

McPherson, J. M. (2001)."*We cannot escape history": Lincoln and the last Best Hope of earth.* Urbana/Chicago: The University of Illinois Press. An exploration of Lincoln's perspective on the importance of the Union.

Murray, P. (1998). *Proud shoes: The story of an American family.*Boston, MA: Beacon Press. A story of the experience of one family, of slavery and survival that recounts the era of pre-civil war through reconstruction.

Stauffer, J. (2008). *Giants: The parallel lives of Frederick Douglass and Abraham Lincoln.* New York, NY: Twelve: Hachette Book Company. A profile of two self-made civil war icons, their leadership and ideals.

Romero, P. W. with Rose, W. L. (2009). *A Black woman's Civil War memoirs: Susie King Taylor.* Princeton, Marcus Weiner Publisher. A narrative portrayal of a black woman's understanding of the civil war.

Pryor, C. R., & Hansen, S. L. (2014). *Teaching Lincoln: Legacies and classroom strategies.* New York, NY: Peter Lang. Historians and classroom teachers' perspective on Lincoln, nationalism, leadership, emancipation and race, and freedom. Includes teachers' lesson plans and reflections on teaching.

Websites

Annenberg Learner. A wide range of resources including photographs, lesson plans text and video resources. https://www.learner.org/
Example: Primary Sources in Teaching American History.
https://www.learner.org/resources/series135.html Keywords: Abraham Lincoln and Civil War.
Gettysburg College. Civil War Institute. https://www.gettysburg.edu/civil-war-institute/
Example: Digital Projects https://www.gettysburg.edu/civil-war-institute/digital-projects/
Ohio Civil War Central http://www.ohiocivilwarcentral.com/resources.php
Links to other resources
Example: Civil War 150th Anniversary, [see Illinois, Ohio, Virginia and others]
https://www.ohiocivilwarcentral.com/link-category.php?rec=7

Resources for Classroom Teachers

C-Span

A range of resource highlighting people and events that precede the civil war. Includes links to film, artifacts, lectures, oral histories and books. https://www.c-span.org/series/?theCivilWar

C-Span Classroom

The *C-Span Classroom* website offers a wide variety of lesson plans and bell-ringer activities linked to video accessible through the site. Bell ringers include short clips of one to two minutes in length; lesson plans utilize multiple short clips. Additionally educators can create clips from longer videos and develop playlists. Videos are narrated by historians and government leaders. A list of titles of particular interest to readers of this volume follows.

Lesson Plans

Major Events leading to the Civil War begins with Missouri Compromise and ends with the election of 1860. Video clips for each event are included and range in length from two to ten minutes.

Dred Scott v. Sanford lesson includes two clips providing background to the landmark Supreme Court case, a video timeline of the case, and segments addressing the questions answered by the Court's decision, Justice Taney's opinion, and the legacy of the case.

Civil War Era and the Constitution Professor Timothy Huebner discusses the Constitutional issues raised during the civil war area with a focus on slavery during the antebellum period, Lincoln's emerging views on slavery, and the work of African Americans to gain their freedom. The lesson contains five clips each addressing a different aspect of the topic.

Bell Ringers

Bleeding Kansas Dr. Jeremy Neely chronicles the clash between pro—and anti-slavery forces in Kansas

The Compromise of 1850 Historian Fergus Borderwich discusses the importance of the compromise to the North's victory in the Civil War.

The Formation of the Republican Party Author and historian Heather Cox Richardson highlights the connections between the Kansas-Nebraska Act and the formation of the Republican party.

The Caning of Charles Sumner Filmed on the floor of the United States Senate, historian Stephen Puleo recounts the caning of Charles Sumner in 1856.

https://www.c-span.org/classroom/

"Have to" History—The American Civil War (Causes). *Blue Cereal Education.*

This website gathers all of the essential information you must know to teach the topic. The post is broken down into the three big ideas of slavery, the election of 1860, and overconfidence as key to understanding the causes of the Civil War. An overview of events leading up to the outbreak of war in 1861 is included. A printable pdf is available for download by educators.

http://bluecerealeducation.com/have-history-american-civil-war-causes
EdSitement: National Endowment for the Humanities
Billed as the "Best of the Hukanites on the Web" *EdSitement* is a collection of unit and lesson plans covering a wide variety of topics relevant to the humanities. All lessons include primary sources related to the topic, students handouts, assessments, and suggestions for extending the activities. Of particular interest to readers of this volume:
"An Early Threat of Secession: The Missouri Compromise of 1820 and the Nullification Crisis"
The lesson focus centers on the debate over the Missouri Compromise in 1820, followed by a consideration of the Nullification as an example of the widening divide between North and South.
"The Kansas-Nebraska Act of 1854: Popular Sovereignty and the Political Polarization over Slavery"
"On the Eve of War: North vs. South"
"The First Inaugural Address (1861)—Defending the American Union"
"Abraham Lincoln, the 1860 Election, and the Future of the American Union and Slavery"

Historic Landmarks

Fort Sumter National Monument; Charleston, South Carolina.
"Decades of growing political tension around the issue of slavery between North and South erupted in civil war on April 12, 1861 when Confederate artillery opened fire on this Federal fort in Charleston Harbor. Fort Sumter surrendered 34 hours later. Union forces would try for nearly four years to take it back" (Citation: https://www.nps.gov/fosu/index.htm, February 20/2019).
St Louis in the Civil War. A range of photographs and sites documenting the role of St. Louis in the civil war, with links to the Old State Courthouse (Dred Scott), The Filed House, Bellefontaine Cemetery, Grant's Farm and other sites. https://explorestlouis.com/itinerary/civil-war-in-st-louis/
Andersonville National Historic Site
As well as the infamous Andersonville Prison, this site in Georgia contains the Anderson National Cemetery and the National Prisoner of War Museum opened in 1998 as a memorial to all American prisoners of war. Exhibits of art, photographs, displays and video presentations at the museum depict the capture, living conditions, hardships of prisoners of war in all periods. Used between February 1864 and April 1865, this prison camp was commanded by Captain Henry Wirz, who was tried and executed after the war for war crimes, including allowing unsanitary conditions and overcrowding to four times its capacity, as well as providing an inadequate water supply and food rations to the approximately 45,000 Union prisoners held there. Nearly 13,000 died of scurvy, diarrhea and dysentery.
https://www.nps.gov/ande/index.htm
Antietam National Cemetery
The Antietam National Cemetery has taken the place of miles of temporary graves constructed right after the single bloodiest day on American soil. The Battle of Antietam,

also known as the Battle of Sharpsburg, was fought on September 17, 1862 near Sharpsburg, Maryland and Antietam Creek. It was the first field army-level engagement to take place on Union soil, during which 22,717 Union and Confederate soldiers died. The battle led President Abraham Lincoln to issue the preliminary *Emancipation Proclamation.*
https://www.nps.gov/anti/index.htm

Appomattox Court House

The Appomattox Court House is a National Historical Park of original and reconstructed 19th century buildings in Appomattox County, Virginia. The village is famous as the site of the Battle of Appomattox Court House fought on the morning of April 9, 1865, followed by the surrender of the Confederate army under Robert E. Lee to the Union commander Ulysses S. Grant at the home of Wilmer McLean, effectively ending the Civil War.

https://www.nps.gov/apco/index.htm
https://www.history.com/topics/american-civil-war/appomattox-court-house
https://www.battlefields.org/learn/civil-war/battles/appomattox-court-house
https://www.battlefields.org/learn/articles/10-facts-appomattox-court-house

Mulberry Plantation

Mulberry Plantation near Camden, South Carolina was the home of Mary Boykin Chesnut, wife of former U.S. Senator James Chesnut, renowned for having kept a detailed diary of her wartime experience in the South, starting with the momentous decision South Carolina made in becoming the first state to secede from the Union. As the wife of a former U.S. senator, her diary provides a personal account of the political and societal realities of life in the Confederacy as well as first-hand accounts of important events like the bombardment of Fort Sumter and the start of the Civil War. Learn of the city's importance to the war's Southern Campaigns and life at that time in the backcountry.

https://www.historiccamden.org
https://www.nps.gov/people/mary-boykin-chesnut.htm

Cherbourg, France

The Civil War spilled over into several other countries including France. On the morning of June 19, 1864, the most fearsome ship afloat, the *CSS Alabama,* weighed anchor for repairs in the harbor at Cherborg, France. For almost two years, the Confederate commerce raider had prowled the seven seas in search of nautical prey as part of their guerrilla tactics against the Union's merchant shipping. The ship had captured or destroyed more than 60 U.S. ships and inflicted more than $5 million worth of losses to the Union's merchant marine trade. The *U.S.S. Kearsarge,* a Union warship was in the area quickly had the elusive vessel cornered and sunk. In 1872, an international arbitration panel ordered Great Britain to pay the United States $15.5 million in damages caused by the Alabama and other British-built Confederate raiders.

https://www.history.com/news/the-civil-war-comes-to-france-150-years-ago
https://www.history.navy.mil/our-collections/photography/wars-and-events/the-american-civil-war—1861-1865/the-battle-of-cherbourg.html

Fairfax, Virginia

The economy of Fairfax County, Virginia was improving in the 1850s; population was increasing, farms were becoming more productive, mills were increasing production, and businesses were growing, all contributing to a growing middle class. As many anti-slavery northerners moved into the area, local power brokers arranged for a vote for secession. With threats of violence, many anti-secession voters stayed away from the polls on May 23, 1861, resulting in a vote of 1,231 for secession and 289 against. The Union quickly built a ring of forts along the Alexandria/Fairfax line to defend Washington, fearing that Confederate troops would try to take the capital city. As both sides took control of railroad lines, they became inaccessible for shipping produce and products, greatly affecting the Fairfax economy. The county became a "no-man's land," with both the Union and the Confederacy claiming victory after the June 1, 1861 raid on the Fairfax Court House. The presence of warring armies plundering their produce, livestock and possessions throughout the war greatly disrupted the lives of Fairfax County residents. The Battle of Ox Hill was the biggest battle in the area, while the Fairfax train depot is best known as the location where the 40-year-old government clerk, Clara Barton, treated hundreds of wounded. Known as the "Angel of the Battlefield," she would go on to establish the American Red Cross.

https://www.fxva.com/275/history-essays/the-civil-war-in-fairfax-county/
https://www.fairfax-station.org/about.html
https://ehistory.osu.edu/biographies/clara-barton-angel-battlefield

Fort Oglethorpe

The Chickamauga and Chattanooga National Military Park is the oldest and largest Civil War park in US. It commemorates the 1863 battles for Chattanooga that marked a major turning point in the war and the Confederate's last major victory. Fort Oglethorpe serves as the entrance to the park, that spans the borders of northwest Georgia and Tennessee, with major units at Chickamauga, Lookout Mountain, Missionary Ridge, Orchard Knob and Signal Point. The Chickamauga Battlefield Visitor's Center includes extensive exhibits on the Civil War experience.

https://fortogov.com
https://www.chattanoogafun.com/listing/chickamauga-%26-chattanooga-national-military-park/868/

Fort Sumter

The Battle of Fort Sumter, from April 12–14, 1861, was the Confederate's opening attack on the Union. The fort held no strategic value to the North as it was unfinished and its guns faced the sea rather than the shore. The battle resulted in a quick win for the Confederacy and proof that further war was inevitable. It was only the first of the many hostilities that were yet to come to this area of Charleston, South Carolina and throughout the nation.

https://www.battlefields.org/learn/civil-war/battles/fort-sumter

Gettysburg

Probably the most well-known Civil War site, the location of one of the war's bloodiest engagements, and one of the most famous speeches (the Gettysburg Address) in

American history. The fighting here proved a crucial turning point in the war in the Union's direction. Its well-maintained battlefields eerily resemble how they looked in 1863. The National Park Services' education programs include Great Task Youth Leadership Programs, Days with Documents, a Civil War Documents Video Series, and teacher workshops.

https://www.nps.gov/gett/index.htm

Glorieta Pass, NM

The Battle of Glorieta Pass, fought from March 26–28, 1862, is the only Civil War battle that took place in the western half of the United States. Dubbed the "Gettysburg of the West" it occurred in the Sangre de Cristo Mountain in what is near present-day Santa Fe, New Mexico. The Pecos National Historical Park explains how the Confederates hoped to extend slavery all the way west to California and north to Colorado, acquiring both land and wealth. Unfortunately for them, Union soldiers were alerted to their plans and destroyed their supply train and most of their horses and mules. Eventually the Confederates had to withdraw entirely from the territory and their western movement stopped here.

https://www.legendsofamerica.com/nm-civilwarbattles/
https://www.battlefields.org/learn/articles/battle-glorieta

Harpers Ferry

Sitting at the confluence of the Potomac and Shenandoah Rivers, this is the site of a pre-war event that helped escalate tensions on both sides. On October 16, 1959 abolitionist John Brown led a raid on the federal armory located at Harpers Ferry, Virginia (now in West Virginia). His band of 16 whites and 5 blacks hoped to create an uprising amongst the region's slaves. The entire countryside was alerted, and combined state and federal troops overwhelmed the raiders in two days. Seventeen men died in the fighting, and Brown and his six surviving followers were hanged before the end of the year. The move backfired. Although the raid was denounced by a majority of Northerner, it convinced Southern slaveholders that abolitionists would stop at nothing to eradicate slavery.

https://www.nps.gov/hafe/index.htm
https://www.britannica.com/event/Harpers-Ferry-Raid

Lincoln Memorial

The Lincoln Memorial is the most recognized landmark relating to the Civil War in Washington, DC. commemorating President Abraham Lincoln, commonly known as the "Savior of the Union." Under some of his most memorable words, sits a huge marble statue of the man that symbolizes the unity, strength and wisdom of the 16th president of the United States and the war that defined him and the country he led through this terrible time of struggle.

https://www.nps.gov/linc/index.htm

Mobile Bay

In late summer 1864, the Union attempted to close Mobile Bay to blockade running vessels from the Gulf of Mexico port city of Mobile, Alabama. On August 3rd, 1,500 Union infantry and cavalrymen laid siege to Fort Gaines on the west of the ship channel. On August 5, Admiral Farragut's Union fleet of eighteen ships, including four ironclad monitors, entered Mobile Bay and received fire from both Fort Gaines and Fort Morgan, east of the channel. Farragut's fleet successfully navigated the narrow, torpedo-filled passage, losing only the ironclad USS Tecumseh. After successfully passing both forts, losing only the ironclad USS Tecumseh, the Union forces forced surrender of both forts and the majority of the Confederate fleet. Essentially shutting down the port, the city of Mobile surrendered, but only three days after General Lee's surrender at Appomattox.

https://www.battlefields.org/learn/civil-war/battles/mobile-bay

Montgomery, Alabama

In 1861, 9,000 people lived in the city. As a transportation center, with steamboats on the Alabama River, stagecoaches traveling east and railroads running northeast and southwest, it was considered the richest city for its size in the nation. On January 11, the State of Alabama seceded from the Union. Less than one month later, delegates of the other seceded states met in Montgomery to form the new Confederate nation. They elected Jefferson Davis as its president. In late February, Davis took the oath of office while standing on the portico of the state capitol in Montgomery. But by May the summer's humid heat, the mosquitoes, the limited number of hotels, and the newly seceded Virginians' offer of their own state capital as the seat of the Confederacy, the move was made. Touring the Capital and the "earliest Confederate white house" provides an interesting juxtaposition from the many Civil Rights landmarks also located within the city.

https://www.battlefields.org/learn/articles/capital-cities-confederacy

http://www.encyclopediaofalabama.org/article/h-1429

Palmito Ranch

Confederate General Lee surrendered at Appomattox on April 9, 1864, triggering a series of formal surrenders in other places throughout the country over the next months. During this battle near the Texas coast on May 13th, that lasted only four hours, Confederate casualties were a few dozen wounded, while Union forces had 115 captured and thirty wounded or killed; clearly a Confederate victory. Ironically, at the same time as this battle, the Confederate governors of Arkansas, Louisiana, Missouri and Texas were authorizing Confederate General Kirby Smith to disband his armies and end the war.

https://www.battlefields.org/learn/civil-war/battles/palmito-ranch

https://tshaonline.org/handbook/online/articles/qfp01

President Lincoln's Cottage

Less well-known than the Lincoln Memorial in Washington, DC is the President Lincoln and Soldiers' Home National Monument, sometimes shortened to President Lincoln's Cottage. During the Civil War, he and his family lived in the cottage from June into November to escape the heat and distraction of life at the White House. As he traveled on horseback, unguarded at all hours of the day and night, between the cottage and the White House he could see the nation's capital transformed by military camps, hospitals, and contraband camps where escaped slaves sought refuge behind a

ring of defensive fort built to protect the city. The refreshing breezes of the location provided relative privacy during a time when he confronted momentous decisions about military strategy, domestic policy, and foreign relations. He and his family also mourned the death of their son, 12-year-old Willie, from typhoid at this location, being evacuated only once when nearby Fort Stevens came under Confederate attack in July 1864.
https://www.lincolncottage.org/the-cottage/
Richmond, Virginia
For the majority of the Civil War, Richmond was both the capital of the Confederacy and its manufacturing hub. The area is home to the Richmond National Battlefield Park, operated by the National Park Service, with its dozen important wartime landmarks including Belle Isle, a war prison used by the Confederacy, and the Tredegar Iron Works. Historic Tredegar is a National Historic Landmark, designated as Richmond's Official Gateway to the Civil War, with various exhibits that explore the causes, course, and legacies of the war from the Union, Confederate and African American perspectives.
https://www.encyclopediavirginia.org/richmond_during_the_civil_war
https://www.civilwarrichmond.com
https://acwm.org/about-us/our-story/historic-tredegar
Vicksburg, Mississippi
When the Union, under Major General Ulysses S. Grant's Army of the Tennessee conducted the bloody six-week campaign and capture of Vicksburg on the Mississippi River during the summer of 1863, they essentially took control of the Mississippi River. Having pushed the Confederate army into Vicksburg itself, Grant launched two major assaults that were repulsed with heavy casualties. On May 25, Grant laid siege to the city. After holding out for more than forty day, with food and supplies nearly gone, and no hope of reinforcements, the Confederates surrendered on July 4. More than 1400 monuments and memorials throughout Vicksburg honor the veterans of this siege. This surrender, along with the Union victory at Port Hudson five days later, effectively split the Confederacy in half and ultimately led to Grant's appointment as General-in-Chief of the Union armies. The Vicksburg National Military Park and the USS Cairo Museum provide the only remaining example of a City Class ironclad and a glimpse into the Brown Water Navy, a term used describe the Union forces patrolling the muddy Mississippi River, and life on board these important vessels.
https://www.battlefields.org/learn/civil-war/battles/vicksburg
https://www.nps.gov/vick/index.htm
https://www.battlefields.org/learn/articles/navies-civil-war

Museums

Abraham Lincoln Presidential Library & Museum; Springfield, Illinois.
"The Abraham Lincoln Presidential Museum brings to life Abraham Lincoln's story through immersive exhibits and displays of original artifacts." (Citation: https://www2.illinois.gov/alplm/museum/About, May 3/2019). The Pre-Presidential

Years Journey (Journey One) exhibit highlights Abraham Lincoln's journey to presidency with the presidential campaign of 1860.

The Gettysburg National Military Park Museum & Visitor Center; Gettysburg, Pennsylvania. The museum experience involves the learning of the Battle of Gettysburg within the context and causes of the American Civil War. https://www.nps.gov/gett/planyourvisit/visitorcenters.htm

National Civil Rights Museum at the Lorraine Motel; Memphis, Tennessee

The exhibit, A Culture of Resistance: Slavery in America 1619–1861, offers a graphic representation of the global impact of slavery in the 17th, 18th, and 19th century. https://www.civilrightsmuseum.org/a-culture-of-resistance

Smithsonian—National Museum of African American History & Culture; Washington D.C.

The Slavery and Freedom exhibit includes objects and first person accounts of both free and enslaved African Americans' contributions to the making of America beginning in 15th century Africa and Europe through United States' Civil War and Reconstruction era. https://nmaahc.si.edu/slavery-and-freedom

Smithsonian—National Museum of American History; Washington D.C.

View artifacts related to the United States' institution of slavery. https://americanhistory.si.edu/treasures/slavery

Appendix: Teaching the Causes of the American Civil War Using Inquiry

All lesson plans use the Inquiry Design Model (IDM) template from the College Career and Civic Life Framework. Teachers are licensed under Attribution-Share Alike 4.0 International (CC BY-SA 4.0) license.

To access resources included in the inquires, please visit the series website at TCTAH.online

Table A1: Why Did the South Secede? By Carly Meutteries

Compelling Question	What led the Confederate States of America to secede from the United States?
Standards and Practices	**National Council for the Social Studies C3 Framework:** D2.His.1.9–12. Evaluate how historical events and developments were shaped by unique circumstances of time and place as well as broader historical contexts. D2.His.3.9–12. Use questions generated about individuals and groups to assess how the significance of their actions changes over time and is shaped by the historical context. D2.His.4.9–12. Analyze complex and interacting factors that influenced the perspectives of people during different historical eras. D2.His.12.9–12. Use questions generated about multiple historical sources to pursue further inquiry and investigate additional sources. D2.His.14.9–12. Analyze multiple and complex causes and effects of events in the past. D2.His.15.9–12. Distinguish between long-term causes and triggering events in developing a historical argument. D2.His.16.9–12. Integrate evidence from multiple relevant historical sources and interpretations into a reasoned argument about the past.
Staging the Question	Examine a map of the United States showing the Union and the Confederacy to analyze and respond to three statements outlining potential reasons for southern secession.

Supporting Question 1	Supporting Question 2	Supporting Question 3	Supporting Question 4
In what ways did states attempt to compromise on the issues of slavery, state sovereignty and territorial expansion?	In what ways did the election of 1860 divide the nation?	What did Southerners say about secession?	What did Northerners say about secession?

Appendix

Table A1: Continued

Formative Performance Task	Formative Performance Task	Formative Performance Task	Formative Performance Task
Construct an annotated timeline detailing the compromises over issues of slavery, state sovereignty and territorial expansion.	Write a paragraph describing the ways in which the election of 1860 divided the nation over the preservation of southern power, the expansion of slavery in the territories and federal regulation of enslaved people in free states.	Create a Venn diagram and construct an evidence-based claim that answers the supporting question.	Complete the Venn diagram and construct an evidence-based claim that answers the supporting question.
Featured Sources	**Featured Sources**	**Featured Sources**	**Featured Sources**
Source A: The Missouri Compromise, Excerpt (1820).	Source A: "Dividing the National Map," editorial cartoon (1860).	Source A: "Declaration of the Immediate Causes Which Induce and Justify the Secession of South Carolina …" Excerpt (1860).	Source A: "The Dis-United States. Or the Southern Confederacy," editorial cartoon (1861).
Source B: Henry Clay's Resolutions for the Compromise of 1850, Excerpt.	Source B: "Election of 1860 Results Map" by Gerhard Peters and John T. Woolley.	Source B: "Who Is Responsible for this War?" by Alexander H. Stephens, Excerpt (1861).	Source B: "South Carolina Topsey in a Fix," wood engraving by Thomas W. Strong (1861).
Source C: The Fugitive Slave Act, Excerpt (1850).	Source C: Election of 1860 Party Platforms.	Source C: "Nashville Convention Speech" by Robert Rhett, Excerpt (1850).	Source C: Letter to Abraham Lincoln from Horace Greeley, Excerpt (1860).
Source D: The Kansas—Nebraska Act, Excerpt (1854).	Source D: "The Union is Dissolved!" Broadside. *Charleston Mercury* (1860).	Source D: "Thanksgiving Sermon" by B.M. Palmer, Excerpt (1860).	Source D: Letter to Abraham Lincoln from the New York Republicans, Excerpt (1861).

Continued

Table A1: Continued

Source E: *Dred Scott v. Sanford*, Excerpt (1857).		**Source E:** "Corner Stone Speech" by Alexander H. Stephens, Excerpt (1861).
Summative Performance Task	**Argument**	Why did the South secede? Construct an argument (e.g., detailed outline, poster or essay) that addresses the compelling question using specific claims and relevant evidence from contemporary sources while acknowledging competing views.
	Extension	Participate in a Structured Academic Controversy by arguing a claim that answers the compelling question.
Taking Informed Action		**Understand:** Research an issue within your own state that created tension between federal and state power (e.g., environmental regulation, energy conservation, civil rights investigations, border control, etc.) **Assess:** Take a position on whether your state or the federal government has the power to govern the issue you selected. **Act:** Draft a letter to your state or federal representative stating your position on the selected issue, including claims and evidence to support your position.

Appendix 171

Table A2: Can Words Lead to War?

Compelling Question	Did the publication of *Uncle Tom's Cabin* change public opinion against the practice of slavery?
Standards and Practices	**National Council for the Social Studies C3 Framework:** D2.His.1.9–12. Evaluate how historical events and developments were shaped by unique circumstances of time and place as well as broader historical contexts. D2.His.3.9–12. Use questions generated about individuals and groups to assess how the significance of their actions changes over time and is shaped by the historical context. D2.His.4.9–12. Analyze complex and interacting factors that influenced the perspectives of people during different historical eras. D2.His.12.9–12. Use questions generated about multiple historical sources to pursue further inquiry and investigate additional sources. D2.His.15.9–12. Distinguish between long-term causes and triggering events in developing a historical argument.
Staging the Question	Consider the power of words and examine a video of students using words to try to bring about positive change.

Supporting Question 1	Supporting Question 2	Supporting Question 3	Supporting Question 4
How Harriet Beecher Stowe describe slavery in *Uncle Tom's Cabin*?	What led Harriet Beecher Stowe to write *Uncle Tom's Cabin*?	How did people in the North and South react to *Uncle Tom's Cabin*?	How did *Uncle Tom's Cabin* affect abolitionism?
Formative Performance Task	**Formative Performance Task**	**Formative Performance Task**	**Formative Performance Task**
Write a summary of the plot of *Uncle Tom's Cabin* that includes main ideas and supporting details from Stowe's description of slavery in the book.	List four quotes in the sources that point to Stowe's motivation and write a paragraph explaining her motivation.	Make a T-chart comparing viewpoints expressed in newspaper reviews of *Uncle Tom's Cabin* and make a claim about the differences.	Participate in a structured discussion regarding the impact *Uncle Tom's Cabin* had on abolitionism.

Continued

Table A2: Continued

Featured Source	Featured Source	Featured Source	Featured Source
Source A: Summary of *Uncle Tom's Cabin*	**Source A:** Harriet Beecher Stowe's concluding remarks to *Uncle Tom's Cabin*.	**Source A:** Review of *Uncle Tom's Cabin* published in the *Boston Morning Post*	**Source A:** Excerpt from Charles Sumner's Senate speech
Source B: Excerpts from *Uncle Tom's Cabin*	**Source B:** Letter from Harriet Beecher Stowe to Lord Thomas Denman	**Source B:** Review of *Uncle Tom's Cabin* published in the *Southern Press Review*	**Source B:** Article by John Ball Jr. published in *The Liberator*
Source C: Illustrations from *Uncle Tom's Cabin*			**Source C:** Sales of *Uncle Tom's Cabin*, 1851–1853

Summative Performance Task	**Argument**		Can words lead to war? Construct an argument (e.g., detailed outline, poster, essay) that discusses the impact of *Uncle Tom's Cabin* using specific claims and relevant evidence from historical sources, while acknowledging competing views.
	Extension		Create an educational video of the argument that responds to the compelling question "Can words lead to war?"

Taking Informed Action	**Understand:** Identify and describe a human rights issue that needs to be addressed (e.g., child labor, trafficking, or poverty). **Assess:** Create a list of possible actions that involve words. This may include letters, editorials, social media, videos, and protests. **Act:** Choose one of the options and implement it as an individual, small group, or class project.

Grant, Lee, and Swan, 2014

Table A3: Caught in the Middle: Kentucky and Causes of the Civil War. By Emily Moses

Compelling Question	How do you pick a side in an argument?	
Standards and Practices	**National Council for the Social Studies C3 Framework:** D2.His.1.9–12. Evaluate how historical events and developments were shaped by unique circumstances of time and place as well as broader historical contexts. D2.His.3.9–12. Use questions generated about individuals and groups to assess how the significance of their actions changes over time and is shaped by the historical context. D2.His.4.9–12. Analyze complex and interacting factors that influenced the perspectives of people during different historical eras. D2.IIis.9.9–12. Analyze the relationship between historical sources and the secondary interpretations made from them. D2.His.14.9–12. Analyze multiple and complex causes and effects of events in the past.	
Staging the Question	Kentucky's economy was deeply invested in the institution of slavery. The Commonwealth held a unique position of bordering the Deep South's plantations and the free North. What side do they choose?	

Supporting Question 1	Supporting Question 2	Supporting Question 3
What were the reasons southern states seceded from the Union?	As a border state, what factors influenced Kentucky's decision of whether or not to remain in the Union	Why did Kentucky elect to remain Neutral? In addition, How did other southern states try to influence that decision?
Formative Performance Task	**Formative Performance Task**	**Formative Performance Task**
List out 4 reasons (from each) South Carolina and Mississippi felt they needed to leave the United States.	Find three quotes in the sources that show the motivation for Kentucky to remain in the Union.	Identify the reasons why the Alabama Commissioner stated it would benefit Kentucky to secede. Then list the reasons why Kentucky decided not to secede.

Continued

Table A3: Continued

Featured Sources	Featured Sources	Featured Sources
Mississippi Declaration of Secession (https://www.battlefields.org/learn/primary-sources/declaration-causes-seceding-states)	"To Orville H. Browning" The Collected Works of Abraham Lincoln. Vol. IV, 1860–1861. P. 531–533.	Letters Exchanged between Stephen Hale and Beriah Magoffin.
South Carolina Declaration of Secession (https://www.battlefields.org/learn/primary-sources/declaration-causes-seceding-states)	"To Beriah Magoffin" The Collected Works of Abraham Lincoln. Vol. IV, 1860–1861. P. 497.	*The War of the Rebellion: A compilation of the Official Records of the Union and Confederate Armies.* Ser.4, Vol. 1, Section 1. P. 4–15 *The Official Records can be found at hathitrust.org

Summative Performance Task	Argument	Construct a T-Chart outlining the political reasons for Kentucky to both secede and remain in the Union. Using those instances, create an argument for Kentucky to remain neutral.
	Extension	Using your argument, please construct a press release stating that Kentucky will remain neutral in the Civil War.

Taking Informed Action		**Understand:** Design a system for rationalizing the two sides of an argument that you can apply to your own life. **Assess:** Think of a current events situation that you think should be examined from both perspectives. **Act:** Draft a letter to your local representative or your local newspaper explaining why it is important to consider all the facts before making a critical decision.

Grant, Lee, and Swan, 2014

Appendix

Table A4: Slavery and Justice. By Emily Moses

Compelling Question	What impact can society have on crime?	
Standards and Practices	**National Council for the Social Studies C3 Framework:** D2.His.1.9–12. Evaluate how historical events and developments were shaped by unique circumstances of time and place as well as broader historical contexts. D2.His.3.9–12. Use questions generated about individuals and groups to assess how the significance of their actions changes over time and is shaped by the historical context. D2.His.4.9–12. Analyze complex and interacting factors that influenced the perspectives of people during different historical eras. D2.His.12.9–12. Use questions generated about multiple historical sources to pursue further inquiry and investigate additional sources. D2.His.14.9–12. Analyze multiple and complex causes and effects of events in the past. D2.His.16.9–12. Integrate evidence from multiple relevant historical sources and interpretations into a reasoned argument about the past.	
Staging the Question	Consider how the brutal, local, chaotic events leading to war, may have society to see a significant uptick in criminal activity.	
Supporting Question 1	**Supporting Question 2**	**Supporting Question 3**
What purpose does a Warrant serve?	How does the Fugitive Slave Act of 1850 determine whose responsible for finding the slave?	Who should dispense Justice?
Formative Performance Task	**Formative Performance Task**	**Formative Performance Task**
Define "Warrant" in your own words and list 4-6 reasons as to why a court would issue a warrant.	Examine the Fugitive Slave Law of 1850 and identify the ways that this law changed.	Read and list the reasons outlined to the governor expressing how law and order will cease without the capture of "Jim Brown."

Continued

Table A4: Continued

Featured Sources	**Featured Sources**	**Featured Sources**
Source A: F.A. Cannon et al., Five Hundred Dollars Reward Source B: 1862 Warrant	Source A: The Fugitive Slave Act (Excerpt) Source B: Effects of the Fugitive Slave Law Lithograph, 1850.	Source A: Robert Glass to Beriah Magoffin Source B: Alex H. Major to Beriah Magoffin

Summative Performance Task	**Argument**	What impact can society have on crime? Consider incident surrounding "Jim Brown." Based on historical sources determine if you would defend or prosecute him were his trial go to court. *Don't tell students about the extension until they submit their argument.
	Extension	If you chose to defend or prosecute Jim Brown in your argument, you now must do the opposite and construct a case with supporting evidence to show the other side.

Taking Informed Action	**Understand:** Describe the legal world that both society and slaves navigated prior to the Civil War. **Assess:** Examine how the Fugitive Slave Law sought to promote the agenda of slaveholders. **Act:** Write a letter to the Governor of Kentucky (Beriah Magoffin) expressing how the Fugitive Slave Law will impact all Americans (this includes all persons regardless of their gender, race, or nationality).

Grant, Lee, and Swan, 2014

Table A5: Passmore Williamson and the Fugitive Slave Act. By Alaina McNaughton and Lindsay Campellone

Compelling Question	How did the Fugitive Slave Act of 1850 challenge the nation's views about slavery?
Standards and Practices	**National Council for the Social Studies C3 Framework:** D2.His.1.9–12. Evaluate how historical events and developments were shaped by unique circumstances of time and place as well as broader historical contexts.
	D2.His.3.9–12. Use questions generated about individuals and groups to assess how the significance of their actions changes over time and is shaped by the historical context.
	D2.His.4.9–12. Analyze complex and interacting factors that influenced the perspectives of people during different historical eras.
	D2.His.9.9–12. Analyze the relationship between historical sources and the secondary interpretations made from them.
	D2.His.14.9–12. Analyze multiple and complex causes and effects of events in the past.
Staging the Question	Construct an annotated timeline detailing state and federal legislation on the issue of slavery.

Supporting Question 1	Supporting Question 2	Supporting Question 3
How did the Fugitive Slave Act of 1850 challenge the laws of Northern states?	How did Passmore Williamson challenge the Fugitive Slave Act of 1850?	Did the results of Passmore Williamson v. John K Kane influence the national conversation on slavery?
Formative Performance Task	**Formative Performance Task**	**Formative Performance Task**
Construct a T-chart that contrasts Pennsylvania state laws with U.S. federal laws.	Develop an evidence-based claim that explains how Passmore Williamson and his abolitionist contemporaries challenged the 1850 Act.	Participate in a structured discussion regarding the political climate following Passmore Williamson's imprisonment.

Continued

Appendix

Table A5: Continued

	Featured Sources	Featured Sources	Featured Sources
	Source A: Pennsylvania Personal Liberty Law, Excerpt (1826)	**Source A:** *Narrative of facts in the case of Passmore Williamson*, Excerpt (1855)	**Source A:** "Southern chivalry—argument versus club's," editorial cartoon. (1856)
	Source B: Pennsylvania Personal Liberty Law, Excerpt (1847)	**Source B:** Passmore Williamson's Prison Visitors' Book, Excerpt (1855)	**Source B:** Dred Scott v Sanford, Excerpt (1857)
	Source C: The Fugitive Slave Act, Excerpt (1850)	**Additional Secondary Source:** "Passmore Williamson, Westtown's Crusading Abolitionist" by David Walter (2018)	
Summative Performance Task		Argument	How did the Fugitive Slave Act of 1850 challenge the nation? Construct an argument (e.g., detailed outline, essay, or poster) that discusses the compelling question using specific claims and relevant evidence from historical sources while acknowledging competing views.
		Extension	Recreate the Passmore Williamson v. John K. Kane (1855) trial in your classroom.
Taking Informed Action		**Understand:** Research unjust laws in your community or state. **Assess:** Evaluate the laws and propose an alternative or new law. Support your decision with evidence. **Act:** Contact your local official or representative with your opinions.	

Grant, Lee, and Swan, 2014

Appendix

Table A6: The Election of 1860 by the Numbers. By Elizabeth Barrow

Compelling Question	Why did Abraham Lincoln win the Electoral College vote in the election of 1860 but not the popular vote?	
Standards and Practices	NCSS Themes: (2) Time, Continuity, and Change; (5) individuals, groups, and institutions; (6) Power, Authority, and Governance; and (10) Civic ideas and practices. C3 Framework Dimensions 1–4	
Staging the Question	Brainstorm other elections where the president-elect won the Electoral College vote but not the popular vote. Do you think this is fair? Why or why not? Be prepared to defend your answer.	
Supporting Question 1	**Supporting Question 2**	**Supporting Question 3**
Who were the candidates running for president in 1860 and what where their platforms?	What were the similarities and differences between the presidential candidates and their platforms?	What were the results of the 1860 presidential election?
Formative Performance Task	**Formative Performance Task**	**Formative Performance Task**
Write a campaign slogan song for one of the presidential candidates.	Make a graphic organizer highlighting the similarities and differences between the presidential candidates and their platforms.	Create a T-Chart indicating states that voted in the Election of 1860 on one side and the results on the other side. Be sure to include how many Electoral College votes each state had in 1860. Optional: Create your own visual.
Featured Sources	**Featured Sources**	**Featured Sources**
Source A: Political cartoon—[Dividing the] national [map]	Source A: Excerpts from the 1860 National Presidential Election Platforms	Source A: 1860 Electoral Map

Continued

Table A6: Continued

Source B: North Iowa Times, May 23, 1860 **Source C:** Excerpts from the 1860 National Presidential Election Platforms.	**Source B:** Presidential Election of 1860: A Resource Guide		
Summative Performance Task	**Argument**	Write a newspaper editorial arguing why Lincoln was able to win the Electoral College in 1860 but not the popular vote.	
	Extension	Compare and contrast the 1860 election results with one of the other elections in which the president-elect did not win the popular vote.	
Taking Informed Action	**Understand:** Research the current presidential election process including the voter turnout rates for presidential elections and off-year elections in your state. **Assess:** Discuss as a group the importance of voting in the democratic process. **Act:** Write a guide for future voters in your state about the election process and why they should care about it.		

   Grant, Lee, and Swan, 2014

Appendix

Table A7: Who Voted for Abraham Lincoln? By Elizabeth Barrow

Compelling Question	Why did some people vote for Lincoln and not others?
Standards and Practices	21st Century Skills NCSS Themes: (1) Culture; (4) Individual development and identity; (5) individuals, groups, and institutions; (10) Civic ideas and practices.
Staging the Question	Based on what you have already learned about Lincoln and the United States, brainstorm who you think would have voted for Lincoln in the election of 1860. Use the quick write/draw template to identify what this individual might say or think.

Supporting Question 1	Supporting Question 2	Supporting Question 3
Who was the average voter for Lincoln in 1860? Consider geography, socio-economic status, job titles, etc.	What issues were important to voters in 1860?	Who could not vote in 1860? If they could vote who would they have voted for?
Formative Performance Task	**Formative Performance Task**	**Formative Performance Task**
Expand upon your quick write/draw by completing a sensory figure template describing what the average voter for Lincoln in 1860 might say, think, feel, hear, and do.	Create a graphic organizer to identify and describe the key issues in the election of 1860.	Using the resources provided, and your own research, identify four individuals who could not vote in 1860. They must represent both the North and the South. Create a mock Facebook profile page for each individual.
Featured Sources	**Featured Sources**	**Featured Sources**
Source A: Political Cartoon—"The national game. Three 'outs' and one 'run'"	Source A: Excerpts from the 1860 National Presidential Election Platforms	Source A: Handout of individuals from the Civil War.

Continued

Table A7: Continued

		Source B: Website: 1860 Census
Source B: 1860 Electoral Map **Source C:** Website: *Abraham Lincoln's Classroom: Abraham Lincoln State by State*		
Summative Performance Task	Argument	Create a mind map outlining why some people voted for Lincoln and others did not. Be sure to include political, social, and economic reasons.
	Extension	Create a "Humans of the Civil War" blog page to highlight individuals who did and did not vote for Lincoln in 1860. Students can role-play by taking on a persona and interviewing each other about their voting history (similar to an exit poll). See Barrow, Anderson, and Horner (2017) for more information about the "Humans of the Civil War" photoblog assignment.
Taking Informed Action		**Understand:** Discuss the political, social, and economic issues are we facing today that are similar to, or different, from the issues relevant in 1860? **Assess:** In groups, develop an argument about why you think we are still facing some of the same issues today. Create a list of the top three issues that need to be addressed in your community. **Act:** As a class, write a declaration about how you will work as a group this year to address one of the identified needs of your community.

Grant, Lee, and Swan, 2014

Appendix

Table A8: The Economic Causes of the Civil War. By Christina Palo and Janine Draschner

Compelling Question	In what ways did economic differences between the North and South help cause the Civil War?
Standards and Practices	**National Council for the Social Studies C3 Framework** D2.His.1.9–12. Evaluate how historical events and developments were shaped by unique circumstances of time and place as well as broader historical contexts. D2.His.3.9–12. Use questions generated about individuals and groups to assess how the significance of their actions changes over time and is shaped by the historical context. D2.His.4.9–12. Analyze complex and interacting factors that influenced the perspectives of people during different historical eras. D2.His.9.9–12. Analyze the relationship between historical sources and the secondary interpretations made from them. D2.His.14.9–12. Analyze multiple and complex causes and effects of events in the past.
Staging the Question	Have students watch the video the Economics of the North and South before the Civil War from the Bill of Rights Institute and take notes, then brainstorm ideas as a class of answers to the compelling question.

Supporting Question 1	**Supporting Question 2**
How had the North developed its own economy separate from the South?	To what extent was the Southern economy dependent upon the North?
Formative Performance Task	**Formative Performance Task**
Create a chart showing the change over time of the Northern Economy from 1800 to 1860 on one side and the Southern Economy on the other side.	Using the questions provided as a guide, work in small groups to organize key pieces of information into broader economic ideas. Draw conclusions as a group as to what extent the Southern economy was dependent upon the North.

Continued

Table A8: Continued

Featured Sources	Featured Sources
Source 1: Total Farms in U.S. (1860) and U.S. Farms 1,000 Acres or More (1860) Maps	**Source 1**: Industry and Economy during the Civil War, Benjamin T. Arrington, National Park Service (first seven paragraphs) https://www.nps.gov/articles/industry-and-economy-during-the-civil-war.htm
Source 2: Manufacturing Establishments in 1860 Map and U.S. Industry in the Early 1800s Map	**Source 2**: The Economics of the Civil War, Roger L. Ransom, University of California, Riverside (optional; informational) https://eh.net/encyclopedia/the-economics-of-the-civil-war/
Source 3: Cotton Production Map and Slaves in the U.S. Map	
Source 4: Railroads in 1851 and 1860 Map	
Source 5: Cities in 1820 and 1860 Maps	
	Argument: Construct a claim and a counterclaim that address the compelling question using historical evidence gained from the supporting tasks to prep for a small group Socratic seminar.
Summative Performance Taskw	**Extension**: Students consider possible economic solutions to avoiding the Civil War. Each student, working individually, comes up with a possible economic solution and makes notes to prepare for a small-group discussion.

Grant, Lee, and Swan, 2014

Contributors

ERIK ALEXANDER is an Associate Professor in the Department of Historical Studies at Southern Illinois University Edwardsville, where he teaches courses on the 19th century United States, especially the Civil War and Reconstruction and Abraham Lincoln. He is the author of numerous articles and book chapters and is currently finishing a book on the history of the Northern Democratic Party during Reconstruction.

ELIZABETH BARROW earned her EdD at the University of North Carolina at Chapel Hill in 2017 in Curriculum and Instruction. She earned her Masters of Arts in History at East Carolina University in 2005. Prior to her move to higher education, Dr. Barrow taught U.S. and World History at the secondary level for nine years. She joined the faculty of Georgia Southern University in the fall of 2017 where she currently teaches in the Middle Grades and Secondary Education Department. Her research interests include social studies teacher education and the influence of study abroad on teacher education.

JOHN H. BICKFORD is a former Mid-Prairie (Kalona, Iowa) teacher and a current Associate Professor of Social Studies/History Education in the Department of Teaching, Learning, and Foundations at Eastern Illinois University (Charleston, Illinois). His BA in History, MA in Education, and PhD in Secondary Social Studies Education are all from the University of Iowa. He teaches and researches about the sources and strategies that facilitate students' history literacy, historical thinking, and historical argumentation. He can be contacted at: jbickford@eiu.edu or @SSHistoryEduc

WHITNEY BLANKENSHIP earned her Ph.D. at the University of Texas at Austin in the fall of 2010 in Social Studies Education. Prior to her move to higher education, Dr. Blankenship taught history and social studies at the secondary level for 17 years. She joined the faculty of Rhode Island College in the fall of 2012 teaching in the Departments of Educational Studies and History for six years before returning to the secondary classroom. Dr. Blankenship is currently teaching history at Meridian World School in. Round Rock, Texas and researching the historical black communities of Austin. She is the editor of *Teaching the Struggle for Civil Rights: 1948–1976*.

MELANIE L. BUFFINGTON earned her M.A. and PhD at The Ohio State University and her B.S. at Penn State University. Prior to that, she was a 7th grade art teacher. She has been on the faculty at Virginia Commonwealth University since 2006 and she teaches a range of undergraduate and graduate courses in the Art Education department. Her research interests include public art, contemporary art, Critical Race Theory, and the intersections of these areas.

LINDSAY CAMPELLONE, a recent graduate of West Chester University, serves as the Education Coordinator at the Chester County Historical Society (CCHS). Here, she oversees the team of volunteer museum educators and coordinates the museum programming.

KEVIN CAPRICE is a PhD candidate in history at the University of Virginia where he studies the American Civil War and its wake in American memory. His dissertation explores the opportunities of the Republican majority allowed by the vacated congressional seats of secessionists, and the after-effects of Republican aspirations for the growing United States throughout the nineteenth century.

DAVID CHILDS is Associate Professor of Social Studies Education and History at Northern Kentucky University (NKU). Dr. Childs was the first African American in the history of his department to receive tenure at NKU. His research is in American history, popular culture and education. He earned his Masters degrees in American History and Social Studies Education at Miami University of Ohio. He also earned his Ph.D. in Education and American history at Miami. He has published extensively in academic journals and encyclopedias. Dr. Childs writes a weekly column for Cincinnati's local NPR station (WVXU) entitled Democracy and Me on civics and American history.

S.G. GRANT earned his Ph.D. from Michigan State University in 1994 in Curriculum, Teaching, and Policy. Before completing his doctorate, Dr. Grant taught high school social studies for ten years and worked as the Social Studies Consultant in the Maine Department of Education. After 15 years at the University at Buffalo, Dr. Grant became the Dean of the Graduate School of Education at Binghamton University where he is currently a full professor. His research interests lie at the intersection of teaching, curriculum, and policy.

DAVID HICKS is professor of Curriculum and Instruction in the School of Education at Virginia Tech. He has a background in curriculum and instruction, the learning sciences, instructional design within immersive environments, and human computer interaction to support designing scaffolds to facilitate learning/training within and across formal and informal spaces. To date he has authored or coauthored more than 70 journal articles, book chapters and conference proceedings. His publications also include 2 co-edited books entitled *Education and the Great Depression: Lessons from a Global History* and *Teaching Difficult History Through Film*.

CHARLOTTE JOHNSON received her B.S. in Education/Integrated Liberal Studies and M.A. in Library Studies/Media from the University of Wisconsin-Madison, leading her to a 40-year carer in school, public, special and academic libraries in Australia and the United States. While serving almost 30 years at Southern Illinois University Edwardsville as the library's Director of User Service and Scholarly Communications Librarian, she also served numerous local, state, national and international professional organizations, speaking at conferences around the world. She was named the Illinois Academic Librarian of the Year in 2012. Since her retirement she has concentrated on publishing independent ebooks and producing and exhibiting her artwork, being named in 2019 by Marquis Who's Who in America as one of the nation's top artists.

MICHAEL E. KARPYN teaches history, economics and U.S. Government at Marple Newtown Senior High School in Newtown Square, PA. He earned his BA in History from Gettysburg College, a Master's degree in Education from The Johns Hopkins University and an EdD in Teaching, Learning and Curriculum from the Graduate School of Education at the University of Pennsylvania. He has served as a summer teacher fellow and sits on the Teacher Advisory Group for the Historical Society of Pennsylvania in Philadelphia, PA. He can be contacted at mkarpyn@gmail.com

BONNIE LAUGHLIN-SCHULTZ is Associate Professor of History and Social Science Teaching Coordinator at Eastern Illinois University. She has a BA in History and Secondary Education from Knox College and a PhD in History from Indiana University. Her research renters on 19th century America and women's history and includes publication of *The Ties That Bound Us: The Women of John Brown's Family and the Legacy of Radical Abolitionism* (Cornell University Press, 2013). She can be contacted at blaughlinschul@eiu.edu

JOHN LEE is a professor of social studies education and department head of the NC State College of Education's Department of Teacher Education and Learning Sciences. He is a co-founder and co-director of the C3 Teachers (http://c3teachers.org) and a writer and member of the leadership team for College, Career and Civic Life Framework for Social Studies Standards.

RYAN A. LEWIS is a social studies teacher at Woodford County High School in Versailles, KY, where he teaches history, government, and sociology. He is also currently enrolled in the Pro Teach doctoral cadre program at the University of Kentucky. His area of interest in the program includes the design and implementation of inquiry-based practices in social studies classrooms and preservice teacher education.

ALAINA MCNAUGHTON is a graduate of Temple University's Master's in Public History Program. She currently serves as the Education Director at the Chester County Historical Society (CCHS). At CCHS, she oversees the K–12 museum education programming, as well as the Southeastern Pennsylvania National History Day regional program and contest.

JAMES MITCHELL is Professor of Teacher Education at California State University, East Bay. He is the Director of the Single Subject Credential Online Program that launched in June 2019. Dr. Mitchell teaches Foundations of Education, Technology in Education and Professional Responsibilities. His research focuses on technology in teacher education, cooperation and conflict resolution as related to HIV/AIDS education and service learning, as well as democratic-citizenship skill development through cooperation in the classroom. Presently, Dr. Mitchell is part of a seven-person team that is collaborating on a project to teach Social Studies using STEM and other subjects, specifically as such teaching relates to Civil Rights. His work focuses on "access for all" in today's political and socio-cultural climate

Contributors

EMILY D. MOSES is a native of Birmingham, Alabama, and a 2018 recipient of an M.A. in History from Mississippi State University. Prior to her graduate studies, she served as a research intern and docent for Sloss Furnace National Historic Landmark in Birmingham, Alabama. From 2018-2019 she worked as a NEH-Funded Research Associate, with the Civil War Governors of Kentucky Digital Documentary Edition (CWGK). Her work with CWGK at the Kentucky Historical Society consisted of conducting annotation research, developing thematic lesson plans for classrooms of all ages and amplifying CWGK's outreach efforts to all audiences. Emily currently Manages a Medical Practice in Birmingham, AL.

CARLY MUETTERTIES is a doctoral candidate at the University of Kentucky in Education Sciences, with a focus on social studies curriculum and instruction. Her research focuses on integrating civic education within all subjects, specifically world history. She is guided by the belief that applying learning to relevant civic matters empowers students to meaningfully engage in civic life. She serves as the Executive Director of the Kentucky Council for the Social Studies and the managing editor of C3Teachers.org, which hosts resources aligned with the *C3 Framework for Social Studies State Standards.*

RICKY DALE MULLINS is an assistant professor of Curriculum and Instruction in the College of Education at Eastern Kentucky University with a focus on social studies education and social foundations. He has experience as a social studies educator, special educator, and an assistant principal. His scholarly focus is a direct result of these experiences; therefore, his work coalesces around the topics of Dewey, Disability, and Democratic Education. Ricky has recently started to work on supporting students in analyzing difficult histories, such as the memory of the American Civil War. With an Appalachian background, he is interested in place-based education within the context of Appalachia. He conducts workshops on place-based education, in which he supports social studies educators in learning how to teach social studies using local historical sources and resources. His work, when considered in its totality, explores how to render social studies education more genuinely inclusive of *all* voices.

WILLIAM R. MUTH is professor of adolescent and adult literacy in the Teaching and Learning Department at Virginia Commonwealth University.

CAROLINE R. PRYOR is Professor of Secondary Education at Southern Illinois University Edwardsville. She is Editor of *Learning for Democracy: An*

International Journal of Thought and Practice, a Wye Fellow of the Aspen Institute and editor-in chief of the book series *Teaching Critical Issues in American History*, Peter Lang Publishers. Dr. Pryor is author of six books of which three concern democratic thought in education: *Democratic practices in education: Implications for teacher education*: Rowman Littlefield, *The mission of the scholar: Research and practice*, Peter Lang Publishers, and *Democratic practice workbook: Activities for the field experience*. McGraw-Hill. Her chapter "European/American influences on democratic practice at the professional development school: Post-baccalaureate students in early field experience," Rowman Littlefield, received the 1998 *Best Paper Award* from the Arizona Educational Research Organization, affiliate of AERA. Other award nominated articles include: Preservice to in-service changes in beliefs: A study of intention to become a democratic practitioner. *Theory and Research in Social Education* and Preservice teachers' attitudes and beliefs about democratic classroom practice: Influences on intentions for pedagogical integration. Current Issues in Education. She has received six *National Endowment for the Humanities* awards for her workshop for school teachers on Abraham Lincoln. Her recent chapter on integrating STEM into the social studies is published in *Project-Based Learning: An Integrated Science, Technology, Engineering, and Mathematics (STEM) Approach* (2nd ed.), Sense Publications was nominated as Exemplary Research in Social Studies to the National Council of the Social Studies. She is the current chair of the Special Interest Group, Democratic Citizenship in Education, of the American Educational Research Association.

GABRIEL A. REICH earned a BA in History from the University of Wisconsin, Madison. He taught in secondary schools in New York City and went on to earn a Ph.D. in education from New York University. He is currently an Associate Professor of Secondary History Education at Virginia Commonwealth University where he began his career in 2007. His research interests focus on the intersection between historical consciousness, collective memory, and the history classroom.

KATHY SWAN is a professor of curriculum and instruction at the University of Kentucky. Dr. Swan served as the project director and lead writer of the *College, Career, and Civic Life Framework for Social Studies State Standards*, co-founder of C3 Teachers, and was a project director on the New York Social Studies Toolkit. Over the past two years, Dr. Swan has co-authored the books, *The Inquiry Design Model: Building Inquiries in Social Studies* (2018) and *Inquiry-Based Practice in Social Studies Education: The Inquiry Design Model* (2017; Routledge). Her latest book is *Blueprinting an Inquiry-Based Curriculum: Planning with the Inquiry Design Model* (2019).

Index

A

Abolitionists 23, 25, 27, 38, 44, 51, 52, 94, 99, 129
   links to primary sources on 154, 155
African Methodist Episcopal Church 30
Allen, Reverend Richard 30
Amistad 43, 118
Anderson, Jeremiah 60
Anderson, Osborne 61
Andersonville Prison 160
Antietam National Cemetery 160
Appomattox Courthouse 161

B

Bell, John 80
Birth of a Nation 16, 93
Bleeding Kansas 44, 77, 92, 159
Breckenridge, John C. 79
Brooks, Preston 91
Brown, Belle 57
Brown, Frederick 51
Brown, Jim 35–40
Brown, John Jr. 53
Brown, John 43–76
   execution of 44, 55, 66, 70, 71
   motivations for raid 46–47
   raid on Harper's Ferry 44–46, 73, 77, 92, 94, 96, 152, 153, 157, 163
   trial of 55
   views of in North 44
   views of in South 45
Brown, Mary 52, 61
Brown, Oliver 58
Brown, Watson 57
Burns, Ken 119

C

C3 Teachers 77, 85–86, 97–98, 107, 117, 136, 139, 144, 149, 150
Calhoun, John C. 118
Calvinism, see "Presbyterian"
Charleston *Mercury* 92, 110, 170
Chesnut, James 161
Chesnut, Mary 161
Coker, Reverend Daniel 30–32
College, Career, & Civic Life C3 Framework
for Social Studies State Standards 9, 64, 77, 85, 86, 97, 117, 149
Common Core State Standards 97–98, 150
Compromise of 1850 38, 44, 77, 92, 109, 159
Constitutional Unionist Party 78, 82
Copeland, John 58–59
Cotton Gin 157

INDEX

CSS Alabama 161
Curry, John Steuart, *Tragic Prelude* 49, 63

D

Davis, Jefferson 95–97, 99, 120–121, 132
  inaugural address of, 1861 7, 8
  views on John Brown 45
  in Election of 1860 79
Declaration of Independence 128
  in Jefferson Davis inaugural address 7
  in Lincoln Philadelphia speech 6–7
  use in Election of 1860 82
Dixon, Senator Archibald 36
Douglas, Stephen A. 78–81
Douglass, Frederick 18, 32, 60, 94, 95, 97, 132, 136
Drayton, Percival 1, 3
Drayton, Thomas 1–2
Dred Scott v. Sanford, 60 U.S. 393, (1857) 51, 77, 78, 92, 142, 155, 159, 170

E

Election of 1860 10, 77–90, 109–110, 138, 139–140, 142, 151, 159, 168–169, 179, 181
  party platforms 78–80, 122, 169
Electoral College 80, 82–83, 83, 86–87, 179
Emancipation Proclamation 17, 84, 152, 153
Emancipationist Memory 13
  definition 17
Everett, Edward 80
Evidence-based arguments 108

F

Fairfax, Virginia 162
Frémont, John C. 78
Fifteenth Amendment 33

Fort Sumter 43, 83, 128, 156, 160, 162
Fourteenth Amendment 33, 94
Fugitive Slave Act, 1850 10, 44, 46, 51, 109, 154, 155, 157, 169, 175, 177

G

Gadsden Purchase 109
Garrison, William Lloyd 25
Gettysburg National Military Park 166
Glass, Robert 38
  letter to Beriah Magoffin 176
Gone with the Wind 16
Grant, Ulysses S. 97, 161
Greely, Horace 17, 19, 112, 169

H

Hale, Stephen F. 119
  letters to Beriah Magoffin 174
Harper's Ferry, Virginia 9, 46–48, 153
  Federal Arsenal at 44, 50
  1859 raid on, see "John Brown"

I

Illinois Senate Race, 1858 81
Inquiry Design Model 135–144, 150, 167

J

Jacobs, Harriet 157
Jefferson, Thomas 128
Jim Crow 33, 83, 93, 99

K

Kansas-Nebraska Act 109, 155, 159, 160, 170
Kelly, John 118–119
Kentucky, 1792 admission to Union 36
  views on slavery 36

Index

as a border state 36
"armed neutrality" 36–37, 40
Know-Nothing Party 78

L

Lies My Teacher Told Me 92
Lincoln, Abraham 95
  1864 election 17
  Cooper Union Speech 81
  election in 1860 1
  first inaugural address 83, 119, 121, 152, 160
  "House Divided" speech 80
  letter from New York Republicans 112
  letter to Beriah Magoffin 121
  response to Horace Greeley, 1862 17, 19
  speech at Independence Hall, 1861 6
  views on slavery, 1862 14, 17
Lost Cause Narrative 36, 99, 129
  definition of 15
Louisville and Nashville Railroad 36
Loewen, James 92, 106

M

Magoffin, Governor Beriah 37
  letters to Stephen Hale 121
Major, Alex H. 37
  letter to Beriah Magoffin 176
Mexican American War 91
Mississippi Declaration of Secession 174
Missouri Compromise 109, 139, 155, 159, 160, 169
Montgomery, Alabama 164
Mulberry Plantation 161

N

New York *Tribune* 17, 62, 92, 112
Northern Democrat 78–79, 82
Norwood, Dr. Walter Alves 35–39
Nullification Crisis 1, 155, 160

P

Palmer, B.M. 111, 170
Payne, Bishop Daniel 30–31
Pennsylvania Personal Liberty Law
  1826 178
  1847 178
Pottawatomie, Kansas 44
  newspaper accounts of John Brown's Raid at 51
  first person accounts of John Brown's Raid at 51
Presbyterian Church, views on slavery 26–27

R

Reconciliationst viewpoint 128, 131–132
Religious beliefs before Civil War 9
Republican Party 45, 78, 81–82, 96, 119
  formation of 159
Republican ticket, 1860 17, 26
Rhett, Robert 169
Richmond, Virginia 165

S

Santa Fe Trail, 1940 film 94
SCIM-C Scaffold 120, 122, 142
Shaara, Michael 120, 121
Shaw, Robert Gould 121
Slavery
  as a cause of the Civil War 4, 14, 15–17, 19–20, 23–24, 78, 129, 132
  biblical references to 26–28
  issue in 1860 election 58–59
  southern religious beliefs on 28–30
  theological arguments against 30–33
  U.S. map of in 1860 5
  walking tour of New York 152
Smylie, Reverend James 28
South Carolina Secession Declaration 83, 95, 96, 106–107, 110–111, 119, 128
Southern Democrat 58–59, 61

Stephens, Alexander 15, 95–96, 97, 99
  Cornerstone Speech, 1861 15, 111, 170
  "Who is Responsible for this War?" 169
Stevens, Aaron 56
Stevens, Henry 56
Stowe, Harriet Beecher 29, 155, 171, 172
Structured Academic Controversy 113, 117, 118, 122, 140, 170
Sumner, Charles 91–92, 159, 172

T

Taking Informed Action, Inquiry Design Model 113
The Killer Angels 120
Thirteenth Amendment 33, 152
Thompson, Ruth Brown 52
Treaty of Guadalupe Hidalgo 109

U

Uncle Tom's Cabin 10, 155, 157, 171–172
Underground Railroad 30, 157
Unionist memory 13, 18–19, 128
  definition of 16, 130–131

V

Van Dyke, Reverend Henry J. 29
Vicksburg, Mississippi 165
Virginia Ordinance of Secession 156

W

Walker, David 32
Williamson, Passmore, trial and imprisonment 177–178
Wilmot Proviso 91

Caroline R. Pryor, Erik Alexander,
Charlotte Johnson, James Mitchell,
and Whitney Blankenship
General Editors

In the United States, the Common Core Standards, the C3 Framework for Social Studies Standards (NCSS), and the 10 themes of the National Curriculum Standards (NCS/NCSS) each pose challenges for teachers preparing to teach skills, content, and critical issues of American history. The problem for many middle and secondary teachers is that textbooks do not contain sufficient primary source documents and varied secondary literature linked to these standards. The volumes in the Teaching Critical Themes in American History series fill this need by providing teachers with history content, pedagogical strategies, and teaching resources. The series is organized around key problems/issues in American history so that teachers can select which critical topics upon which they might want to concentrate.

Middle and Secondary pre- and in-service educators will find the books in this series essential for developing and implementing American history and social studies curriculum in diverse and complex classrooms. Teachers will find the books in this series valuable as they search for methodologies and material that will help them address the Common Core Standards in the social sciences and history. Community College history instructors can also find the books in this series helpful as supplementary texts in their U.S. history survey courses. The practical—not to mention exciting—implementation of perspectives offered in each title is a key feature of this series.

This series will address topics such as the formation of the American Republic, the problem of slavery in America, causes of the Civil War, emancipation and reconstruction, America's response to industrialization, the New Deal, the fight for Civil Rights, and more. The series editors invite proposals for edited volumes in American history and social studies, along with articles and lesson plans for both the topics above, and other topics of the series.

For additional information about this series or for the submission of manuscripts, please contact any of the series editors.

Caroline R. Pryor | Erik Alexander
capryor@siue.edu | eralexa@siue.edu
Charlotte Johnson | James Mitchell | Whitney Blankenship
shypoke09@gmail.com | MitchellCSUEB@aol.com | whitney@blankenship.com

To order other books in this series, please contact our Customer Service Department: peterlang@presswarehouse.com (within the U.S.) or order@peterlang.com (outside the U.S.). You may also browse online by series at www.peterlang.com.

www.ingramcontent.com/pod-product-compliance
Lightning Source LLC
Chambersburg PA
CBHW061446300426
44114CB00014B/1857